# Take-Home Leveled Readers

Advanced Level

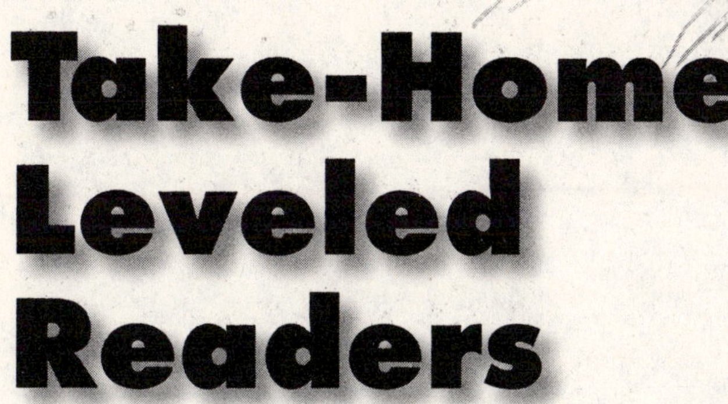

# Science

PEARSON

Scott Foresman

Editorial Offices: Glenview, Illinois • Parsippany, New Jersey • New York, New York
Sales Offices: Needham, Massachusetts • Duluth, Georgia • Glenview, Illinois
Coppell, Texas • Sacramento, California • Mesa, Arizona

sfsuccessnet.com

ISBN: 0-328-19735-1



2 3 4 5 6 7 8 9 10 V004 13 12 11 10 09 08 07 06 05

# Table of Contents

# To the Teacher

Scott Foresman provides three Leveled Readers for every chapter of *Scott Foresman Science*, Grades 1–6: a *Below-Level Leveled Reader*, an *On-Level Leveled Reader*, and an *Advanced Leveled Reader*.

All three readers teach the same science concepts, same vocabulary, address the same target reading skill and contain the same graphic organizer as the corresponding student edition chapter, just at three different reading levels—providing access to important science content for all students. The On-level and Advanced readers also use additional examples to enrich the chapter and extend ideas

This book contains reproducible copies of the Advanced Leveled Readers for Grade 6. These are designed for you to reproduce and send home with your students as appropriate. Encourage students to share these books with parents or family members in order to practice reading skills and reinforce science content.

Online versions of these and other readers are also available through the Scott Foresman Leveled Reader Database.

# Insects and Spiders

by Clara Morales

| Genre | Comprehension Skill | Text Features | Science Content |
|---|---|---|---|
| Nonfiction | Compare and Contrast | • Glossary<br>• Captions | Classifying Living Organisms |

Scott Foresman Science 6.1

# What did you learn?

1. Why do scientists consider insects and spiders successful?

2. Define arthropod and name three types.

3. What are two ways in which spiders catch their prey?

4. **Writing** in Science Insects and spiders go through changes from when they hatch from eggs to when they are adults. What process do insects and spiders go through and how are they similar and different? Use examples from the book to support your answer.

5. **Compare and Contrast** How are insects and spiders alike, and how are they different?

**Vocabulary**

adaptation
bacteria
biosphere
classification
fungi
nonvascular plants
species
vascular plants

**Extended Vocabulary**

antennae
arthropod
cephalothorax
larva
metamorphosis
ommatidia
pedipalps
pupa
thorax

**Picture Credits**
Every effort has been made to secure permission and provide appropriate credit for photographic material.
The publisher deeply regrets any omission and pledges to correct errors called to its attention in subsequent editions.

Photo locators denoted as follows: Top (T), Center (C), Bottom (B), Left (L), Right (R), Background (Bkgd).

7 (B) ©Jerry Young/DK Images; 8 (B) Mark Moffett/Minden Pictures.

Scott Foresman/Dorling Kindersley would also like to thank: 6 (CB), 9 (TR), 11 (CB), 15 (BL) Jerry Young/DK Images.

Unless otherwise acknowledged, all photographs are the copyright © of Dorling Kindersley, a division of Pearson.

ISBN: 0-328-13972-6

# Glossary

**antennae** — long, slender projections on the front of insects that act as the main sense organs

**arthropod** — an animal with a hard outer shell, a segmented body, and jointed limbs

**cephalothorax** — the front section of a spider's two body sections

**larva** — the stage in an insect's development after it hatches from an egg

**metamorphosis** — the change an insect goes through, from hatching from an egg to becoming an adult insect

**ommatidia** — the lenses in the compound eyes found on insects

**pedipalps** — leglike limbs on the front of spiders used for grasping and crushing prey

**pupa** — the stage in an insect's development when it goes into a protective casing, sometimes called a cocoon, and emerges as an adult

**thorax** — the section of an insect that the legs and wings are attached to

3

# Insects and Spiders

by Clara Morales

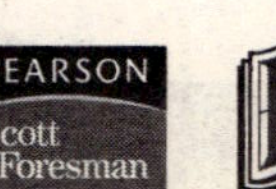

A shield bug parent looks after its young.

Millions of different living things make their home on Earth. The part of Earth that supports living things is called the biosphere. Scientists have named and studied millions of living things, but there are still huge numbers of organisms yet to be discovered.

In the biosphere, different living things depend on one another. For instance, some plants depend on animals for pollination or carbon dioxide. At the same time, animals depend on plants for food. Many plants and animals depend on other living things to survive.

The characteristics that help an organism to survive and reproduce in its environment are called adaptations. Each different living thing has special adaptations to help it survive. This makes for a wide variety of living things.

Despite all these differences, groups of living things are also alike in many ways, often sharing the same characteristics. Organisms that have many of the same characteristics may be part of the same species. A species is a group of similar organisms whose members mate with one another and produce offspring, making possible the continuation of their species.

You may be wondering how it is possible to keep track of so many different living things and species. Scientists group living things according to their similarities. This is called classification. Organisms are grouped, or classified, by their structure, feeding habits, and how they reproduce.

beetle

Wolf spiders attach their cocoons to themselves and carry them. Once the spiderlings emerge, they stay on the mother's back until they can live on their own.

Whatever they do to help their young, insects and spiders are doing something right. They are thriving in the biosphere, far outnumbering other groups in the animal kingdom. In some forests, scientists think there may be thousands of species of insects and spiders. The variety of species is stunning, ranging from colorful dragonflies to huge tarantulas and microscopic dust mites. So the next time you see a spider or insect, consider that they are, by many measures, the most successful types of animals on Earth.

A cave spider looks after her cocoon of eggs.

## Caring for Young

Once a female has laid her eggs, she often leaves them. However, many insects will leave their eggs near a food source so that their young can eat when they hatch. Some females lay their eggs inside a plant for protection.

Other insects will wait for their young to hatch and stay with them. The shield bug is an example of an insect with this trait.

Spiders try to lay their eggs in places that will be free from predators. Often the female spider will leave the cocoon on a plant or other place to which it is attached. Sometimes other spiders will look after the cocoon. Other types of spider mothers will stay with their cocoon until the young spiders emerge. Some raise their young on their webs and feed them while they grow.

Classification has different levels. The first level, called kingdom, is very broad. There are six kingdoms of living things. Some scientists put bacteria into two kingdoms. Bacteria are single-celled organisms that do not have true nuclei. The organisms of one kingdom, archaebacteria, live in certain hot springs. The organisms of the other kingdom, eubacteria, or true bacteria, live in many different environments. Some of them even live in your own body! Many types of bacteria actually help your body and do not cause diseases.

Another kingdom is the protists. This includes unicellular organisms such as algae. Another kingdom is called fungi. Fungi are many-celled organisms that grow in wet, dark places and give off chemicals that break down the organisms on which they grow. Fungi can look like plants, but they are not plants. Plants are in another kingdom.

The kingdom of plants is made up of vascular and nonvascular plants. Vascular plants have cells that form tubes for carrying water and nutrients through the plant. Nonvascular plants do not have these tubes. They pass materials through one cell at a time and, as a result, do not grow very large.

Animals also make up a kingdom and are classified into groups. In this book, you will learn about two types of animals: insects and spiders. They belong to a group of animals called arthropods.

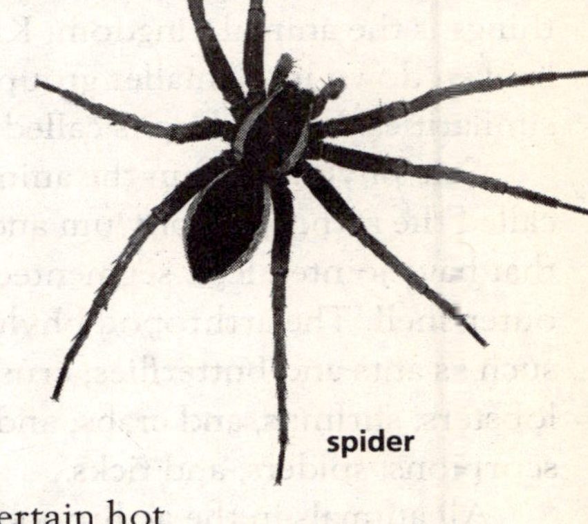

# Living Things

As you know, one of the six kingdoms of living things is the animal kingdom. Kingdoms are also broken down into smaller groups based on similarities. Each group is called a phylum.

One phylum within the animal kingdom is called the arthropod phylum and includes animals that have jointed legs, segmented bodies, and a hard outer shell. The arthropod phylum includes insects, such as ants and butterflies; crustaceans, such as lobsters, shrimps, and crabs; and arachnids, such as scorpions, spiders, and ticks.

All animals in the arthropod phylum share certain characteristics. Most are small, and some you can't see without the help of a microscope. They all have an exoskeleton, or a hard outer shell. This exoskeleton protects and supports their bodies. Arthropods don't have bones or an internal skeleton that some other animals have.

The bodies of arthropods are made up of different parts, or segments. Each segment has a different purpose. The abdomen, for example, contains most of the digestive and reproductive organs. Arthropods have jointed legs. That means the legs have joints, so they can bend. The joints help them leap, swim, walk, and dig. As a result, arthropods can be agile movers.

The spider is an arachnid and belongs to the arthropod phylum.

The tiger beetle is an insect and part of the arthropod phylum.

There are two types of this change; complete and incomplete. In a complete metamorphosis, an insect grows in four stages, from an egg to a larva, then to a pupa, and then to an adult. In an incomplete metamorphosis, the insect goes through three stages, skipping the pupa stage. Dragonflies go through an incomplete metamorphosis, as you can see here.

During a complete metamorphosis, insects hatch from their eggs as larvae. They look very different from their parents and eat different foods. As they grow, they move into a new phase called the pupa. In a protective casing, the pupa changes greatly and comes out of the structure looking like an adult insect.

Butterflies go through a complete metamorphosis. The female lays eggs. The eggs hatch and caterpillars come out. As they grow, they make a protective casing around their bodies. In time, the casing breaks and an adult butterfly will come out.

An oak silk moth caterpillar begins to make its cocoon.

When the adult dragonfly has fully emerged, it leaves its old skin behind.

adult dragonfly

# Reproduction

Spiders and insects do not reproduce in the same way. A spider's young hatch from eggs as immature adults. After mating with a male spider, the female spider will lay her eggs. Some spiders cover the eggs in a cocoon, a silky case that protects the eggs as they grow. Spiders can lay as many as a thousand eggs at one time, but only a small number will survive.

In time, the eggs hatch inside the cocoon. The new larvae then shed their shells twice and become spiderlings, or young spiders. As the young spider continues to grow, it will shed its outer shell several times before it becomes an adult spider.

Most insects lay eggs. And like spiders, they can lay many, numbering in the thousands. Also like spiders, not many eggs will survive. Insects lay eggs in or on plants and in other living things. Once young insects hatch from their eggs, they go through something called a metamorphosis, during which they change.

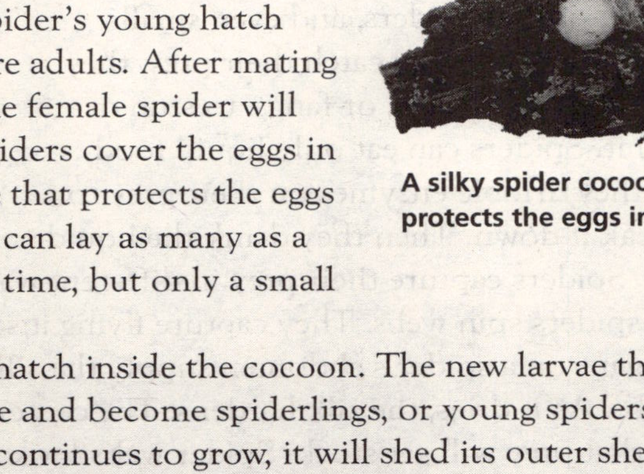

A silky spider cocoon protects the eggs inside.

**Southern Hawker Dragonfly Metamorphosis**

dragonfly egg

A nymph hatches from the egg and lives in water.

The nymph's skin splits and the adult dragonfly emerges.



Arthropods are thought to be the most successful animals on Earth because they have been on Earth longer than other animals. Also, there are more of them than any other type of animal. And there are still more to be discovered! Spiders and insects vary greatly in size and shape, and this helps them to survive in many different habitats. For instance, both insects and spiders live in deserts, woods, mountains, and near water.

Insects account for almost half of all known animals. Even though insects can be bothersome to humans, they play a very important role in nature. For example, they pollinate plants. Without insects, many plants would have trouble reproducing.

Spiders also thrive in the biosphere. There are 40,000 species of spiders. Like insects, spiders carry out important tasks in the environments in which they live. In this book, you will learn more about the characteristics, similarities, and differences among spiders and insects.

You can see the jointed legs and hard outer shell of this crab spider.

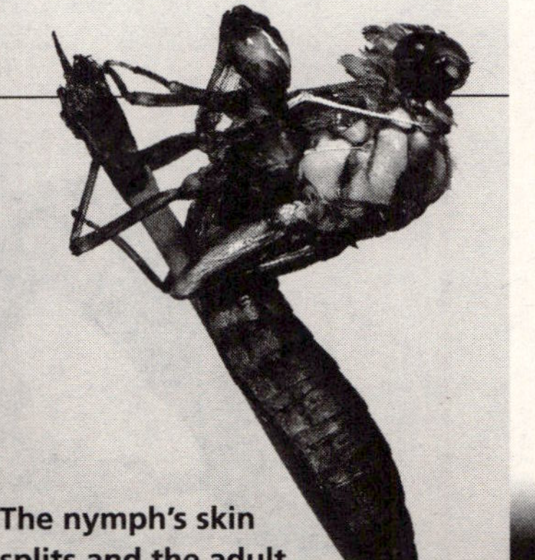

The atta ants shown here are carrying leaves back to their nest. Notice the segments in their bodies.

# Structure And Movement

Insects and spiders, like other arthropods, have a hard outer covering and jointed legs. As spiders and insects grow, they shed the exoskeleton and grow a new one to cover their larger body. During this process they are at risk of an attack since their outer shell provides protection.

Spiders are often mistakenly referred to as insects, but they are not insects. They have a different body structure. Spiders' bodies have two sections. One section contains the head and thorax. The other section is the abdomen. Spiders have eight legs and eight eyes.

The front section of a spider is called the cephalothorax. It contains two biting mouthparts, or chelicerae; two poison glands; two pedipalps, or leglike limbs; four pairs of legs; and eight eyes. The chelicerae, on the front of the mouth opening, are two small, knifelike structures that spiders use for biting prey. Spiders use pedipalps for grasping and crushing prey.

Spiders are carnivores. They eat insects, other spiders, and ever small animals. Once they catch their prey, they use their chelicerae, or fangs, to stun or kill it. Spiders can eat only liquid food, so they dribble enzymes on their prey to break it down. Then they drink the liquid.

Spiders capture their prey in different ways. Some types of spiders spin webs. They capture flying insects in their webs. Organs on a spider's abdomen supply the silk for making the webs. As it dries, the silk hardens. The center of the web is sticky so that prey will get stuck. Spider webs look fragile, but they are very strong, supporting many times the spider's weight. Spiders weave them in different shapes and designs.

Not all spiders spin webs. Some wait for their prey to pass by. Tarantulas will stay very still until they pick up scents and sounds from their prey with the hairs on their legs. When the unlucky animal passes by, the spider will pounce on it, stun or kill it, and eat it.

**This fly is sponging up food remains on a fork.**

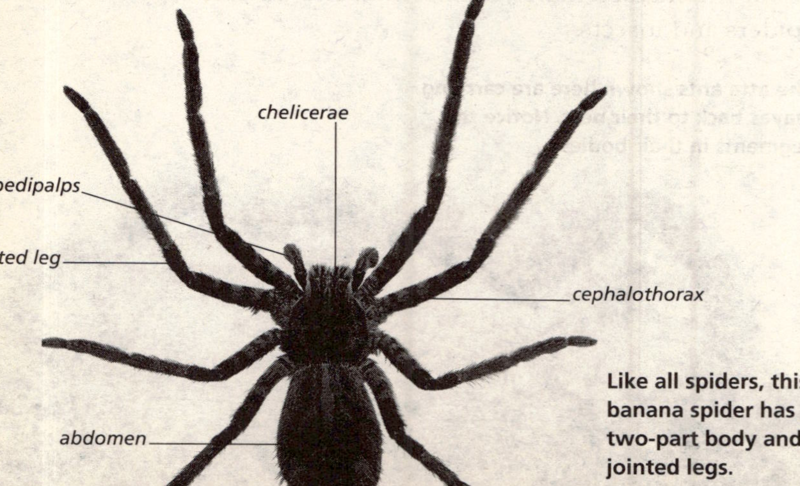

**Like all spiders, this banana spider has a two-part body and jointed legs.**

**The Mexican red-rumped tarantula has caught a grasshopper.**

# Food

Insects eat a wide variety of foods. About half of all insects are plant eaters, living on wood, leaves, and nectar. Other insects hunt for their food and eat small animals. Some insects, such as fleas and lice, are parasites that live off the blood of other organisms. Dung, dead creatures, clothes, feathers, and paper make up the diet of other insects.

Insects have mouthparts that have changed over time to meet the needs of their diet. Many plant-eating insects have jaws with sharp edges. These edges move from side to side, helping the insect
to eat plants. Grasshoppers have this kind of jaw.

Other insects, such as butterflies, have a tubelike tongue, called a proboscis, instead of a jaw. Butterflies sip nectar from plants through their proboscis.

Other insects, like houseflies, often dissolve their food before they eat it. Their saliva contains enzymes that break down food. Flies cover their food in saliva and suck it up after it has dissolved.

This black and yellow butterfly feeds on the nectar from this flower.



Insects' bodies have three parts: a head with antennae, a thorax, and an abdomen. Insects have six legs and usually two pairs of wings. The brain and sense organs are inside the head. The legs and wings are attached to the thorax. Food is digested in the abdomen, and the insect's reproductive organs are located there too.

All spiders and insects have jointed legs. They have many muscles in their legs too. This strength and flexibility makes spiders and insects agile. Usually they move quickly and into small and hard-to-reach places.

In addition, certain insects and spiders have special leg adaptations that help them carry out certain tasks. For example, grasshoppers have strong back legs that help them jump.

Insect and spider legs may end in claws, bristles, or adhesive pads. For instance, some insects and spiders have special tufts on the bottom of their legs that help them walk on smooth surfaces and even upside down.

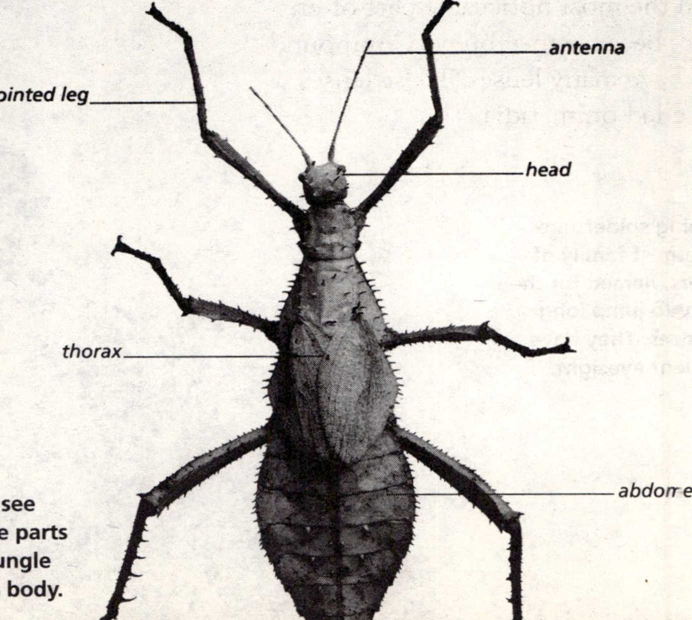


You can see the three parts of this jungle nymph's body.

**May beetle**

# Senses

The major sense organs of an insect are in its head and are called antennae. Antennae are long, thin, and covered with tiny sensitive hairs. They can be very simple or very complex, depending on the insect.

Insects use their antennae for feeling, smelling, and sometimes tasting and hearing. They can use them to pick up scents of food or mates, and odors of predators and other threats.

Some insects use their antennae for hearing too. For example, mosquitoes can detect sounds as well as smell with their antennae. Some also sense heat and moisture, helping insects find mates and enemies.

Insects have compound eyes. They are often the most noticeable part of an insect because they bulge. Compound eyes have many lenses. These lenses are called ommatidia.

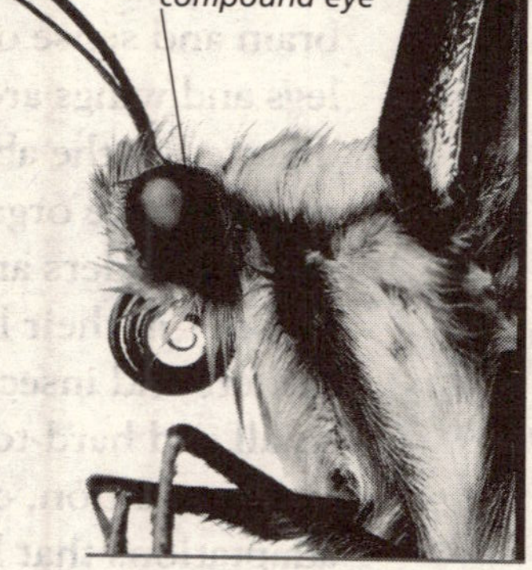


**This butterfly has long, thin antennae with small hairs for smelling, feeling, and tasting.**

**Jumping spiders are the largest family of spiders, named for their ability to jump long distances. They have excellent eyesight.**

**This raft spider has hairs on its pedipalps that are sensitive to vibrations and touch.**

The ommatidia are spread all over the large eyes, allowing insects to see all around them. They make detailed images in the insects' brain. An insect's vision depends on the number of ommatidia. Insects with few ommatidia have poor vision, while insects with many ommatidia have strong vision. Most insects also have three other eyes, called ocelli, which detect levels of light, although they can't form images in the insect's brain. They often tell an insect when to be active and when to rest.

Spiders do not have compound eyes. Their eyes have only one lens. Most spiders have two or four pairs of eyes, grouped in one, two, or three rows. The way the eyes are lined up differs among different types of spiders. The eyes are found on the cephalothorax.

Spiders also use other sensory organs. They have hairs all over them, on their four pairs of legs and pedipalps, that they use to sense vibrations and touch. Their ability to feel through these hairs allows spiders to feel the environment around them and "hear" a predator or prey nearby.

In addition, spiders have another kind of hair on their legs that they use to taste things. Spiders use these hairs for finding food. They use other body structures to eat their food.

Science

# EPIDEMIC

by Lillian Duggan

| Genre | Comprehension Skill | Text Features | Science Content |
|---|---|---|---|
| Nonfiction | Make Inferences | • Captions<br>• Glossary | Cells |

Scott Foresman Science 6.2

# What did you learn?

1. Name two types of microorganisms that cause infectious diseases.

2. What animal was the main source of plague?

3. What helped put an end to cholera in Europe and North America? Why?

4. **Writing** in Science  Travel has been a major cause of epidemics for hundreds of years. Write to explain how travel and epidemics can be linked. Include details from the book to support your answer.

5. **Make Inferences** Last year, a woman received her first flu vaccine. Will she be protected against the flu this year?

**Vocabulary**

chromosome
diffusion
DNA
endoplasmic reticulum
mitochondria
mitosis
organelle
osmosis
ribosome

**Extended Vocabulary**

cholera
endemic
epidemic
immunization
outbreak
pandemic
toxin

**Picture Credits**
Every effort has been made to secure permission and provide appropriate credit for photographic material. The publisher deeply regrets any omission and pledges to correct errors called to its attention in subsequent editions.

Photo locators denoted as follows: Top (T), Center (C), Bottom (B), Left (L), Right (R), Background (Bkgd).

3 NIBSC/Photo Researchers, Inc.; 5 (TR, CR, CR) ©American Museum of Natural History/DK Images; 6 (TR) The Art Archive; 7 ©David Woodfall/Getty Images; 8 (B) Science Museum, London/HIP/The Image Works, Inc.; 10 (B) ©Peter Turnley/Corbis; 11(TR, CR) John Lepine/The Science Museum, London/DK Images; 12 ©Bettmann/Corbis; 13 ©Kin Cheung/Reuters /Landov, LLC.

Unless otherwise acknowledged, all photographs are the copyright © of Dorling Kindersley, a division of Pearson.

ISBN: 0-328-13975-0

## Glossary

**cholera** — infectious disease of the stomach and intestines

**endemic** — existing all the time in certain places

**epidemic** — an infectious disease that has spread across a large distance and lasted for years

**immunization** — making people immune or resistant to a specific disease

**outbreak** — a sudden increase

**pandemic** — an epidemic that has spread over an entire country or continent, or throughout the entire world

**toxin** — a harmful chemical



# EPIDEMIC

by Lillian Duggan

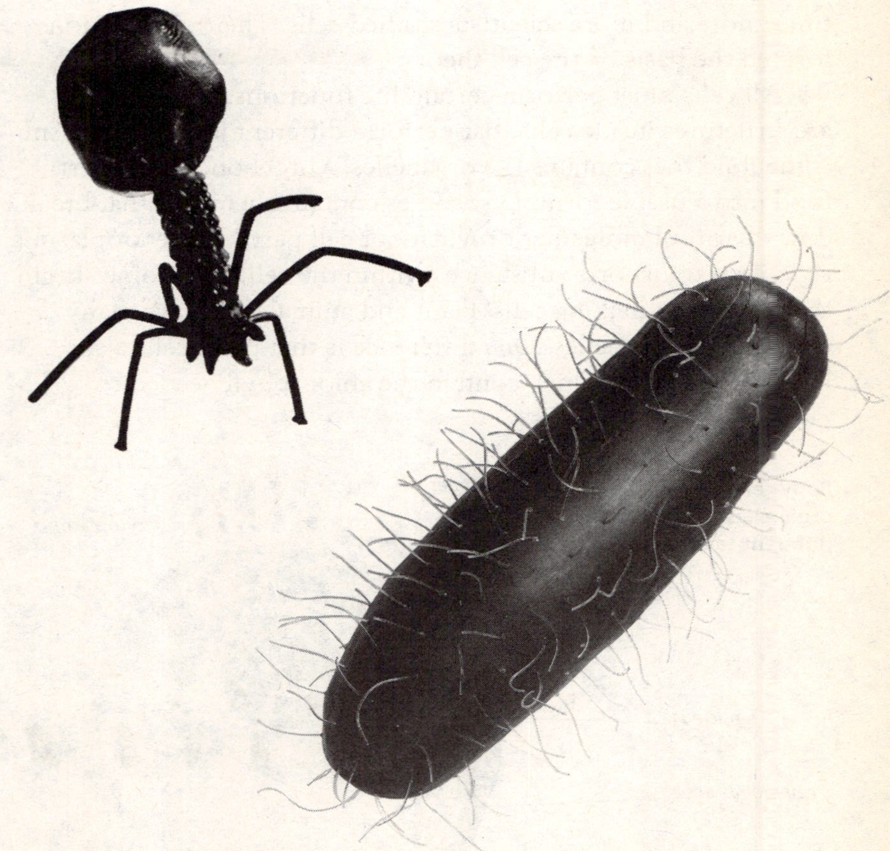

# What You Already Know

All living things are made of cells. A cell is the smallest unit that can carry out the activities necessary for life. Some organisms are made up of only one cell. Each part of a single-celled organism does a particular job. In multicellular organisms, different cells perform different jobs.

Cells were first discovered in 1655 by Robert Hooke. Over time, more and more scientists studied cells. Their observations formed the basis of the cell theory.

All cells must perform certain life functions. Organelles are structures inside cells that perform different jobs. Cytoplasm is the fluid that contains the organelles. Mitochondria convert food into a usable form. Lysosomes contain chemicals that break down harmful molecules or worn-out cell parts. The endoplasmic reticulum transports substances within the cell. Ribosomes begin the process of making cells. Plant and animal cells have many of the same organelles. One difference is that plant cells also have chloroplasts, which contain the chlorophyll needed to perform photosynthesis.

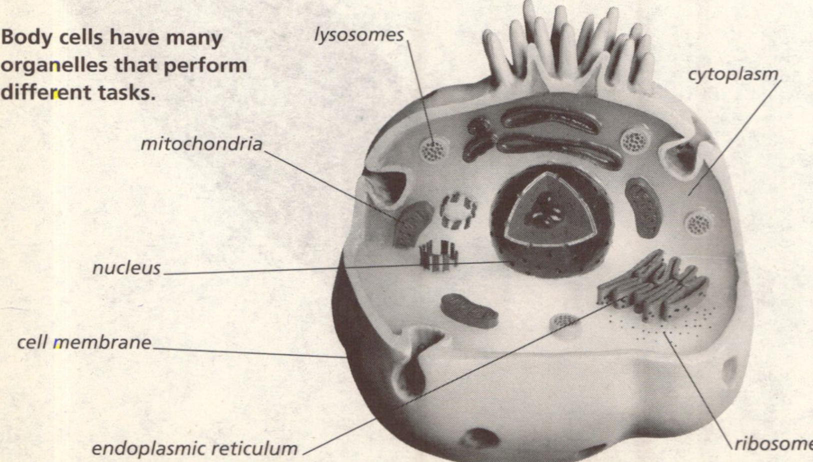


**Body cells have many organelles that perform different tasks.**

Other ways to help prevent the spread of diseases include regular hand-washing and maintaining clean drinking water. Much of the water supply in towns and cities passes through a water treatment facility before it reaches homes. Dirt and other particles are removed from the water, and chemicals may be added to kill harmful microorganisms.

Epidemics occur when infectious diseases spread from person to person over large distances. Epidemics can last many years. Unsanitary conditions, changes in microorganisms, travel, and population growth lead to the quick spread of epidemics. Plague, cholera, and influenza all have cost millions of lives. However, good sanitation and immunization have helped to reduce their impact. These methods of fighting disease are still used today to keep people healthy.

**Regular exercise can help to boost your immunity to disease.**

**Fruits and vegetables are part of a healthy diet.**

# Fighting Infection

Doctors have worked to fight infections by immunizing people. Immunization is making people immune, or resistant, to a specific disease. Vaccination is the most common way of immunizing people.

Vaccines usually are injected into the arm. When the body detects the vaccine, it makes antibodies to fight the disease. Later, if the same disease-causing microorganism enters the body again, the immune system "remembers" these antibodies. It makes the antibodies again, and they destroy the disease. People also can keep their immune system strong by exercising regularly, eating healthy foods, and getting plenty of rest.

**Many people receive immunizations during childhood.**

Cells need substances such as nutrients, salts, and water in order to perform life functions. Nutrients and salts move into and out of the cell by diffusion. When diffusion takes place, a substance moves from an area of higher concentration to an area of lower concentration. Water moves into and out of a cell by osmosis. Osmosis is diffusion across a membrane.

Cells must remain small so that materials don't have to travel too far for life functions to continue. As a cell grows, there isn't enough surface area to allow materials to move into and out of the cell. When cells get too large, they divide. Cell division starts with mitosis, which is the division of the cell's nucleus. DNA is material located in the nucleus that stores information about an organism's growth and development. During mitosis, DNA curls tightly to make rod-shaped bodies called chromosomes. Mitosis ensures that each new cell gets the correct number of chromosomes.

When cells are healthy, they function properly. But sometimes cells come under attack by foreign invaders such as viruses and bacteria. In this book you'll learn more about viruses and bacteria and how the diseases they cause can spread around the world.

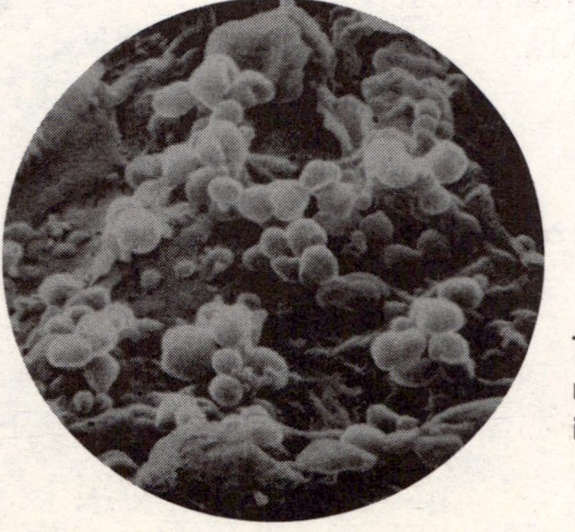

**The measles virus (blue) multiplies through mitosis in an infected cell.**

# Epidemic!

Suppose you wake up and realize your throat is sore and your nose is running. Your body has been invaded by a virus. Lucky for you, this virus is not very dangerous. It causes only the common cold, one of many infectious diseases that are caused by microorganisms such as viruses and bacteria. Microorganisms, also known as microbes, can be carried by animals or humans, or through the air. This is one way infectious diseases can spread.

Viruses are the smallest microorganisms. Many viruses consist of DNA surrounded by a protein coat. A virus can survive only when it is inside the cells of a living being, called a host. When a virus encounters a host cell, it injects its DNA into the host's cytoplasm. The viral DNA enters the cell nucleus and instructs the cell to make copies of the virus. The host cell is destroyed. Copies of the virus are released and can infect other cells.

Bacteria are tiny, single-celled organisms that live just about everywhere. Many bacteria are helpful to humans, but some cause disease. Bacteria enter the body through the mouth, the nose, or cuts in the skin. Once inside, they multiply. When their numbers are high enough, bacteria can cause an infection to begin. Some infections are caused by toxins. Toxins are harmful chemicals that certain bacteria release into the body.

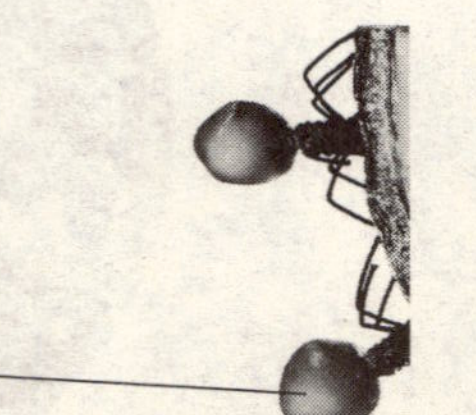

**A virus attacks a host cell and multiplies.**

*1. The virus encounters a host cell.*

Researchers closely followed the spread of the pandemic of 1957–1958. It began in Southeast Asia where animals such as ducks, chickens, and pigs live in close contact with humans. Since flu viruses move easily between animals and humans, these conditions led to many outbreaks.

The virus left Southeast Asian cities such as Hong Kong and Singapore on ships and airplanes. Within six months, it spread around the world.

Today, we have vaccines to help protect us from the flu. Doctors recommend that people who are especially susceptible to the flu be vaccinated regularly. But flu infection can be difficult to stop. Vaccines give people immunity to a particular strain. Having immunity from one strain does not prevent infection from another strain. Flu viruses can change very quickly into new strains against which people do not have immunity.

**Wearing a surgical mask may help prevent the spread of flu infection.**

# Influenza

Influenza, commonly known as the flu, is a viral disease. It causes symptoms such as fever, aching muscles, and coughing. Like all viral diseases, the flu cannot be cured—medicines only ease the symptoms. Most people's bodies can handle the flu. However, young children, the elderly, and people with respiratory problems may be severely affected.

The flu often breaks out in epidemics. Two flu pandemics have occurred in the recent past, one between 1918 and 1920 and the other between 1957 and 1958. The pandemic of 1918–1920 spread around the world. Many of the soldiers serving in World War I were affected. Fifteen million people died in the war, but influenza killed at least twenty million!

When people started living in urban communities, infectious diseases became a threat because they could pass easily from person to person. Many infectious diseases affect a small number of people and last for a short period of time. But sometimes infectious diseases spread across large distances, infecting many people and lasting for years. These diseases are called epidemics. If an epidemic spreads throughout a country, a continent, or the entire world, it is called a pandemic. Other infectious diseases are endemic, meaning they exist all the time in certain places.



An army isolation hospital in Maine in 1918 housed many flu victims.

# What causes an epidemic?

Epidemics thrive in crowded places. Infectious diseases have the opportunity to spread easily when many people live, work, or travel in close quarters. Countries with large populations living in small areas are more likely to experience epidemics.

One reason some diseases spread easily is that symptoms don't appear right away. When people are first infected with a virus, they usually don't even know it. Infected people might ride on a crowded train before beginning to feel any symptoms. By the time they feel ill, they may already have infected other people.

How are epidemics able to start and then disappear? One reason is that microorganisms are constantly changing. After a new infectious disease surfaces, people build resistance to it over a long period of time. The immune system learns to recognize the disease and fight it. But bacteria and viruses can also adapt. They change into new strains that the immune system can't fight, and people therefore become infected quickly.

Crowded slums like this one were common in nineteenth-century England.

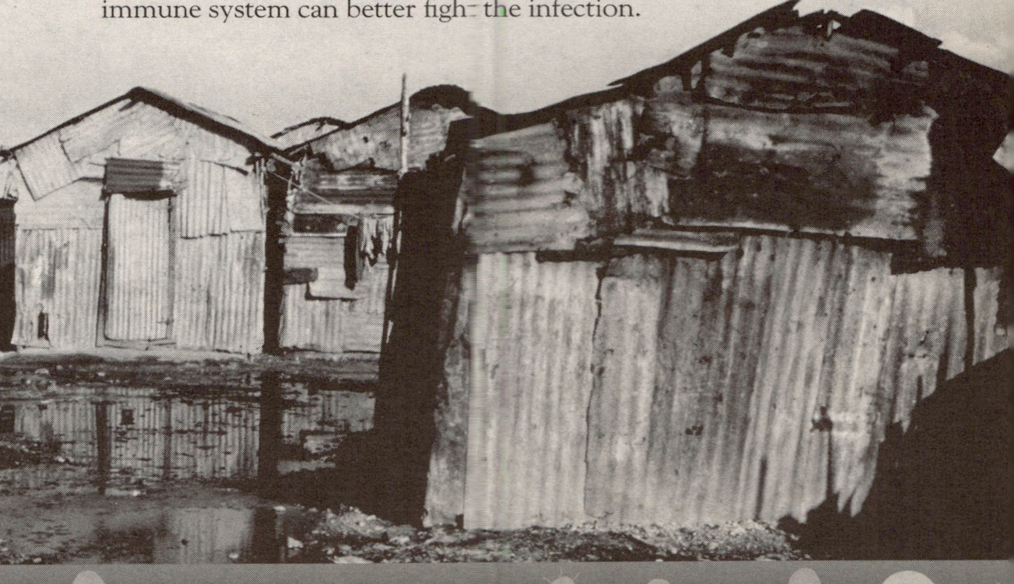

Infectious diseases can spread easily in a crowded commuter train such as this one.

An outbreak in London in 1854 led people to realize that poor sanitation caused the cholera bacteria to thrive. Sanitation and drinking water conditions then improved in Europe and North America, putting an end to the cholera epidemic in these regions.

Some places still have outbreaks of cholera. People may live in areas where sanitation is poor and drinking water is contaminated. In 1991, a foreign ship released thousands of gallons of cholera-infected water into a harbor in Lima, Peru. Foods that were washed or cooked in the contaminated water became infected. Cholera quickly spread throughout Latin America.

Today, cholera victims can be treated with a simple rehydration kit. The kit contains powdered medicine and a dosing spoon. Once the body is rehydrated, the immune system can better fight the infection.

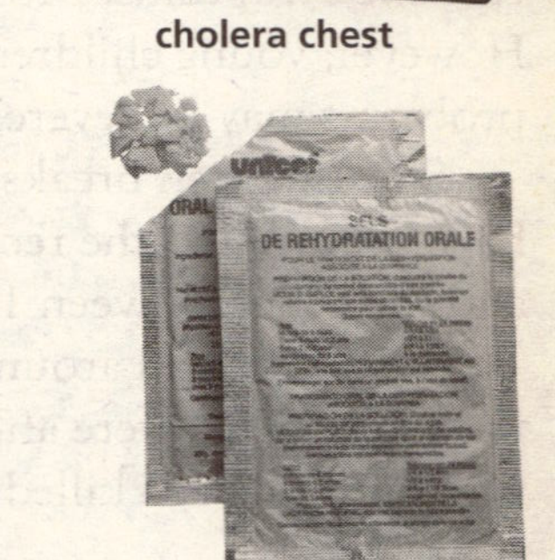

cholera chest

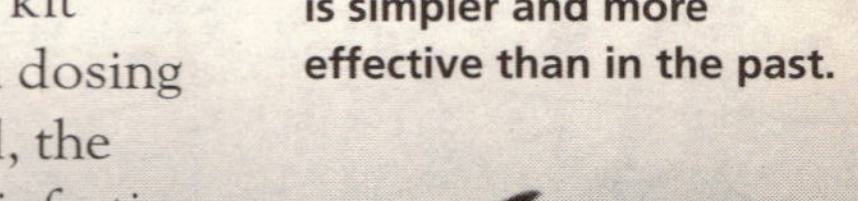

rehydration kit

Cholera treatment today is simpler and more effective than in the past.

# Cholera

Cholera occurs when water is contaminated with the cholera bacterium. When these bacteria enter the body, they multiply in the intestines and release toxins. Symptoms of cholera include vomiting and diarrhea. These can lead to dehydration, which is the loss of body fluids and salts.

The first cholera epidemic began in the early 1800s in India. Sailors and traders who visited India became infected. When they set sail for other lands, they took the deadly disease with them. The epidemic first spread to Asia and the Middle East. By 1832, it reached Europe and the United States.

Like plague, people did not know what caused cholera. For years, they were unable to stop it. All they could do was treat the symptoms. Many travelers carried chests containing medicine to reduce symptoms. Drinking fluids also helped to guard against dehydration.

In places made up of makeshift houses built in unsanitary conditions, cholera outbreaks still occur.

Other factors also contribute to the spread of disease. Water pollution results in ideal conditions for disease-causing microorganisms to live and breed. Polluted water has led to epidemics of diseases such as cholera.

Travel has been a major cause of the spread of epidemics for hundreds of years. When merchants and traders began exploring new lands in the 1300s, they brought diseases with them. Christopher Columbus's journey to the New World resulted in the deaths of many people from diseases such as smallpox and measles.

As the human population increases, people and animals live closer and closer together. This has made people more susceptible to diseases carried by animals. In tropical areas around the world, forests have been cut down to make room for farms and cities. These tropical forests had been home to disease-transmitting mosquitoes for hundreds of years. Today, when people make plans to cut down forests, they must take special measures to reduce the threat posed by these insects.

If people drink polluted water, they can become very ill.

# Plague

Epidemics of infectious diseases have occurred throughout history. Some epidemics are recurrent, meaning they have appeared more than once. Perhaps the most famous recurrent epidemic are those caused by plague. Over the past fifteen hundred years, four major plague epidemics have come and gone. The first began in Egypt in the sixth century.

Starting in the 1300s, a second great epidemic, known as the Black Death, swept through the Middle East and Europe. In medieval Europe, many people lived in crowded and unsanitary conditions, allowing plague to spread rapidly. The populations of many cities were cut in half. When plague hit, fear spread. Many people abandoned their homes. When a third outbreak, known as the Great Plague, reached London in 1665, royalty and wealthy people fled the city to seek safety in the country. Unfortunately, rural areas were as unsafe from plague as the cities were. The Great Plague took close to 100,000 lives in London alone.

People were unable to stop plague because they didn't know what caused it. During the 1600s, some believed plague was caused by foul air. They carried little pomander boxes of aromatic substances. Some looked to other healers for a cure.

Black rats that lived on ships carried plague around the world.

Several outbreaks occurred throughout Europe until the cycle ended in 1750. However, a fourth epidemic began in China a century later. As it spread worldwide, it became a pandemic.

After hundreds of years of recurring epidemics that killed millions, the cause of plague and a cure were finally found. Scientists discovered that plague is caused by black rats that carry a certain bacterium. The bacterium spreads it to fleas that live on the rats. The fleas then pass the bacteria on to humans when they bite. Since black rats live near people, the fleas are able to find hosts easily. In 1896, a vaccine was developed to protect people from plague. A vaccine is a weakened form of a disease that helps the immune system defend itself.

Occasional outbreaks of plague have occurred in recent history. During the Vietnam War, plague hit the country of Vietnam. Another epidemic broke out in India in 1994, killing about fifty people. Thanks to the vaccine and to modern antibiotics, these outbreaks do not have the devastating effects of plague epidemics of the past.

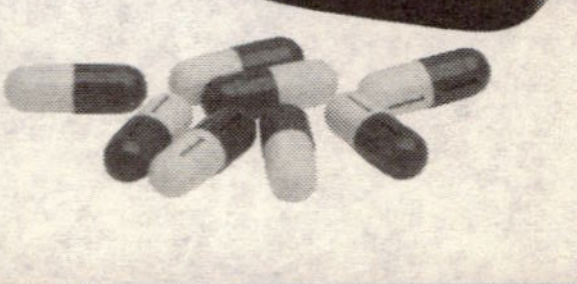

Pomanders, like this one, were thought to help keep the plague away.

Today, people infected with plague are treated with antibiotics.

# Continuing the Species

by Beth Parlikar

| Genre | Comprehension Skill | Text Features | Science Content |
|---|---|---|---|
| Nonfiction | Sequence | • Captions<br>• Maps<br>• Glossary | Reproduction |

**Scott Foresman Science 6.3**

PEARSON
Scott Foresman

DK

ISBN 0-328-13978-5

90000

9 780328 139781

scottforesman.com

# What did you learn?

**Vocabulary**

asexual reproduction
egg cell
fertilization
gene
heredity
meiosis
selective breeding
sexual reproduction
sperm cell

**Extended Vocabulary**

allele
dizygotic
genome
molecule
monozygotic
propagate
protein
replication
somatic cell

1. What is the difference between a gene and an allele?

2. How does a mutation cause a new trait?

3. How are monozygotic and dizygotic twins different?

4. **Writing** in Science  Genes are very important in determining our traits. Write to explain how genes are related to traits and how new traits can appear in individuals. Include details from the book to support your answer.

5. **Sequence** What is the sequence of steps taken by people who wish to breed a new type of organism with certain traits?



**Picture Credits**
Every effort has been made to secure permission and provide appropriate credit for photographic material.
The publisher deeply regrets any omission and pledges to correct errors called to its attention in subsequent editions.

Photo locators denoted as follows: Top (T), Center (C), Bottom (B), Left (L), Right (R), Background (Bkgd).

Scott Foresman/Dorling Kindersley would like to thank: 7 (TR) NASA.

Unless otherwise acknowledged, all photographs are the copyright © of Dorling Kindersley, a division of Pearson.

ISBN: 0-328-13978-5

# Glossary

| | |
|---|---|
| allele | one of two or more versions of the same gene |
| dizygotic | developing from two separately fertilized eggs (zygotes); this term is used to refer to fraternal twins |
| genome | all of the genetic information that an offspring inherits from its parent(s) |
| molecule | a tiny particle consisting of two or more atoms |
| monozygotic | developing from one fertilized egg (zygote); this term is used to refer to identical twins |
| propagate | to cause a plant or animal to reproduce |
| protein | a class of molecules composed of amino acids; supports growth or function of organisms |
| replication | the production of precise copies of materials such as molecules |
| somatic cell | any cell of the body, excluding the sex cells |





# Continuing the Species

by Beth Parlikar

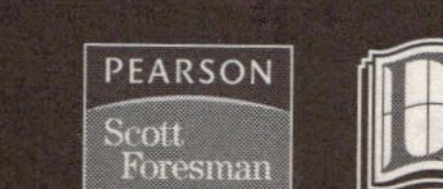

PEARSON
Scott Foresman

DK

# What You Already Know

All organisms inherit many of their traits from their parents in a process called heredity. The instructions for making an organism are found in its DNA. DNA forms long strands called chromosomes in every cell. Each species has a certain number of chromosomes. Chromosomes are divided up into sections called genes. Each gene gives the instructions for making a molecule that contributes to a trait.

DNA looks like a twisted ladder, with rungs made up of materials called bases. The bases come in pairs, and the order of the pairs determines the instructions the cell gets. During mitosis, the ladder divides in half and gets copied, forming two ladders of DNA. A mutation happens when an error is made in copying the DNA, changing the instructions given by a gene.

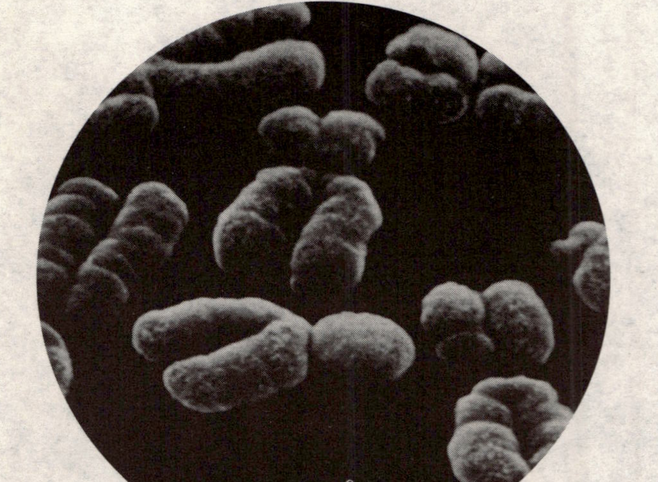

This highly magnified photo shows pairs of chromosomes made up of DNA.

# Conclusion

Although all people are very closely related in their DNA sequence, each person is also unique. This is a result of sexual reproduction, which creates new combinations of genes in every new individual. This is very different from asexual reproduction, in which each offspring is an exact copy of its parent.

Sometimes people inherit many traits from their parents. Other times new traits may show up. These might be recessive traits that were hidden in our parents' genomes, or they might be the result of new mutations in the cells that formed us. Monozygotic, or identical, twins are a special case because they have the exact same DNA. This means that they have many identical traits, but events in their lives can make them develop unique traits as well.

Scientists are now working to understand the secrets contained within the human genome sequence. They hope to learn what instructions our many genes give to our cells, and how changes in those instructions can lead to differences in traits. In the future, it is hoped that cures for diseases will be found using the knowledge gained from studying our genes.



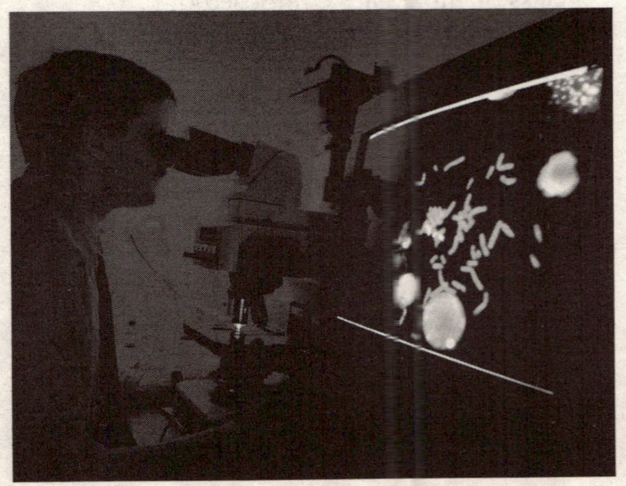

Scientists are still working to unlock the secrets of our chromosomes.

# The Human Genome

Many people think that if we can decode the instructions given by our genes to our cells, we can learn how the body works, and maybe even figure out how to prevent diseases. The Human Genome Project was started in 1990 to figure out the exact pattern of our DNA. The human genome is the full set of DNA carried by each person in every one of his or her cells. Although all individuals have some differences in their DNA which give them unique traits, we are all pretty much identical at the DNA level. This includes people from all races and cultures.

In 2003, fifty years after the discovery of the structure of DNA, scientists finished figuring out the human genome sequence. Now they are beginning the hard part: discovering what the sequence tells us about ourselves.

**Every human body cell has 23 pairs of chromosomes, for a total of 46. The sex cells have only one of each.**

Species survive over the generations because parents pass their traits on to their offspring. Organisms can reproduce by either asexual or sexual reproduction. In asexual reproduction there is only one parent, which makes a copy of itself through the process of mitosis.

In sexual reproduction, sex cells from two parents combine to form a zygote in a process called fertilization. An egg cell from the female parent combines with a sperm cell from the male parent. Offspring produced by sexual reproduction have unique DNA traits because they have a mixture of the mother's and father's DNA. This is an important advantage of sexual reproduction because there is a greater chance of the species surviving. The advantages of asexual reproduction are that it can happen quickly, does not use energy for making sex cells, and it requires just one parent.

Selective breeding is used to develop plants or animals with desirable traits by choosing a few parents with those traits. For example, selective breeding has resulted in dog breeds with different traits.

In this book you will learn about what makes you unique, what makes identical twins alike, how we inherit many physical traits from our parents, and the effect of mutating genes. You will also learn about the latest scientific findings about genes, heredity, and the continuation of the species, such as our own.

**There are many varieties of dog breeds due to selective breeding.**

# Continuing the Species

Many people look a lot like one or both of their parents. Some may even look very similar to an aunt, uncle, or grandparent. Do you have your mother's hair, your father's nose, or your grandfather's height? Do people tell you that your brother or sister looks a lot like you? If so, there is a good explanation: heredity.

Heredity means that we inherit traits from our parents. The information for these traits is carried in the nucleus of each of our cells by a chemical called DNA. DNA comes in long strands. The strands are divided into small sections called genes. The patterns of chemicals contained within these genes instruct our cells to make certain molecules. These molecules might help to determine our eye color or the shape of our ears. Our genes also help determine how healthy we will be or which diseases we may get during our lives.

**Many family members have traits in common.**

## Test for Color Blindness

Color blindness can be caused by mutations in genes on the X chromosome. Look at the illustration. Can you see the number 68? If you can, then you do not have color blindness.

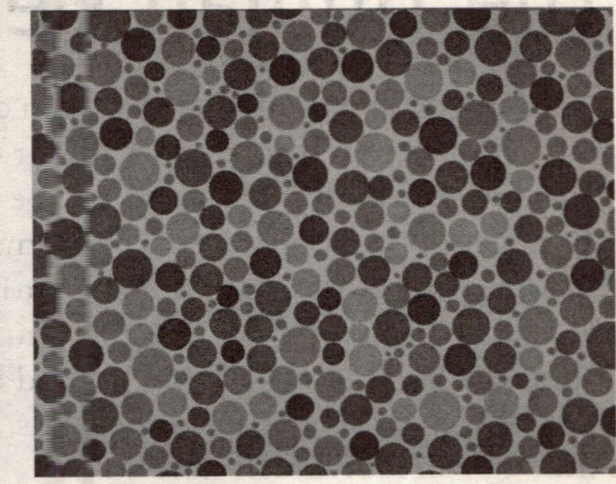

Unfortunately, there are also many mutations that have negative effects. Many defects and diseases are caused by mutation of a single gene. One defect that can be caused by a single gene mutation is color blindness. The gene for color vision is on the X chromosome. Females have two X chromosomes, while males have one X and one Y chromosome. If a color vision gene is mutated on a male's single X chromosome, he will be color blind. In order for a female to be color blind, both copies of her color vision genes must be mutated. It is much less likely for a person to inherit two mutant copies than to inherit just one. That is why more men than women are color blind.

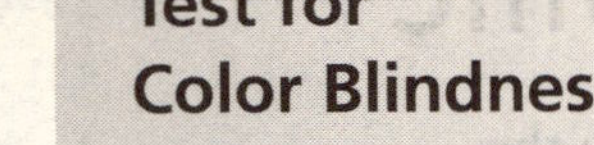

# Mutation

As you read earlier, DNA is constantly dividing and making exact copies of itself. But sometimes the copies don't come out quite right. Most of these mistakes make no difference in the function of the cell, because they don't happen in a part of the DNA that contains a gene. If a mistake happens in a part of the DNA that contains a particular gene, the instructions given by that gene to the cell can be changed. In some cases, the protein usually made by that gene might not be made anymore. If the mistake happens in a sex cell, the offspring created by that cell will inherit the mistake in the DNA. When a change happens in the DNA inherited by an offspring, and this change affects a trait, it is called a mutation.

Some mutations have good effects. They might make the offspring bigger or healthier or better adapted to the environment. Mutations can also be neutral. A mutation could make someone have red hair when the rest of the family has dark hair.

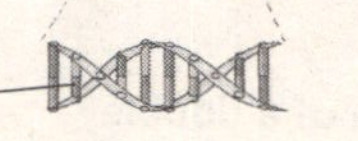

Some of these mice have been affected by mutation.

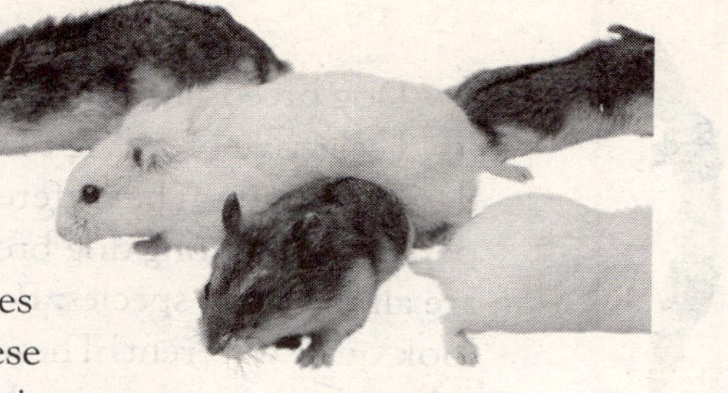

Albino rabbits have mutations affecting fur and eye pigmentation.

Genes are grouped together on chromosomes, which are very long strands of DNA. Chromosomes are found in the nuclei of all of our cells. Except for sex cells, each cell in our body contains forty-six chromosomes. The chromosomes come in pairs, with one half of each pair coming from each parent. This means that each of our cells has two copies of every gene.

Scientists have figured out the sequence of the DNA making up the human chromosomes. The collection of all the genes on all the chromosomes is known as the genome. So far scientists have identified about 30,000 genes in the human genome. This information can help us learn more about the causes of hereditary diseases and thus help us cure them.

## Structure of a Cell

*Cells contain many parts, including the nucleus.*

*The nucleus contains all the pairs of chromosomes.*

*A chromosome is a very long piece of DNA that coils up on itself.*

*DNA strands get wound up tightly so the chromosomes will fit into the nucleus.*

*Genes are pieces of chromosomes that carry particular instructions.*



27

# Genes and DNA

Every cell contains all of the instructions needed to make the organism of which the cell is a part. These instructions are contained in a chemical called DNA, or deoxyribonucleic acid. DNA forms very long strands, called chromosomes. The chromosomes are found in the nucleus of each cell. Each somatic (body) cell has two copies of each chromosome. One of those copies originally came from the mother, and the other came from the father. In humans there are twenty-three pairs of chromosomes, or forty-six chromosomes altogether.

DNA molecules have the shape of a double helix, which looks like a twisted ladder. The rungs of the ladder are made of pairs of chemicals called bases. There are four different bases, and each base can pair up with only one other base. As you can see in the picture, Adenine (A) pairs only with Thymine (T), and Cytosine (C) only with Guanine (G). These patterns of different pairs of bases are like a code for the information contained in the DNA. Short segments of this code are called genes. These different genes control an organism's characteristics.

Your body is constantly renewing itself by creating new cells. It does this through a process called mitosis, in which cells divide and make an exact copy of themselves. Before cells divide they need to copy all of their DNA so that the new cell gets a full set of instructions. During DNA replication, the double helix gets split right down the middle, and each split-off half generates a new half, leaving two new strands of DNA.

Thymine (T) pairs with Adenine (A).

Cytosine (C) pairs with Guanine (G).

**DNA takes the shape of a double helix, similar to a twisted ladder.**

Dog breeds are another good example of how people have used selective breeding to develop new types of organisms with desirable traits. The differences in size, color, body shape, and personality among dog breeds make it difficult to believe that they are all the same species. For example, a toy poodle and a collie look quite different. These breeds were created when people selected dogs with traits that they liked and bred them together. From the offspring were then selected the healthiest dogs with those traits, and the breeding continued this way through the generations. If a farmer wanted a large dog to protect his sheep, he would get the two largest dogs he could find and breed them together. If this was done again and again for generations, the dogs would become very large.

**Breeding dogs with certain traits has created different dog breeds.**





28

# Mixing the Genes

Humans have known about the advantage of changing traits for thousands of years and have put it to good use. For example, the earliest farmers chose to grow wheat plants with characteristics that made them easier to farm. Wild wheat plants pop open and drop their seeds all over the ground, which makes it almost impossible for people to gather them up in large amounts. Thousands of years ago, farmers found a wheat plant that didn't pop open and drop its seeds. They bred this useful plant, and farming became easier. Scientists today are still trying to breed wheat plants with better resistance to diseases, insects, and drought, and with better nutritional value.

Some crop plants have been developed much more recently. Pink grapefruit is one example. About seventy years ago, farmers in Florida and Texas discovered pink grapefruits growing in the orchards with the normal white grapefruits. The farmers selected the plants that grew pink grapefruits and propagated them, and today pink grapefruit is a very common and popular variety.

Breeding developed new types of fruits, such as pink grapefruit and orange tomatoes.

Adenine (A) pairs only with Thymine (T).

Guanine (G) pairs only with Cytosine (C).

Genes allow cells to function and determine an organism's characteristics by directing cells to make proteins. Proteins are molecules that perform a variety of jobs in cells. They form fibers such as hair and muscle. They help to digest food and convert it into energy. Proteins repair cells when they get damaged, and they direct the processes of mitosis and meiosis.

How do genes determine an organism's characteristics by making proteins? They do it in a number of complex ways. One simple example is flower color. If the cells of a plant contain a copy of a gene that makes a protein that can make a red pigment, then the flowers will be red. Another plant might have a gene that makes a protein that makes a paler pigment. That plant's flowers will be pink.

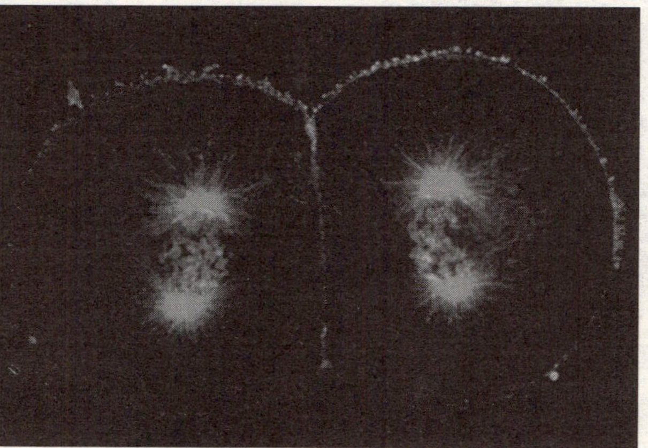

Body cells multiply through the process of mitosis.

# Heredity

While many people look a lot like one or both of their parents, children and their parents are never identical. This is because offspring get a mixture of their parents' DNA. Half of the DNA comes from the mother and half from the father. Each gene that determines a trait has two copies in every cell. It is the combination of those two copies that decides what the trait looks like in the offspring.

Maybe you look very different from your parents and siblings. Or maybe in some ways you look more like an aunt or uncle than like one of your parents. This is not at all unusual. Although all the siblings in a family get half of their parents' DNA, they don't necessarily get the same half!

Some characteristics can be handed down through many generations.

Changing environments are the biggest problem for organisms that use asexual reproduction. Although the identical offspring will do well as long as the environment stays the same, they probably will not do very well if it changes. Environments change often, due to droughts, storms, fires, and other events. Since asexual offspring are almost always exactly like their parents, there is almost no chance that they'll be born with a new trait that will help them deal with the new conditions. They could even die off if conditions change too much.

Sexual reproduction takes more energy and time than asexual reproduction does. It also requires two parents of opposite sexes, which can be a problem if there aren't many members of the species in an area. But sexual reproduction has one big advantage: each and every new offspring has a different set of traits. So some individuals are better suited to their environment than others. If conditions change, some members of the species are bound to be able to do well in the new situation.

## Advantages and Disadvantages

| Sexual | Asexual |
| --- | --- |
| ☑ offspring have new combinations of genes that can help them survive in different conditions | ☒ offspring have little genetic variation and may not survive changing environmental conditions |
| ☒ can take a lot of energy and time | ☑ requires little energy or time |
| ☒ requires two parents | ☑ requires only one parent |

# Sexual or asexual?

Why do many organisms use asexual reproduction to ensure the continuation of their species, while others use sexual reproduction? The answer seems to be that each type of reproduction offers advantages and disadvantages.

Asexual reproduction has many good points. In many cases it can be completed very quickly. It also does not use up very much of the parent's energy. This means that one parent can have a large number of offspring in a short time by reproducing asexually. Another advantage to asexual reproduction is that it only requires one parent. Even if there is not another member of the species anywhere nearby, a lone individual can reproduce. Finally, asexual reproduction produces offspring that are exact copies of the parent. If the parent is successful in a particular environment, there is a good chance that its offspring will survive too, as long as conditions don't change.

The buff wax cap fungus can reproduce sexually or asexually.

Aphids reproduce sexually and asexually. They make young quickly by asexual reproduction, but also mate and lay eggs before winter.

*newly cloned aphids*

Sperm and egg cells combine to form a zygote.

The process that determines which parts of the DNA are put into the sperm or egg cell is random. On top of that it is random which egg and sperm come together to form the zygote. When you look at it this way, it's not at all surprising that some people look different from their family members. This is true for all sexually reproducing forms of life. For example, purebred dogs may look much like their parents, but there are always some differences.

You could say that no two individuals are genetically identical. However, there is one exception to this rule: identical twins.

These kittens look similar to their mother, but they are not identical to her or to each other.

# Twin Life

Twins are born in about one out of every seventy births. Two-thirds of twins are fraternal or dizygotic. Fraternal twins are conceived when two *(di)* eggs are fertilized, each by a different sperm. The two zygotes develop together and are born at the same time, but aside from that they are no more alike than any other siblings.

About one-third of twins are identical, or monozygotic. Monozygotic twins come from one *(mono)* zygote. This means that one sperm fertilized one egg to create a zygote. But instead of going on to form a single baby, the zygote split into two cells, each of which developed into a separate baby. Because they come from the same original cell (the zygote), monozygotic twins are genetically identical.

identical twins

Potato plants have a very good strategy for keeping their species going. They can reproduce either sexually or asexually. Most potato plants can make seeds if their flowers get pollinated. However, most farmers prefer to reproduce their potato plants by using the potatoes like "seeds." If the flowers don't get fertilized, each "eye" on a potato can grow into a whole potato plant. This way the new plant is a genetic copy, or clone, of the plant that made the potato.

The whiptail lizard may have the most surprising way of reproducing. Lizards are complex animals that usually use sexual reproduction. But some species of whiptails can have babies without the need for sperm cells. These species are all female. They lay eggs that contain all the necessary chromosomes and develop into normal, female lizards. The only difference is that no sperm are needed to fertilize the egg, and all the offspring are clones: they have the same DNA as their mother.

Potato plants can reproduce sexually using their flowers, or asexually through the buds or "eyes" on the potato.

Some species of whiptail lizards reproduce asexually.

32

# Asexual Reproduction

So far we've focused on humans, who have offspring by sexual reproduction. Many life forms use asexual reproduction to carry on their species, resulting in offspring genetically identical to the parent. For example, all bacteria reproduce asexually. Because each bacterium is just a cell, it can reproduce by simply going through mitosis once, making two cells from the original one. Bacterial reproduction can happen in just twenty minutes! Such quick reproduction is a big advantage in keeping a species going.

Some other organisms that reproduce asexually do so in different ways. Hydra are simple animals that live in the water. They make their homes on the bottom of lakes and eat things that float by. Hydra can reproduce asexually by growing a baby hydra on their side, as shown in this picture. When the new hydra grows big enough, it falls off and starts a life of its own. As with bacteria, the new hydra has exactly the same DNA as its parent, and will grow up to have the same characteristics.

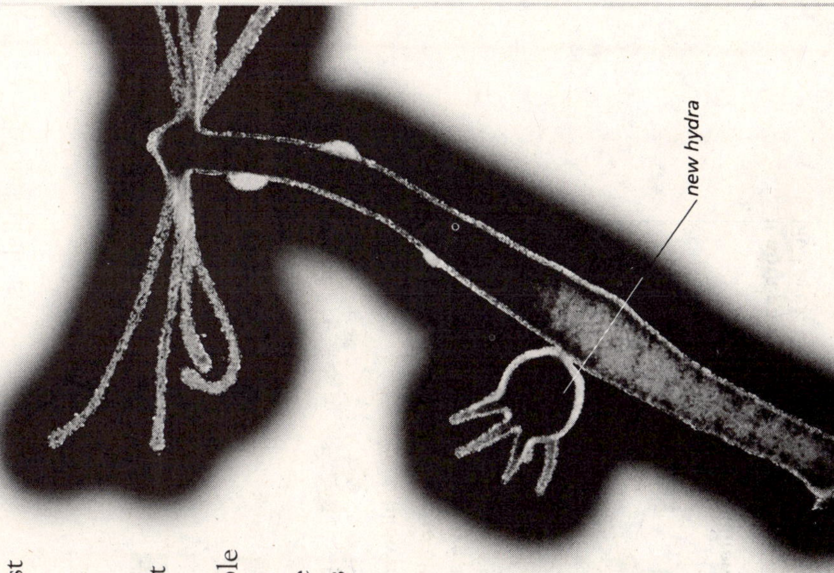


**Hydra reproduce asexually by budding. The new hydra shown here will fall off and grow up to look like its parent.**

## Identical and Nonidentical Twins

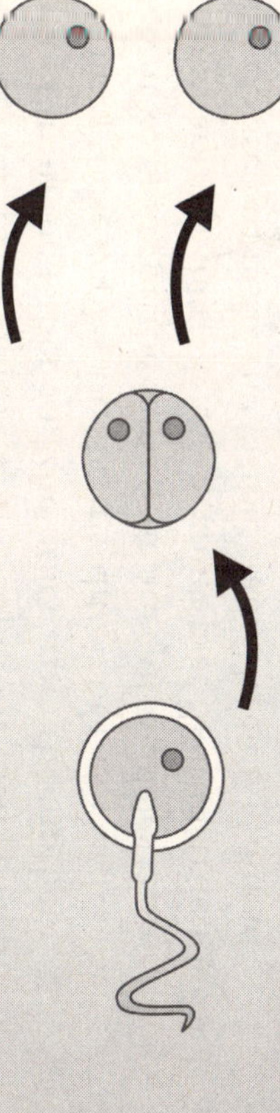

**Fraternal, or dizygotic, twins are conceived when two sperm fertilize two eggs at the same time. This forms two nonidentical zygotes.**

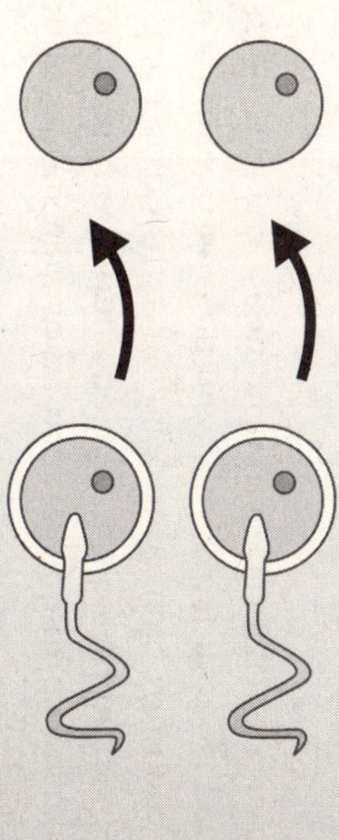

**Identical, or monozygotic, twins occur when a single fertilized egg splits into two separate zygotes. These zygotes have the same DNA.**

Because they have exactly the same DNA, monozygotic twins look identical to each other and often have similar personalities. Slight differences in appearance between identical twins are actually common, and are caused by events that happen while the babies are developing or after they are born. One thing that is always different between identical twins is their finger prints. They tend to be similar but are never exactly the same. So while they may be genetically identical, monozygotic twins are still unique!

Scientists study twins to help learn which traits are mainly determined by genes and which are due to an individual's nutrition, upbringing, and other environmental factors. For instance, studies of twins have shown that diabetes, a very harmful disease, is largely, but not entirely, caused by genes.

# Dominant vs. Recessive

Let's think more about why some people look different from their parents. You may know someone who has blond hair, even though both of that person's parents have dark hair. You may think this is a bit strange. Also, you may know that in most parts of the world, dark hair is more common than blond or red hair. Why is this so?

The answer goes back to genes. Hair color is a visible trait, something that we can easily see by looking at a person. Yet the genes a person carries in all of his or her cells are the cause. We learned earlier that people have two copies of each gene, one inherited from the father and the other from the mother. Sometimes these copies are slightly different from each other. Different versions of the same gene are called alleles. Some alleles are dominant to other alleles, meaning that their instructions will always be used to make the visible trait. The nondominant version is called a recessive allele.

Dark hair is a dominant trait, while blond hair is recessive.

Let's think about what this means for hair color. Suppose that the gene for hair color has two versions. One allele gives the cell instructions to make dark hair, and the other allele tells the cell to make blond hair. Each person gets two genes for this trait, one from the mother and one from the father. If either one contains the dark hair allele, the hair will be dark, because the dark allele is dominant. If both are dark, the hair will also be dark. This is how a dominant trait is expressed. The hair will only be blond if both genes are for blond hair, because the blond allele is recessive.

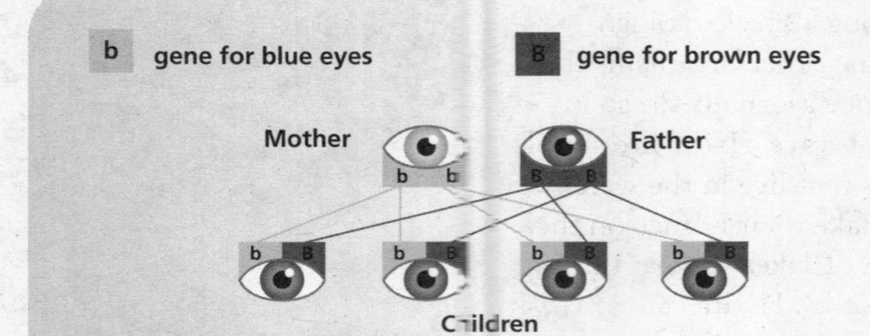


Brown eye color is dominant to blue eye color. If one parent has two copies of the brown eye allele, all of the children will have brown eyes, even if the other parent has blue eyes.

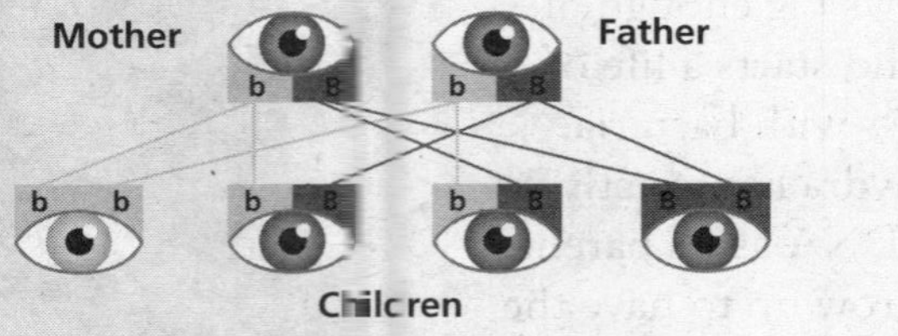

If both parents have brown eyes but carry the recessive allele for blue eyes, they can have children with either blue or brown eyes.

Science

# Body Imaging

by Mary McLean-Hely

| Genre | Comprehension Skill | Text Features | Science Content |
|---|---|---|---|
| Nonfiction | Cause and Effect | • Captions<br>• Maps<br>• Glossary | Body Systems |

Scott Foresman Science 6.4

PEARSON
Scott Foresman

ISBN 0-328-13981-5

9 780328 139811

90000

scottforesman.com

**Vocabulary**

alveoli
antibody
endocrine gland
enzyme
gland
hormone
impulse
neuron
pathogen

**Extended Vocabulary**

compound microscope
computed tomography
  scanning
contrast medium
electron microscope
endoscope
magnetic resonance imaging
positron emission tomography
radionuclide scanning
ultrasound imaging

# What did you learn?

1. Who was Galen?

2. How does an X-ray machine work?

3. What are some uses for ultrasound imaging?

4. **Writing** in Science  EEG and ECG are two tests that have some similarities. What are these similarities? What are the differences? Use examples from the book to support your answer.

5. **Cause and Effect** How has the endoscope changed the way many medical procedures are done and the recovery time patients need following the procedure?



**Picture Credits**
Every effort has been made to secure permission and provide appropriate credit for photographic material. The publisher deeply regrets any omission and pledges to correct errors called to its attention in subsequent editions.

Photo locators denoted as follows: Top (T), Center (C), Bottom (B), Left (L), Right (R), Background (Bkgd).

1 Simon Fraser/Photo Researchers, Inc.; 3 International Museum Of Surgical Science, Chicago/DK Images; 4 Charles Walker/Topfoto/The Image Works, Inc.; 5 Alinari Archives/Corbis; 7 (CR) Science Museum, London/DK Images; 8 (T) David Morbey/©The Natural History Museum, (BL) Omikron/Photo Researchers, Inc.; 9 David M. Phillips/ The Population Council/Photo Researchers, Inc.; 10 ©Science Museum, London/DK Images; 11 (TR) Mediscan/ Visuals Unlimited; 12 Zephyr/Photo Researchers, Inc.; 13 Larry Mulvehill/Photo Researchers, Inc.; 14 Gabe Palmer/Corbis; 15 Custom Medical Stock Photo; 16 (BR) S. Grover/Custom Medical Stock Photo; 17 M. English/ Custom Medical Stock Photo; 18 (BL) Simon Fraser/Photo Researchers, Inc., (BR) ©Science Museum, London/DK Images; 19 Tim Beddow/Photo Researchers, Inc.; 20 A. Pasieka/Photo Researchers, Inc.; 22 (BR) David M. Martin, M. D. / Photo Researchers, Inc., (CR) Science Museum, London/DK Images; 23 (TR) Science Museum, London/DK Images.

Unless otherwise acknowledged, all photographs are the copyright © of Dorling Kindersley, a division of Pearson.

ISBN: 0-328-13981-5

# Glossary

| | |
|---|---|
| **compound microscope** | a microscope that has two lenses— an eyepiece lens and an objective lens |
| **CT scanning** | computed tomography scanning; uses X rays and a computer to make 3-D images of internal organs |
| **contrast medium** | a liquid or other substance that will show up inside the body on an X ray or other type of body imaging |
| **electron microscope** | a microscope that uses beams of electrons to create images of objects too small to be seen by other microscopes |
| **endoscope** | a thin, flexible tube with a light on the end that doctors use to look inside different body cavities |
| **MRI** | magnetic resonance imaging; a method that uses nuclear magnetic resonance to make pictures |
| **PET** | positron emission tomography; injects radioactive tracer into a patient to show processes in the body |
| **radionuclide scanning** | a method that uses radioactive material and X rays to find abnormal activity in the body |
| **ultrasound imaging** | high-frequency sound waves are directed into a part of the body, producing an echo that is then made into an image |



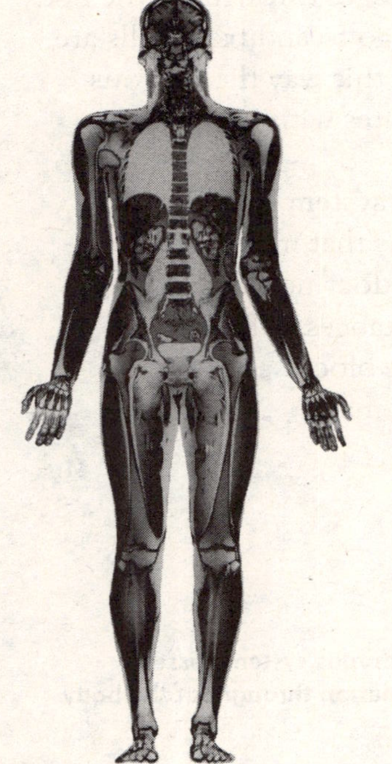

# Body Imaging

by Mary McLean-Hely

# What You Already Know

As you know, cells are the building blocks of your body. Groups of the same cells make up tissues. Groups of tissues make up organs. Groups of organs make up organ systems. The major body systems are the circulatory, digestive, endocrine, excretory, immune, muscular, nervous, reproductive, respiratory, and skeletal systems.

The nervous and endocrine systems control and communicate with all of the other body systems. In the nervous system, nerve cells, called neurons, pass messages throughout the body. The messages that go to and from cells are called impulses. In this way the nervous system communicates with the cells, and vice versa.

The endocrine system is made up of glands, or organs that make chemical substances. The endocrine gland releases these substances, called hormones, into the blood. Hormones control many body functions.

**The nervous system passes information throughout the body.**



## The First Endoscopes

In the early 1800s, doctors first made attempts to look inside the body. Early endoscopes, like the one shown here, were rigid and used a candle for light.

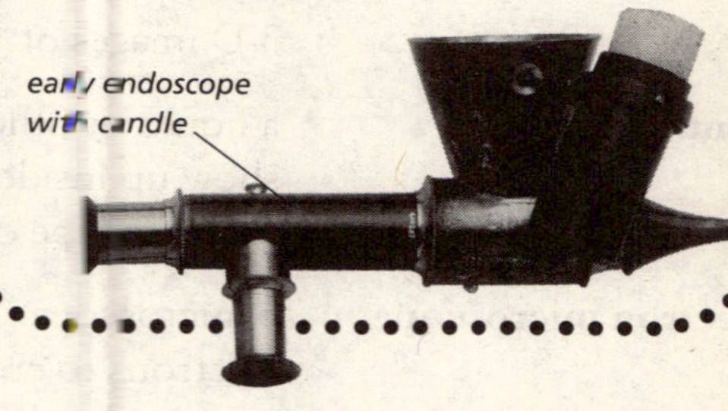

tip of endoscope, which goes inside body

early endoscope with candle

The doctors can make a small opening and insert the endoscope. While watching through the endoscope, they use tiny instruments to complete the surgery. Smaller incisions usually mean a shorter recovery time for the patient.

Body imaging is a complex part of medicine. It offers doctors many ways to see details in the human body that were previously impossible to see. Body imaging allows doctors to diagnose and treat illness, disease, and damage more accurately, thus saving lives. X rays, ultrasound, CT, PET, radionuclide scanning, MRIs, ECG, EEG, and endoscopy all have different applications that help doctors diagnose different problems. And body imaging technology is always improving. In the future, doctors will be able to see even better into the human body.

# Endoscopes

Another tool scientists use to see inside the body is called an endoscope. It is a small tube with a light on the end that doctors can use to look inside different body cavities.

An endoscope is a thin, flexible tube with a lens and light on the end. The tube takes pictures inside the body. A doctor can look at these pictures as the endoscope is moved around. The doctor inserts the endoscope through an opening in the person's body such as the mouth. Sometimes the endoscope is inserted through an incision in the skin. Usually patients are given a local anesthetic so that they don't feel any pain from the procedure.

Doctors also use endoscopes to perform surgery. Small surgical instruments can fit through the endoscope tube. This enables doctors to see inside a patient's body and perform delicate surgical procedures without making a large cut.

**The endoscope is a long, flexible tube with a lens, light sources, and eyepiece.**

*eyepiece*

*Light source attaches here.*

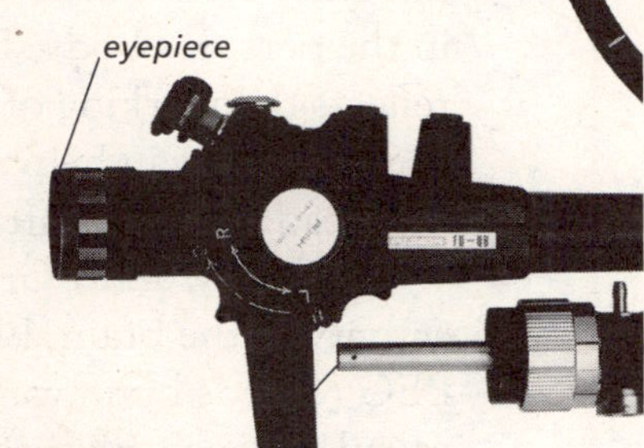

**endoscopic view of the vocal cords**

Another system that contains glands is the digestive system. In the stomach, glands make substances called enzymes that break down proteins.

The respiratory system carries oxygen into the body and removes carbon dioxide. When you breathe in, air moves into your lungs. From there it goes into smaller and smaller tubes. At the end of all these tubes are tiny sacs, called alveoli. The circulatory system works together with the respiratory system. Oxygen enters the blood stream and is carried to the cells. Carbon dioxide moves from the blood into the alveoli and is sent out of the body.

The immune system fights disease. It is constantly fighting off pathogens, organisms that cause disease. One way your body fights pathogens is by producing a type of white blood cell. These cells make antibodies, which are chemicals that kill specific pathogens.

In this book, you will discover how doctors find out what's going on in the different body systems. You will find out how doctors can see into the body and check on how things are working.

**This is an X-ray of a hand.**

# Before Body Imaging

Why do people get sick? What is the cause of a disease? Does diet play a part in health? People have had questions about health for thousands of years. People come up with theories that they try to prove. Over time, as they find out more about the human body, their theories change.

People have tried since ancient times to understand and explain what happens inside the human body. Not being able to see inside, thinkers came up with theories that today seem funny. At the time, however, people took these theories very seriously.

One such theory is that of the "four humors." Greek thinkers came up with this theory in 400 B.C. to explain health and personality. A bodily fluid represented each humor. The four fluids were phlegm, blood, yellow bile, and black bile. The four humors were also connected with seasons, personal traits, organs in the body, and elements in nature.

For hundreds of years, people believed diseases were caused by imbalances in the humors. They thought that good health was the result of the humors being in balance.

The four humors—phlegmatic, sanguine, choleric, and melancholic—were thought to affect the body's health.

# ECG and EEG

An electrocardiogram, or ECG, records the electrical activity in the heart on a screen and on paper. For an ECG, electrodes are put on a person's body. Then the person may need to walk or lie flat while the electrodes take in information about an electrical current in the person's body. This current reflects the working of the heart. In this way an ECG can help show activity that may lead to a heart attack.

Similarly, an EEG, or electroencephalogram, records electrical activity in the brain. Electrodes are put on a person's head. An EEG records brain waves and is often used to diagnose a disease called epilepsy. EEG can also detect brain damage and can chart the different stages of sleep.

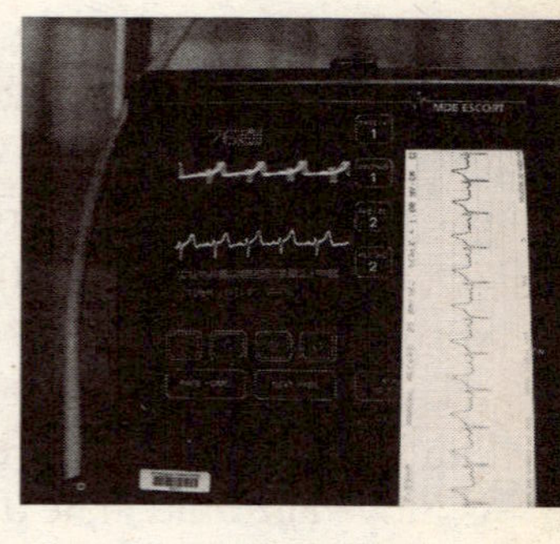

The ECG monitor shows electrical activity in the heart.

**The different stages of sleep as detected on an EEG**

falling asleep

deep sleep

dreaming (REM sleep)

# Radionuclide Scanning

Radionuclide scanning is another form of internal imaging. In this kind of scan, a doctor can inject a small amount of radioactive material into a patient, or the patient can drink it.

A scanner that makes use of X rays reads the levels of radioactivity in organs. Different types of tissue will look different on the scan. In this way doctors can find any abnormal activity in the organs and can make sure that organs are acting the way they should be.

Different types of radionuclide scanning are used for different parts of the body. This type of scanning, shown below, is used on the stomach, liver, bladder, intestines, bones, and other parts. Radionuclide scanning can be used to detect liver cirrhosis, bone cancer, and many other conditions.

In this radionuclide scan of hand bones, the bones are colored orange.

Many drawings of human anatomy appear in the notebooks of Leonardo da Vinci, including this study of the workings of the eye.

The Greeks used this theory to devise medical techniques. One treatment was bloodletting, in which a person was cut in order to bleed. It was thought that this let out the harmful fluids in the body.

An ancient Greek doctor named Galen wrote a book on the four humors called *On the Temperaments*. Galen is one of the most famous ancient doctors. He studied organs by dissecting animals, and wrote books that had a great impact on medicine for hundreds of years.

Much later, in the 1500s, a man who is known for his artistic brilliance, Leonardo da Vinci, studied the human body. Through studying people, da Vinci learned about the circulation of blood and the workings of the human eye. He recorded these studies in his notebooks.

Today it's hard to imagine that people believed that something like bloodletting would help a sick person. Someone living at the time of Galen or da Vinci, though, would have had a hard time believing that a machine could see inside your body! Today we have a whole range of machines that enable us to see into the body.

# Microscopes

Why do scientists use microscopes? To see tiny skin cells, minute antibodies, pathogens, and more. They use them to see things that are too small to be seen otherwise.

One important purpose of microscopes is their use by doctors to see human cells and tissues. Doctors take specimens from their patients. Then they look at the sample through a microscope. This way, they can see what is happening in the cells and tissues.

But how do microscopes help? Microscopes magnify images of tiny objects. There are different types of microscopes. One type is a compound microscope. It has two lenses, an eyepiece lens and an objective lens. Each lens is at an end of the top of the microscope.

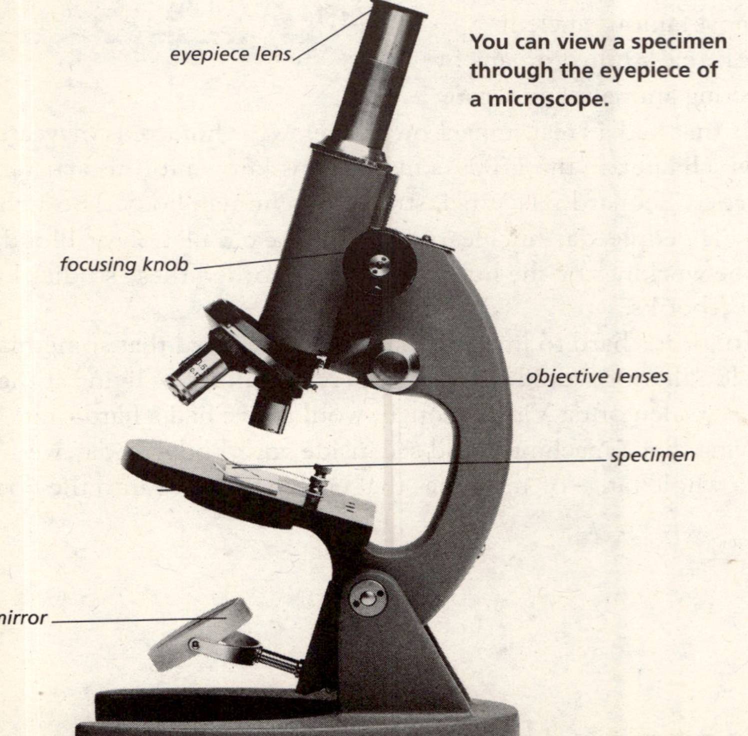


**You can view a specimen through the eyepiece of a microscope.**

# PET

Another way of getting pictures of internal tissues is positron emission tomography, or PET. In PET a radioactive tracer is injected into a patient. A glucose compound is also injected at the same time.

When the positrons from the radioactive tracer hit electrons in tissues, photons are produced. These photons can be recorded by a scanner. This information is used to create a picture of the tissues. The PET can show different processes and reveal data about them, which can help the doctor diagnose disease.

PET scans are often used for getting pictures of the brain. They are useful for diagnosing brain tumors and strokes. They also can be used to detect cancer and heart disease. Different colors on the scan show different levels of activity in an organ. Doctors use this information to tell what is happening in that organ.

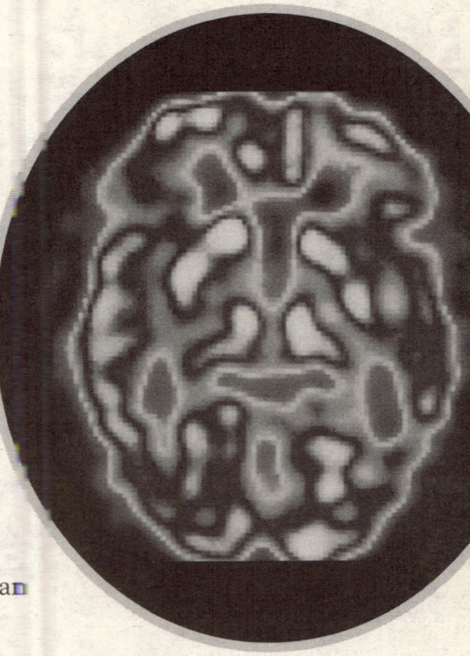

**This PET scan shows brain activity: blue represents low, and yellow represents high.**

# MRI

Magnetic resonance imaging, also known as MRI, is another method doctors use to see inside a patient's body to diagnose illnesses and conditions. MRI makes thin section pictures of any part of the body from any direction. Doctors can use the images to carefully examine internal organs, such as the heart.

MRI uses the principles of nuclear magnetic resonance to make pictures. MRI places the body in a magnetic field and emits radio waves. It stops and then records the body's electromagnetic transmissions. It uses this information to make an image or a map of the body. It makes a picture in a similar way to the CT scan. MRI pictures are very detailed. They are often used for scans of the brain and nervous system.

This MRI scan gives a very detailed image or a colorful map of the body.

An MRI helmet is used when a child's brain needs to be scanned.

Between the two lenses is the focusing knob. This knob adjusts distance between the two lenses so that the specimen is in focus. The specimen rests on a base through which light passes. This light is reflected from the mirror below. When the two lenses are used together, a specimen can be magnified up to two thousand times.

## The First Microscopes

In the 1600s, a Dutch scientist, Antonius van Leeuwenhoek, created a double-convex lens microscope that could magnify objects nearly three hundred times. Microscopes in most schools are based on this one made in Holland. Robert Hooke, an English scientist, also built a microscope in the 1600s. He used it to study the structure of plant cells.

Hooke's microscope

You can observe magnified sweat crystals through a microscope.

# Electron Microscopes

As you know, compound microscopes use more than one lens to magnify. Some objects, however, are too small to be seen with a compound microscope. For these objects scientists use electron microscopes. Electron microscopes do not use light. They use beams of electrons. They can create images of objects, such as viruses, which are too small to be seen by other microscopes.

One type of electron microscope is the scanning electron microscope, or SEM. Using electrons, SEMs can magnify something up to two million times.

A scientist observes a magnified image of an object on a monitor created by using an SEM.

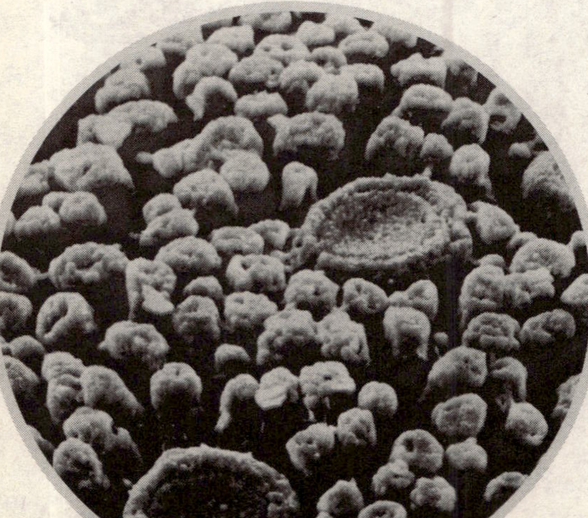

Tiny surface projections on a tongue, called papillae, look like this when seen through an SEM.

Another important difference between a basic X ray and a CT scan is the kind of picture each produces. Basic X-ray images are 2-D, or flat. CT scans make 3-D pictures of parts of the body. This provides doctors with more information to diagnose patients accurately.

As with X rays, contrast medium is used in CT scans. A patient may drink a contrast medium or a doctor may inject one. The contrast medium will make certain organs show up better on the scan.

Doctors use CT scanners to look at the brain after an accident or a stroke. Scanners are also used to see the abdomen, chest, spine, and pelvis.

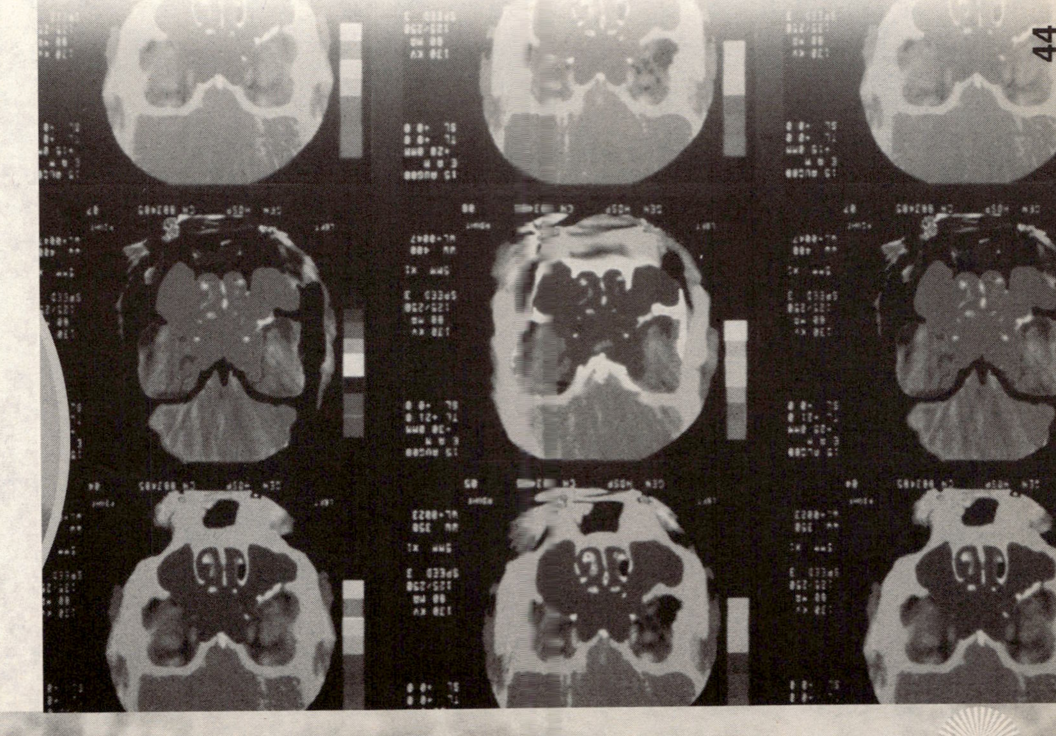

Results of a colorized CT scan of a patient's head

# CT Scanning

CT stands for computed tomography. It is also known as computed axial tomography, or CAT scanning. CT scans use X rays and a computer to make three-dimensional, or 3-D, pictures of the inside of the body.

Sir Godfrey Newbold Hounsfield and Allan MacLeod Cormack developed the CT scan in the late 1960s and 1970s. The first scanners were very slow, often taking several hours. Newer scanners work in just seconds.

In a CT scan, a person lies on a table that moves through the tunnel-like scanner machine. Inside the scanner, beams of X rays are sent through the patient. A detector picks up the X rays. As the person moves through the scanner, the beams and detector move all the way around the body. All the rays picked up by a detector are transformed into 3-D pictures by a computer.

CT scans use X rays, but they provide more detailed pictures than basic X rays. X rays show bones and dense parts of the body; CT scans can show small details and soft tissue in a cross section.

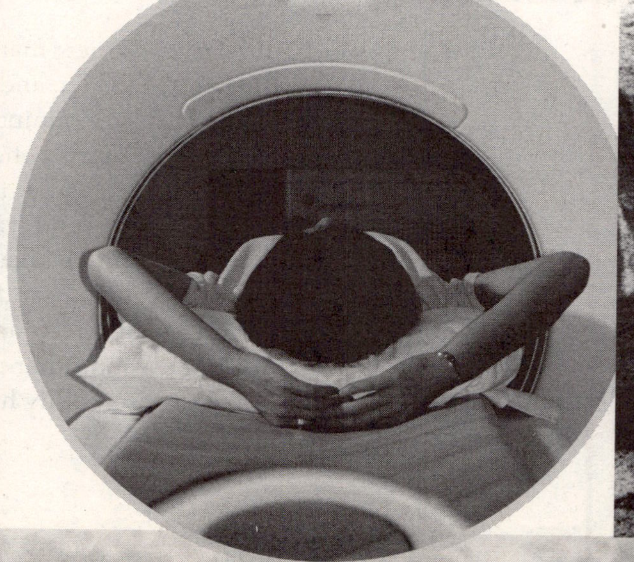

Beams of X rays will be directed at the patient inside the CT scanner. The X rays and detectors move around the patient.



The object that is being magnified first needs to be treated specially to activate the electrons. The electrons are beamed through a column that focuses them on the object. The beam is passed over the object. As it moves, electrons are bounced off the object. The microscope records the movements of the electrons, making a picture. This picture appears on a monitor that scientists view.

A second kind of electron microscope is the transmission electron microscope, or TEM. A TEM directs a beam of electrons through an object. When the electrons reach the object, they are sent in various directions depending on what they hit. The electrons that pass through are recorded and projected on a screen or photographic plate. Scientists read these pictures. TEMs can magnify something up to one million times.

**Magnified image of epithelia, microvilli, and bacteria as seen with a TEM.**

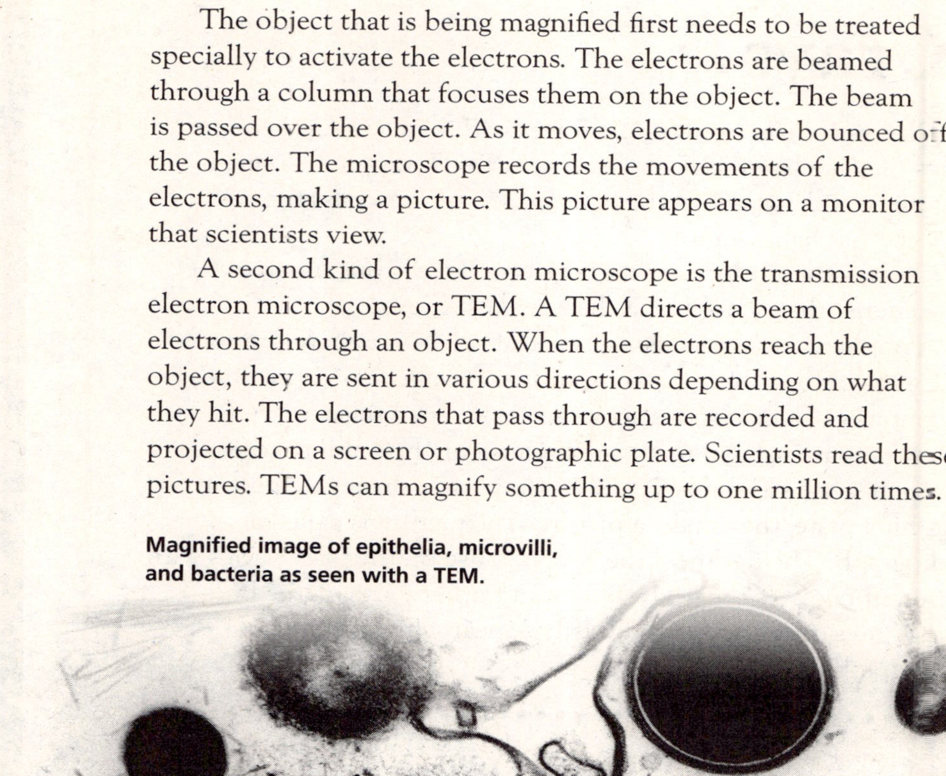

# X rays

X rays are electromagnetic waves with high energy. In some ways they are like the light we can see. But X rays have a much shorter wavelength than the light we see and can pass through objects that light cannot.

X rays are produced when high-speed electrons hit an object. The energy that is not lost as heat makes X rays.

People make X rays using a special tube. X rays are produced in a glass bulb with no gases or air inside, called an X-ray tube. It contains two electrodes, an anode, and a cathode.

X rays are used in medicine because of their ability to pass through some substances. When X rays pass through a person and hit a plate, they make a picture. The picture is called a radiograph. The darkness the X rays cause on the plate varies with different parts of the body. Bones and other parts of the body that X rays cannot penetrate easily appear white on the radiograph.

## The First X rays

Wilhelm Conrad Roentgen, a German physicist, discovered X rays by accident in 1895. He was working with an object called a Crookes tube, similar to the X-ray tube shown below. During his experiment, he noticed that the tube was producing invisible radiation. He won the Nobel Prize for his discovery.

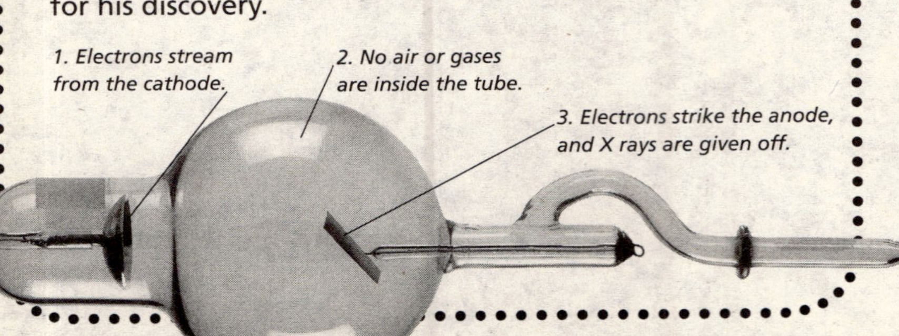


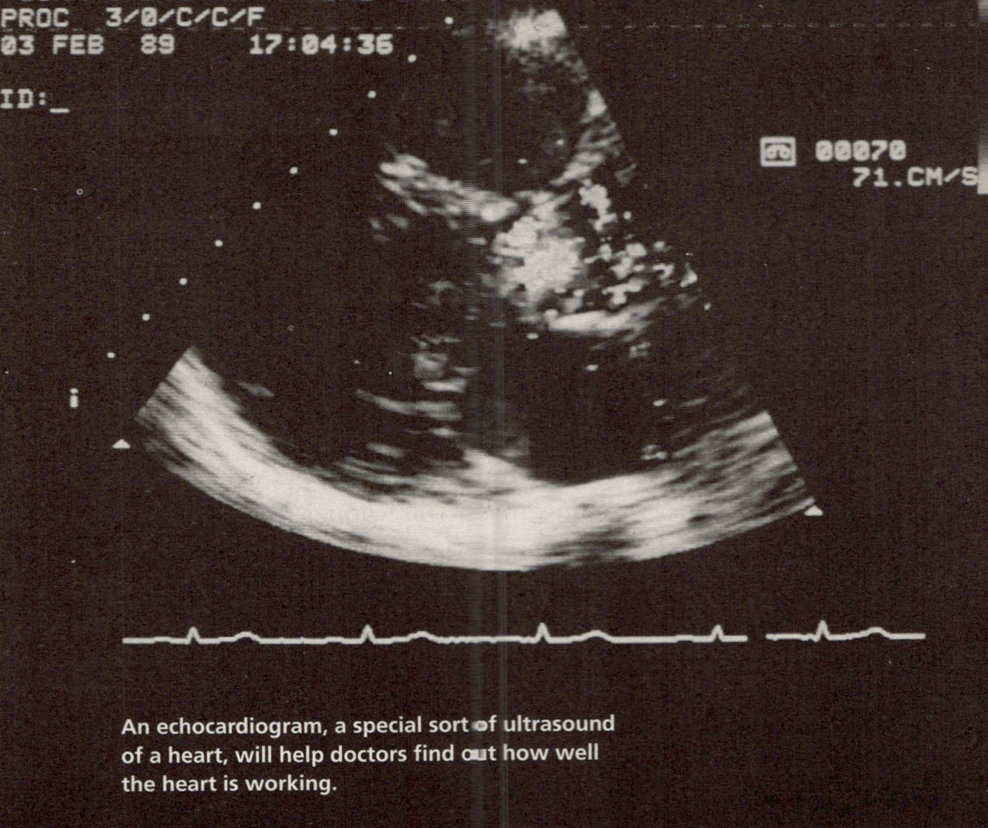


An echocardiogram, a special sort of ultrasound of a heart, will help doctors find out how well the heart is working.

Ultrasound can be used to view many different parts of the body, such as the heart, bladder, and brain. It cannot be used on bone or parts of the body containing air, such as the lungs, because these tissues do not conduct the waves.

One widespread use of ultrasound imaging is for viewing a fetus during pregnancy. Ultrasound waves are not harmful as X rays are, so many pictures can be taken. Doctors use the ultrasound to check the health, size, and due date of the baby. Sound waves used in ultrasound tests are safe because they do not damage living tissues. X rays and other radiations used in diagnostic therapy might cause bodily harm if not used properly.

# Ultrasound

Another diagnostic method for seeing inside the body is ultrasound imaging. In ultrasound imaging, high-frequency sound waves are directed into a part of the body. The sound waves are so high that the human ear cannot hear them.

The body tissues that come in contact with the ultrasound waves reflect the sound. These reflected sound waves are used to make either a static picture or a moving picture of the tissues.

Ultrasound is performed with a scanner. The part of the scanner that comes in contact with the body is called the transducer. It sends the sound waves and receives the echoes back. The pictures made from the reflected sound waves are projected onto a monitor. Still images can also be printed.

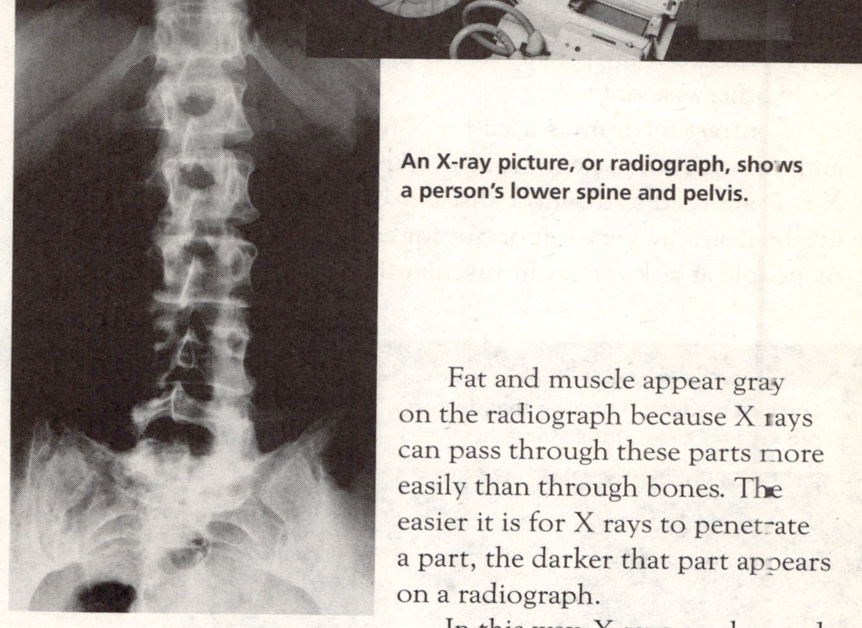

A man's head is being X-rayed.

An X-ray picture, or radiograph, shows a person's lower spine and pelvis.

The ultrasound scan will give an image of this man's throat.

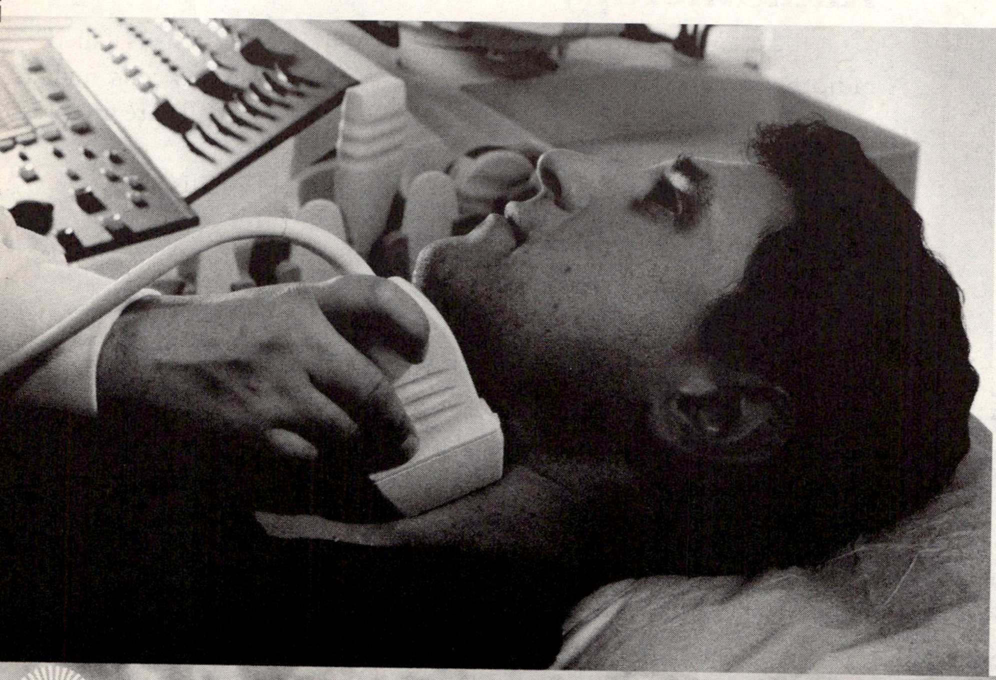

Fat and muscle appear gray on the radiograph because X rays can pass through these parts more easily than through bones. The easier it is for X rays to penetrate a part, the darker that part appears on a radiograph.

In this way, X rays can be used to take pictures of organs inside the body. Bones and soft tissues, such as muscles, show up in the picture. Doctors use these pictures to determine if bones are broken or if there are problems in the tissues. This is called diagnosing an illness or condition. Using X-ray images is called diagnostic radiology.

When a person gets a radiograph, a beam of X rays passes through a part of the body. The X rays are then captured on film. Doctors read the pictures to aid in their diagnosis. The doctor will often share the results of the X-ray image with the patient.

# Contrast X-rays

Sometimes doctors need to see organs that cannot be revealed by X rays. In this case, doctors give people contrast medium, a liquid or other substance that will show up on the X-ray.

A person must drink or inhale contrast medium, or a doctor will inject it. As the contrast medium travels through an organ or system, an X-ray picture is taken. The contrast medium will be visible on the X-ray picture. It will show parts of the person's body otherwise not seen.

Contrast medium is used for X-raying parts of the stomach and intestines, muscle joints, the spine, and blood vessels. Such X-rays are used to diagnose diseases of the torso. Scans that focus on the heart are very important for early diagnosis and treatment of people at risk for cardiovascular disease.

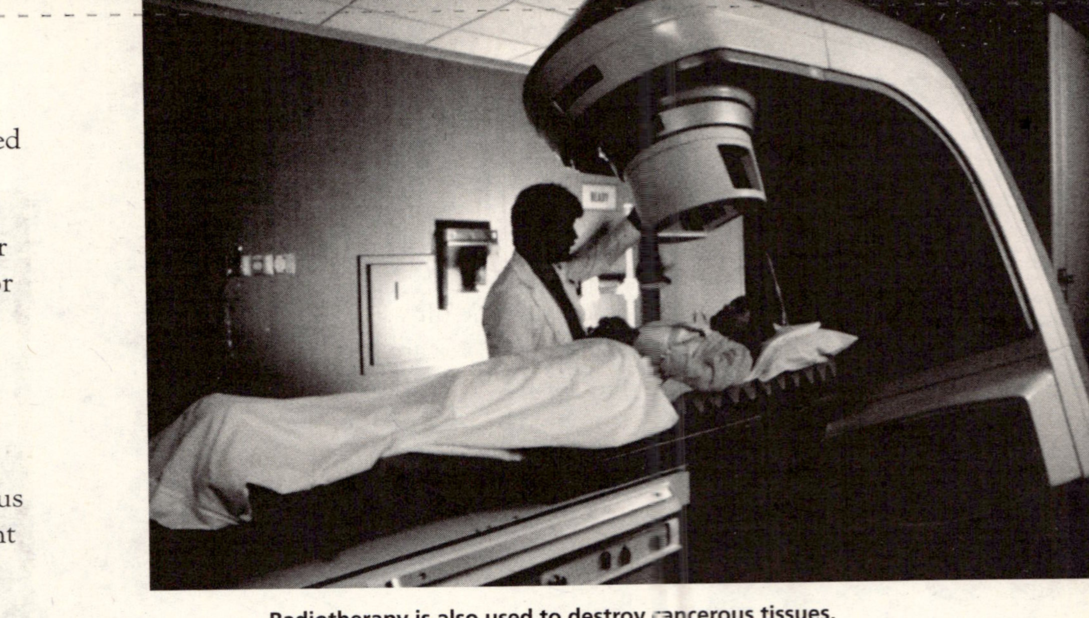

Radiotherapy is also used to destroy cancerous tissues.

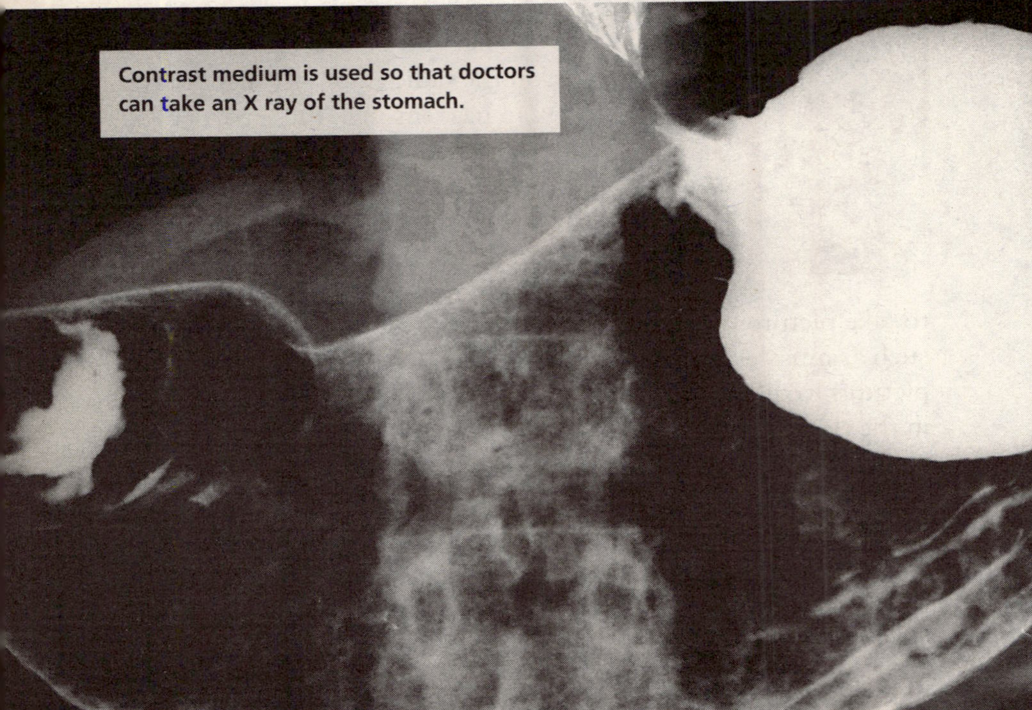

Contrast medium is used so that doctors can take an X ray of the stomach.

# Radiotherapy

This power of X rays can be used to help people. This is called radiotherapy. Doctors can use X rays to destroy diseased cells such as cancerous tissues. In this type of therapy, cancerous cells are given a dose of radiation that kills them.

Radiotherapy, used in the treatment and relief of diseases, makes use of deep tissue-penetrating rays, which react physically and chemically with diseased cells to destroy them. But there are other forms of radiotherapy, which use infrared and ultraviolet rays. These therapies use heat lamps to relieve pain and inflammation of the tissues, such as in the treatment of neuritis and arthritis.

X rays, however, can have some negative effects. Powerful X rays can harm healthy living tissue. For example, they can badly burn skin that is exposed to them too long. Doctors who use X rays take certain precautions. X rays are aimed at a specific part of the body. Other parts are covered with protective materials. X rays are taken in a special room that keeps all the harmful rays contained in one place.

# TOP CROPS

**by Patricia Walsh**



| Genre | Comprehension Skill | Text Features | Science Content |
| --- | --- | --- | --- |
| Nonfiction | Compare and Contrast | • Captions<br>• Glossary | Plants |

**Scott Foresman Science 6.5**

# What did you learn?

| Vocabulary | Extended Vocabulary |
| --- | --- |
| cellular respiration | cholesterol |
| epidermis | crops |
| guard cell | cultivating |
| phloem | exports |
| photosynthesis | famine |
| stoma | fertile |
| transpiration | fiber |
| tropism | herb |
| xylem | kernel |
| | nutrition |

1. What process makes energy-providing glucose in plants? Explain the process.

2. Which of the five top crops is native to, or originated in, America?

3. If you wanted to grow a very high-producing crop in a wet environment, which of the top crops would you choose? Explain your choice.

4. **Writing** in Science  Look back at the photograph of the combine harvester on page 10. It is used to harvest wheat. Using what you learned, do you think a combine harvester can be used to harvest other grain crops? Tell why or why not.

5. **Compare and Contrast** Choose two crops that you read about in this book. Then use a Venn diagram to show the differences between and similarities of the two crops.

**Picture Credits**
Every effort has been made to secure permission and provide appropriate credit for photographic material. The publisher deeply regrets any omission and pledges to correct errors called to its attention in subsequent editions.

Photo locators denoted as follows: Top (T), Center (C), Bottom (B), Left (L), Right (R), Background (Bkgd).

9 (TL) David Young-Wolff/PhotoEdit; 12 (B) Garry Black/Masterfile Corporation.

Scott Foresman/Dorling Kindersley would also like to thank: 14 (TL) Stephen Oliver/DK Images.

Unless otherwise acknowledged, all photographs are the copyright © of Dorling Kindersley, a division of Pearson.

ISBN: 0-328-13984-X

# Glossary

| | |
|---|---|
| **cholesterol** | a white, crystalline substance found in animal fat |
| **crops** | food products grown or gathered for use |
| **cultivated** | helped plants grow by labor and care |
| **exports** | goods sent out of one country for sale and use in another country |
| **famine** | lack of food; starvation |
| **fertile** | that produces crops easily |
| **fiber** | any part of food that cannot be digested |
| **herb** | a flowering plant on which the above-ground stem does not become woody |
| **kernel** | a grain or seed of wheat, corn, or other cereal plant |
| **nutrition** | food used by plants and animals for growth and energy |





# TOP CROPS

by Patricia Walsh

# What You Already Know

Roots, leaves, and stems are the parts of a vascular plant. The roots anchor a plant and absorb water and minerals from the soil. The leaves make food for the plant in the form of glucose, or sugar. Stems provide support and transport for the water, minerals, and glucose that the plant needs.

Xylem are the long, narrow cells that move water and minerals from the roots through the stems to other parts of the plant. Phloem carry the glucose from the leaves to the rest of the plant.

The epidermis, or outer layer of the leaves, has small holes in it that allow water and gases to pass in and out. Each small hole is called a stoma. Around each stoma are two guard cells that open and close the stoma. When the stoma is open, gases from the air enter the leaf and water exits the leaf. The loss of water is called transpiration. As the water moves out of the leaf, more water is drawn up from the roots.



young runner bean plant

These women are selling bananas at a street market in India.

A banana does not really grow on a tree, although the plant it grows on looks like a tree. The banana plant is actually a giant herb that is related to the lily and orchid families. People in many tropical countries also use the large leaves of the banana plant. They use the leaves to roof their homes and to make bags, baskets, and mats.

Bananas provide much of our needed fiber, potassium, and vitamin C. They contain no fat. A banana is a healthful food that can be eaten at any meal.

The world's farmers produce an abundance of food. Among the crops they grow are rice, corn, wheat, potatoes, and bananas. These top crops help feed people all over the world. Scientists, through research, continue to develop new varieties of food plants that are resistant to diseases and plagues. Food producers constantly strive to increase the productivity of their plants and make the food they grow more abundant, healthful, and nutritious.

The process in which plants make glucose is called photosynthesis. This requires a green substance in plants called chlorophyll. During photosynthesis, chlorophyll uses light energy from the Sun, carbon dioxide from the air, and water to create its own energy food, called glucose. As a result of making glucose, the plant releases oxygen.

When a plant makes more glucose than it needs, it stores the energy as sugars and starches. To release the stored energy, the plant breaks down the sugars and starches in a process called cellular respiration. This process produces carbon dioxide, water, and energy.

Plants use energy to respond to their environment. They bend, twist, droop, and turn as they grow toward or away from something in their environment. This movement is called tropism.

Plants are important because many living organisms get energy from consuming plants. Plants are a source of energy for people. In this book you will read about five important plants that people cultivate and eat.

# Bananas

Peel 'em, cook 'em, or fry 'em. Any way you slice it, bananas are one of the world's most popular fruits. Bananas were brought to the New World by Spanish explorers. It is believed that the very first banana roots were planted in fertile Caribbean soil in 1516. Bananas probably got their start in the Malaysian jungles of Southeast Asia.

Yet banana history goes back much further. Bananas probably got their start in the Malaysian jungles of Southeast Asia.

Americans got their first taste of bananas at the 1876 Philadelphia Centennial Exhibition. At this fair, bananas wrapped in foil sold for ten cents each. Today, Americans eat about four million tons of bananas each year. These bananas are grown in the South and Central American countries of Colombia, Costa Rica, Ecuador, Guatemala, Honduras, Nicaragua, and Panama. In all, more than eighty-five countries around the world grow bananas, with Uganda, Brazil, and India producing the most.

**53**

Bananas are grown on plantations throughout much of South and Central America.

# Farming Beginnings

About ten thousand years ago, people moved from gathering plants to growing, or cultivating, them. This was a huge step forward for civilization. By growing the food they needed, people no longer had to wander in search of food. Farmers settled in one place. They cleared land and planted seeds. They began growing and improving crops. Villages sprang up near these farms because food was available. By choosing seeds from the healthiest and most productive plants, farmers improved their crops. Food-producing plants became bigger and better.

In the United States there was a revolution in farming beginning around 1850. As cities and industry grew, many people gave up farming and moved to the cities. There were fewer people growing their own food, so farms became bigger and more productive. A single farm no longer fed only the farm family. Now farm crops were raised and sold to feed many, many others.

In the following pages we'll take a look at five important crops: rice, corn, wheat, potatoes, and bananas. These top crops provide a major source of nutrition for the people of the world.

The edible part of the potato plant grows below the ground.

Later the potato was introduced to other parts of Europe when the Prussian ruler Frederick the Great saw potatoes as a solution to the recurring problems of famine. He ordered his people to plant and eat potatoes. A young French chemist found himself eating and liking potatoes when he was held prisoner in Prussia. When he returned to France, he convinced King Louis XVI and Queen Marie Antoinette that the potato was a good thing. The king and queen and the people of France soon agreed and demanded more potatoes. You can thank Thomas Jefferson, our third President, for bringing french fries to the United States. Jefferson introduced Americans to this new potato dish when he served "fries" with a White House dinner.

Today potatoes, which were brought to North America by Irish immigrants, are grown throughout the United States. They are grown on huge potato farms in states such as Washington and Idaho, and they are grown in home gardens. But the world's leading potato producer is Russia, which grows about one-third of all the world's potatoes.

Mashed and baked potatoes are popular potato dishes.

# Potatoes

Did you know that the average American eats 120 pounds of potatoes a year? That works out to almost 365 potatoes per person, or one potato a day. A potato is a healthy source of carbohydrates and proteins. Potatoes are fat free and cholesterol free. They are high in potassium, vitamin C, other vitamins, and fiber.

The origin of potatoes can be traced back thousands of years to the Andes Mountains of South America. In the mountains, at heights of ten thousand feet above sea level, the Aymara Indians developed more than two hundred varieties of potatoes. Around 1570, Spanish explorers of South America returned to Europe with the first potatoes. At first, potatoes were grown as medicinal plants. The Spanish had noticed that sailors who ate potatoes did not suffer from the disease called scurvy.

Potatoes are cultivated throughout the United States, and all over the world.

# Top Crops

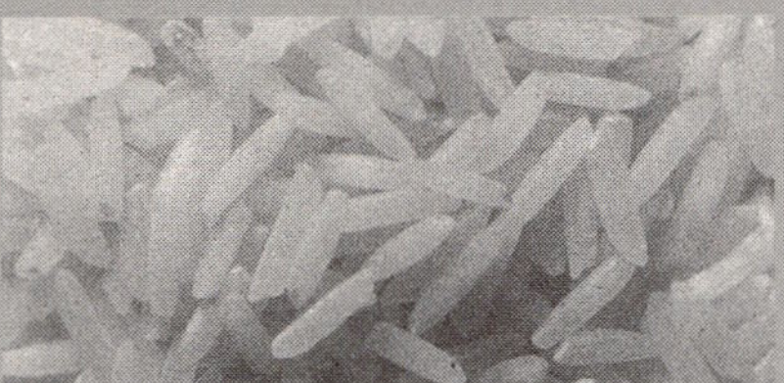

**Rice:** cultivated for more than 5,000 years in China

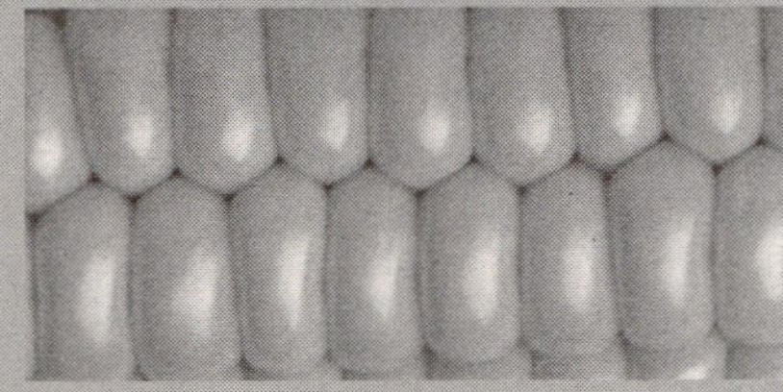

**Corn:** fossilized pollen grains found in Mexico could be 80,000 years old

**Wheat:** domesticated by nomadic hunter-gatherers in the Middle East, 8000 to 6000 B.C.

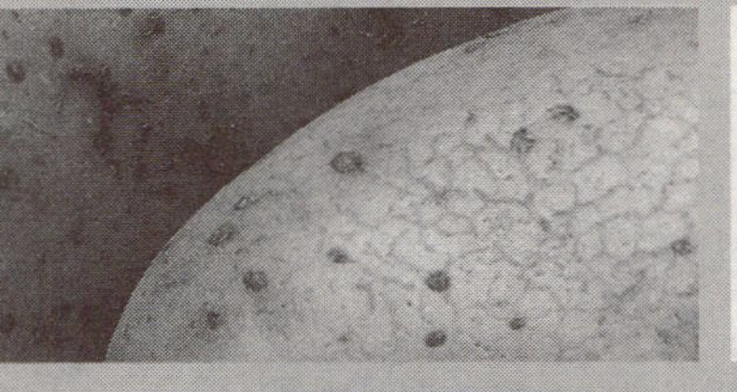

**Potatoes:** native to the Andes and domesticated by pre-Columbian cultures at least 4,000 years ago

**Bananas:** of Malaysian origin, believed to be the first fruit farmed by man

# Rice

Rice is brown or white and has short, medium, or long grains, but there are thousands of different varieties of rice. You can eat it steamed or fried. You can eat it in rice pudding or sushi. Are you surprised to learn that it is one of the most important foods in the world? Half of the world's people depend on rice for the most important part of their diet.

Rice has almost no fat or cholesterol and very little sodium, or salt. It is a good source of essential amino acids, vitamins, and minerals. Brown rice is more nutritious than white rice because it is minimally processed. It contains fiber, bran, vitamins, and minerals not found in white rice.

Rice is cultivated in more than one hundred countries and on every continent except Antarctica. It is most often grown at sea level, but it grows also at elevations ranging from two thousand to nine thousand feet above sea level. Rice thrives in a hot, wet climate, and when it grows, it produces! A single rice seed can yield, or produce, more than three thousand grains of rice, making it one of the top crops.

Rice is one of the leading crops in the world. It is grown in more than 100 countries.



It is thought that the first humans chewed the raw wheat kernel. Later people figured out that they could pound the kernels to make flour. They mixed the four with water and baked it to make the first flat bread. Columbus brought wheat to the West Indies on his second voyage to the New World, in 1494. The Spanish brought wheat to Mexico around 1510. By 1582 wheat was being grown in what is now the southwestern United States. Three hundred years later, Eastern European immigrants brought a hardy winter wheat to Kansas. This wheat is now the type most often grown in the United States.

Today the United States, China, India, the former Soviet Republics, France, Canada, and Australia are the top wheat-producing countries. Of the forty-two states in the United States that grow wheat, Kansas is the top producer. The United States produces far more wheat than it needs, so it exports about 50 percent of all its wheat to feed people and livestock around the world.

Pasta, made from wheat, is a favorite food in the United States. More than 600 pasta shapes are produced worldwide.

# Wheat

Wheat is the most widely cultivated grain in the world. More foods are made with wheat than with any other cereal grain. You'll find wheat in bread, crackers, tortillas, pasta, cookies, pizza, and breakfast foods, to name a few. Pour out a bushel of wheat and you'll find about one million kernels. A bushel of wheat can be used to make about forty-two loaves of white bread. It can also be used to make about ninety loaves of the more nutritious whole-wheat bread.

Cultivation of wheat probably began in western Asia around 8000 to 6000 B.C. This was when people discovered that they could grow wheat during the summer, store it for food in the winter, and plant seeds in the spring.

Wheat is the most widely cultivated grain in the world. It grows in forty-two states in the United States.

Japanese family eating rice— rice is eaten with different kinds of meals.

Not much is known about the first use of rice as food, but there is evidence that people have been eating rice for more than five thousand years. The first known mention of rice was by a Chinese emperor in 2800 B.C. The practice of cultivating rice spread from China to ancient Greece to Persia and to the Nile Delta.

Rice was probably brought to America by accident. It is believed that in 1694, a storm-damaged ship on its way to Madagascar arrived in Charles Towne harbor, Charleston, South Carolina. The colonists repaired the ship and the grateful captain gave them a gift of yellow seeds called "Golden Seede Rice." The fresh tidal waters of the Carolinas and Georgia were ideal for growing this rice. The soil was rich, flat, and fertile, and tides flooded the area twice a day. By 1700 rice was a major crop in the colonies. It was said at the time that there was more rice to ship to England than ships to carry it. Today in the United States, the major rice-producing states are Arkansas, California, Louisiana, Texas, Mississippi, and Missouri.

# Corn

Corn grew in America and was harvested by Native Americans long before the first colonists arrived in the New World. The Native Americans shared their corn and their knowledge of growing it with the colonists. Having corn helped the colonists survive their first winter. Since then, there's been a corn explosion!

Today farmers grow corn on every continent except Antarctica. In the United States, twice as much corn is grown as any other grain. The agricultural area known as the Corn Belt is made up of a dozen states: Iowa, Illinois, Nebraska, Minnesota, Indiana, Wisconsin, South Dakota, Michigan, Missouri, Kansas, Ohio, and Kentucky.

Sweet corn is the kind of corn you eat when you have corn on the cob, canned corn, or frozen corn. Popcorn, a favorite companion to a movie, is a special variety of corn.

In the United States, corn is the top crop.

Corn on the cob is one way corn is served.

Even though you can find more than one thousand foods that contain corn or corn products in your grocery store, people do not eat most of the corn crop. It is used for livestock feed and in manufacturing. This corn is called field or dent corn.

When you see fields of corn, you're probably looking at rows and rows of dent corn. Horses, poultry, hogs, and catfish are raised on corn. Dent corn is used to make starches, oils, and even an alternative fuel called ethanol. Dent corn is also used in the making of crayons, paints, and paper. Diaper a baby and you might have just used an absorbent corn product. Sip a soda and you've probably just enjoyed corn syrup sweetener. Box up your grandmother's teacups and you could be using packing peanuts and cardboard that include a corn product. Corn products have more than thirty-five hundred different uses, and more are being found each day.

sweet corn

cornflakes

tortilla chips

taco

# FORESTS
## Around the World

by Charles Miller

Science



| Genre | Comprehension Skill | Text Features | Science Content |
| --- | --- | --- | --- |
| Nonfiction | Main Idea and Details | • Captions<br>• Map<br>• Glossary | Biomes |

**Scott Foresman Science 6.6**

PEARSON
Scott Foresman
scottforesman.com

ISBN 0-328-13987-4
9 780328 139873
90000

# What did you learn?

1. Why do some animals in deciduous forests hibernate?

2. What adaptations help conifers survive the winter?

3. Why do few plants grow on the floor of the tropical rain forests?

4. **Writing** in Science The type of biome that exists in an area depends on its climate. What kind of adaptations do trees need to make to take advantage of differences in temperature and light in various climates?

5. **Main Idea and Details** What do you think is the main idea of the second paragraph on page 14? Identify details that support the main idea.



**Vocabulary**

abiotic factor
biome
biotic factor
community
ecosystem
environment
population

**Extended Vocabulary**

canopy
conifer
coniferous forest
deciduous forest
dormant
hibernate
migrate
rain forest
understory

**Picture Credits**
Every effort has been made to secure permission and provide appropriate credit for photographic material. The publisher deeply regrets any omission and pledges to correct errors called to its attention in subsequent editions.

Photo locators denoted as follows: Top (T), Center (C), Bottom (B), Left (L), Right (R), Background (Bkgd).

Opener: Jon Arnold/Alamy Images; 1 Tim FitzHarris/Minden Pictures; 9 (B) Jon Arnold/Alamy Images; 12 (B) Frans Lanting/Minden Pictures; 15 Frans Lanting/Minden Pictures.

Unless otherwise acknowledged, all photographs are the copyright © of Dorling Kindersley, a division of Pearson.

ISBN: 0-328-13987-4

# Glossary

| | |
|---|---|
| **canopy** | a covering of leaves high above the forest floor that absorbs most of the sunlight |
| **conifer** | a tree that produces seeds in cones and does not flower |
| **coniferous forest** | the forest of the north, centered around conifers and adapted to long, cold winters |
| **deciduous forest** | the forest of the temperate regions, in which trees lose their leaves and stop growing in winter |
| **dormant** | that does not grow or produce food |
| **hibernate** | to be in an inactive condition in which the body functions slow down |
| **migrate** | to travel to a different biome |
| **rain forest** | the forest of the tropics, which is in continual growth and has the most diversity |
| **understory** | the layer of plants growing between the forest floor and the canopy |

# FORESTS
## Around the World

by Charles Miller

# What You Already Know

Every part of Earth's surface, atmosphere, and oceans is home to living organisms. An organism's environment is all of the things around it that affect how it lives and grows. The abiotic factors of the environment include all of the nonliving things, such as sunlight, air, water, and even temperature. The biotic factors are the living parts of the environment. Both types of factors are important to the survival of an organism.

The different species in a particular area interact with one another and with the environment around them. A population is a group of individual organisms of one species that live in an area. Humans can be classified as part of a population. You are part of the human population of your neighborhood, your state, the entire country, and the Earth.

# Forests at Risk

The type of forest that grows in a particular region depends on its climate. In the coniferous forests of the far north, success depends on developing a way to survive the winter. In the deciduous forests, many of the plants and animals take advantage of the changing seasons. The tropical rain forests provide food and shelter to more species than any other biome on Earth.

The central part of any forest is its trees. Unfortunately, many of the world's forests have disappeared or are threatened. Half of the tropical rain forests have been cut down in the last half century. Some of them have been cut for lumber and others to provide farmland. Because of the large number of different species and how they interact, it is almost impossible to restore a tropical rain forest that has been cleared. Many coniferous forests have also been cut down for lumber, paper manufacturing, and other wood products. Once the trees have been removed, erosion of the land by wind and water can cause problems that make it hard for the forest to regrow. Most of the original deciduous forests have been cut down for lumber and to clear fields for farming. Because this type of forest grows quickly, many of these forests have recovered, but without careful controls, even these forests are at risk.

**Hidden beneath the canopy of this rain forest live an incredible number of plants and animals.**

This squirrel monkey's tail is useful for life in the branches.

Many primates, such as monkeys and apes, live among the trees. Large mammals, such as hippopotamuses, rhinoceroses, and even elephants, live on forest floors. Large cats, including jaguars and leopards, prey on other animals, from frogs to antelope.

Rain forest animals have many interesting adaptations. Toucans and parrots have beaks that are designed for particular types of food. Some insects and reptiles protect themselves by making poisons. Poisonous animals are often very brightly colored, so that a predator knows they are dangerous.

Chameleons change the color of their body to blend into their environment and hide from predators. The sloth, which lives in the South American forests, moves slowly through the trees. It hangs upside down looking for fruit. Algae grow in the sloth's fur, giving it a green color and making it difficult to detect.

The red-eyed tree frog has huge, brightly colored eyes that scare away predators.



There are as many different populations in an area as there are species. For example, a pine forest has a population of pine trees, but it also has populations of many species of birds. A community is a group of populations that interact with each other in a particular area. The trees and birds are both part of the pine forest community.

The entire community of living things and the nonliving parts of the environment are called an ecosystem. Ecosystems can be small, such as a dead log and the organisms that inhabit it. They can also be an entire forest, including the dead log and its inhabitants.

Similar ecosystems can occur in many places if environmental factors are similar. For example, forests of pine trees exist in many places in North America. Similar forest ecosystems occur in many parts of Europe and Asia. A biome is a large group of ecosystems with similar climates and organisms.

In this book you will read about three types of forest biomes. You will learn about many of the populations of animals and plants that live in these biomes.

# Forest Biomes

What do you think of when you hear the word *forest*? Although ancient forests were dominated by very tall ferns or mosses, the main characteristic of a modern forest is its trees. In a forest, trees provide food, shelter, and oxygen for many communities of organisms. The types of organisms that live in a forest ecosystem are often determined by the kinds of trees that grow there.

A forest includes much more than just the trees, though. The living parts of the forest—the biotic factors—also include shrubs and grasses, mosses, and other plants. Animals, from tiny insects to large mammals, depend on these plants and affect how they grow. Microorganisms that break down leaves into soil are an essential part of a forest.

Forests cover about thirty percent of the land surface of Earth. There are three major types of forest: deciduous forests, coniferous forests, and rain forests. Deciduous forests have trees with wide leaves that fall off in the winter. They are located in the middle latitudes of the Northern Hemisphere.

**Forests Around the World**

Deciduous

Coniferous

Rain forest

The forest biomes form rings around the land masses of Earth.

Deciduous forests grow rapidly, beginning new growth each spring.

The canopy and understory are home to an incredible number of plants and animals, many of which never leave the trees. Some plants, including orchids and bromeliads, live in the trees, collecting nutrients from small pockets of decaying leaves. Colorful birds such as toucans and parrots, large butterflies and moths, and a wide variety of small reptiles and mammals move through the canopy looking for food and protection from predators. There are so many species in the rain forests around the world that scientists are constantly discovering new ones.

The bottom layer of the rain forest has very few plants because so little light reaches the forest floor, which is covered with wet leaves and decaying plants. The hot and moist environment is the perfect place for fungi, bacteria, and other microorganisms. Large insect populations also live on the forest floor.

Many exotic birds, such as parrots, live in the canopy of the rain forest.

The warm, wet climate of the rain forest is perfect for boa constrictors and other reptiles.

# Rain Forests

The tropical rain forests make up a hot, wet biome located near the equator all around the world. In this climate, plants grow all year round, with no dormant period. Instead of summer and winter, the tropical seasons are the rainy season and the dry season. The temperature never drops below freezing. As you can see in the photo, the rain forest is full of lush, green growth.

The tropical rain forest grows in layers. The upper canopy is formed by trees that grow up to 130 feet tall. In the emergent layer giant trees grow sparsely to about 250 feet tall. Thick vines climb up the trunks of the trees into the canopy and compete with the trees for sunlight. Below the canopy is the middle layer, called the understory, made of vines, smaller trees, ferns, and palms. Many of the plants have huge leaves to capture as much light as possible.

The main feature of coniferous forests is trees that produce seeds in cones. Trees in coniferous forests have needlelike leaves that remain on the trees throughout the winter. In general, coniferous forests grow farther north than deciduous forests.

A rain forest grows where temperatures are warm and where it rains throughout most of the year. Rain forests have very dense plant growth and the trees do not lose their leaves in the winter. Most rain forests are located near the equator and are known as tropical rain forests. Along the northwest coast of North America, where the ocean causes some areas to be warmer and wetter, there are some temperate rain forests.

The rain forest contains layers of plants that compete for sunlight.

Coniferous forests are adapted to the cold, snowy areas of the north.

In the rain forest plants grow tall, competing for sunlight.

# Deciduous Forests

Deciduous forests grow in the temperate regions, between the cold polar area and the hot tropics. The plants and animals in this biome have adapted to cold winters and hot, rainy summers. If you live near a deciduous forest, you have seen leaves like those pictured below. The trees have broad leaves that gather a lot of light during the growing season. Leaves form a canopy, which is a covering high in the trees that blocks much of the light. The floor of the forest is covered with communities of plants, such as azaleas and mosses, that have adapted to decreased sunlight.

Trees use the light, heat, and moisture of the summer to grow and produce seeds. In autumn, when the amount of sunlight decreases, the leaves stop producing food for the tree, change color, and then drop to the ground. When this happens, the forest loses its canopy. If the leaves remained on the tree all winter, enough snow could collect on the leaves to break the branches. During the winter, the trees become dormant, which means that they do not produce food or grow.

Acorns and other deciduous tree seeds provide food for many animals, as well as start new trees.

Leaves changing color at the end of the growing season is a sign of a deciduous forest.

Birds of prey, including this American kestrel, thrive on the many small animals that live in ponds and bogs.

Even in areas with little rain, the northern forests still have a lot of ponds and bogs. In spring, the melting snows provide a lot of water, which evaporates slowly in the cool climate. The wet environment is the perfect home for a large insect population. Many species of birds, such as grosbeaks, flycatchers, and warblers, fly to the northern coniferous forests in summer to feast on these insects. When the weather becomes cold, these birds migrate, or move from one place to another, flying south to a warmer climate for the winter. Many seed-eating birds, such as finches and sparrows, stay all year long.

Other animals of the forest adapt to the cold winters in several different ways. Some, such as hares and other small mammals, burrow underground during winter to escape the cold. Others, such as bears and bats, store food in their bodies as fat in summer and autumn, when there is a lot of food, and sleep during much of the winter. Wolves, mink, and wolverines grow thick winter coats so they can hunt even in cold weather.

Many predators, such as this bobcat, grow a thick, insulating coat for the winter.

The shape of conifers is one adaptation to the cold, snowy climate. The branches bend downward and snow falls off the tree before it becomes heavy enough to break the branches. The needles usually are a dark color that absorbs the maximum amount of heat from the Sun, and they do not fall off the tree in winter. Because the summers are short, this allows the plant to start photosynthesis as early in the spring as possible.

The trees in a coniferous forest tend to grow close together and are very densely covered with needles. Because of this few plants grow on the ground. Mosses and lichens are common, but flowering shrubs are rare. Many insects and fungi live in the bark of the trees or in decaying logs of dead trees. Fungi, important decomposers in these forests, are also eaten by insects and other animals. One of the main sources of food for animals in the forest is the seeds produced in the cones of the trees.

In the spring, before the canopy returns, many smaller plants, such as the bluebells in the photograph on this page, use the extra sunlight to grow rapidly on the forest floor. Many small forest plants flower early in the growing season before the canopy is complete.

Within the canopy, insects and caterpillars feed on the nutrient-rich leaves. In turn, they become meals for warblers and other birds that live in the canopy. The sounds of insects and songbirds give the forest a feeling of constant activity.

**Bears of the coniferous forest grow fat from eating smaller animals, seeds, and berries, and then they are inactive all winter.**

Many different kinds of animals live in a deciduous forest. The decaying leaves on the ground provide nourishment for mushrooms and other fungi. The leaves are also home and food for animals such as insects and worms. Other small animals—toads, spiders, moles, and birds—eat the plants and animals on the forest floor. Larger animals that are common in this biome include skunks, raccoons, coyotes, deer, and bears.

After the trees lose their leaves, the food supply of the deciduous forest decreases until spring growth begins. Forest animals have to adapt to this shortage. Some birds and butterflies fly to warmer climates until the spring brings new food. Some animals move to a sheltered place. During the winter their body functions slow down, or they enter a similar state resembling sleep. Other animals, such as squirrels, chipmunks, and blue jays, store extra food in the warm months and then retrieve it in winter.

This woodpecker finds insects inside trees, digging them out with its strong beak.

Deer eat low-growing plants, acorns, and young trees.

# Coniferous Forests

Coniferous forests are located in a band around the northern parts of the continents of North America, Asia, and Europe. The organisms of these forests must be able to survive long, very cold winters. Most of the trees in these forests are conifers—trees that have long, narrow, evergreen leaves, often called needles. These leaves have waxy coatings that decrease water loss in the winter, when the frozen ground keeps the tree from getting water. Conifers include pines, spruces, and firs. They are called conifers because they produce cones instead of flowers.

Look at the photograph at the bottom of the page. You can see that all the trees have a similar shape—wide at the bottom and coming to a point at the top. Can you think of a reason why that is a good shape for a tree in a place with heavy snow?

The needle-shaped leaves and the cone full of seeds show that the stone pine is a conifer.

Life Science

# Predator and Prey

by Kristin Cashore

| Genre | Comprehension Skill | Text Features | Science Content |
| --- | --- | --- | --- |
| Nonfiction | Predict | • Captions<br>• Glossary | Ecosystems |

Scott Foresman Science 6.7

# What did you learn?

**Vocabulary**

competition
decomposer
energy pyramid
host
parasite
succession
symbiosis

**Extended Vocabulary**

bioluminescence
carnivore
carrion
echolocation
ecology
nocturnal
savanna
scavenger

1. Why are predators at the mercy of their prey?

2. What need do all desert animals have in common?

3. What adaptations are common to many animals in polar regions?

4. **Writing** in Science  Sea creatures have different adaptations for survival in the oceans. Write to explain how some sea creatures use trickery to catch their prey or escape their predators. Include details from the book to support your answer.

5. **Predict** In this book you have read about many different kinds of predators. What makes humans the most dangerous predators? Use examples to expand on your answer.

# Glossary

| | |
|---|---|
| **bioluminescence** | the ability of an animal to use chemicals in its body to produce light |
| **carnivore** | a meat-eating animal |
| **carrion** | dead or decaying flesh |
| **echolocation** | a sensory system used by animals such as bats and dolphins. The animals emit a sound and listen for its echo. They use the echo to determine the location and size of objects |
| **ecology** | the study of the relationship between living things and their environment |
| **nocturnal** | sleeping during the day and waking at night |
| **savanna** | a flat grassland in a tropical or subtropical area |
| **scavenger** | an animal that eats dead or decaying matter |

# Predator and Prey

by Kristin Cashore

PEARSON
Scott Foresman

DK

# What You Already Know

Every species of animal or plant has a unique set of adaptations that suits its particular environment. These adaptations develop over many generations and can take the form of structures, behaviors, and body processes. Organisms are either producers, consumers, or decomposers of energy, and energy travels from organism to organism within an ecosystem.

An energy pyramid helps us to visualize the passage of energy through an ecosystem. The pyramid shows that every time energy passes from one organism to another, some energy is lost. In fact, only 10 percent of the energy at one level moves up to the next level. Because of this, the organisms at the top of the pyramid must eat many organisms to get the energy they need. This is why there are many small species at the bottom of a food pyramid but only one predatory species at the top.

Competition is the struggle among organisms to survive in an ecosystem with limited resources. When organisms have similar needs, competition for food, water, or territory arises. Even plants compete for water, space, minerals, and sunlight.

# Protecting The Environment

Every ecosystem has animals that have the right adaptations for their habitats. Some animals are predators and some are prey, but every living thing is affected by the actions of humans. Humans use up far more of the Earth's energy than any other species. Much of the energy we use creates pollution, which changes the environment and affects all of the Earth's ecosystems. When these changes affect even one organism, the impact trickles down to all parts of the ecosystem. For example, overfishing is causing the depletion of many fish species in our oceans, which in turn affects other animals in the ecological chain.

Humans have incredible power to change the environment. This means that we also have incredible responsibility. You can do your part by recycling, by staying informed about alternative sources of energy, and by making mindful decisions. By protecting the environment, you can help maintain the natural balance between predators and prey.

Reforestation helps to regenerate ecosystems and protect the environment.

Bottlenose dolphins hunt in groups called pods. When hunting in dark areas, they use echolocation to "see" their prey. This means that they produce a small sound, such as a click, and then listen for its echo. The echo tells the dolphins the size, shape, and location of nearby fish, and the dolphins move in for the kill.

Other predators such as jellyfish and sea anemones use stinging tentacles to catch their prey. They feed on drifting sea life called plankton and small shellfish.

The ocean is a dangerous place for predators and prey; you never know what strange skill an animal will use to survive!

This shrimp doesn't have much defense against a stinging sea anemone.





Symbiosis is a close, long-term bond between organisms that benefits at least one of the organisms. Symbiosis can be mutualistic, commensalistic, or parasitic. In parasitic symbiosis, the parasite benefits from the relationship, but the host is harmed. In mutualistic symbiosis both organisms benefit. In commensalistic symbiosis the parasite benefits and the host is neither helped nor harmed.

Materials such as nitrogen, carbon, and water are constantly recycled and reused in the Earth's ecosystems. Ecosystems change over time, either naturally or as a result of human behavior. Natural changes can occur quickly, or they can occur slowly in a process known as succession. Succession is a series of predictable changes that occur in an ecosystem over time.

The pollution people cause has a tremendous impact on ecosystems. The best solution to pollution is prevention, through recycling, education, and mindfulness.

In every ecosystem there is a delicate balance between predator and prey. Each species has unique survival adaptations that suit its particular ecosystem. In this book you will learn about the adaptations that help both predators and prey survive in their ecosystems.

Bears are predators who compete to catch salmon.

# Ecosystems

An ecosystem is made up of a community of plants and animals that live together in a certain habitat. All living things belong to an ecosystem. Every living thing depends on some aspect of its ecosystem for energy. Energy moves through the ecosystem from one organism to another. The study of the relationship between living things and their environment is called ecology, and the scientists who specialize in this study are called ecologists. Every organism has adaptations that allow it to survive in its particular ecosystem. A jellyfish cannot survive on land, and a tomato plant cannot survive in the ocean. An organism without adaptations appropriate to its ecosystem will probably not survive long.

Every ecosystem requires a special balance of consumers and producers, predators and prey. Every organism in an ecosystem is crucial. Each plays an important role in the food chain, and each has a place in the energy pyramid of the ecosystem. If one species becomes endangered or extinct, other species in the ecosystem will be affected.

A caiman floats through the water while sneaking up on its prey. A caiman would not do well in a waterless ecosystem.

This shoal of fish is working together to protect itself from sharks, whales, and other predators.

74

# Oceans

The ocean is the largest ecosystem on Earth, and there are more animal species in the ocean than on land. The constant give-and-take between predators and prey contributes to the success of the ocean ecosystem.

Many species of fish, such as herring, feed on phytoplankton, which are tiny plant organisms and algae. Others feed on smaller fish and crustaceans. Many ocean animals have adaptations to protect themselves from the great ocean predators. For example, fish swim together in large shoals to protect themselves from predators such as sharks, toothed whales, and tuna.

Some sea creatures have ingenious ways of hunting and protecting themselves. The stargazer is a fish that buries itself under the sand, with only its eyes showing. When its prey passes above, the stargazer leaps out and grabs it!

An octopus can change color and texture to camouflage itself. It can also eject a cloud of ink, which confuses its attacker while the octopus makes a getaway.

The anglerfish lives in the dark depths of the ocean. In a process called bioluminescence, it uses chemicals in its body to create a light on the top of its head. This light attracts prey, and the anglerfish attacks!

The light of the anglerfish attracts its prey, like the lure on the end of a fishing line.

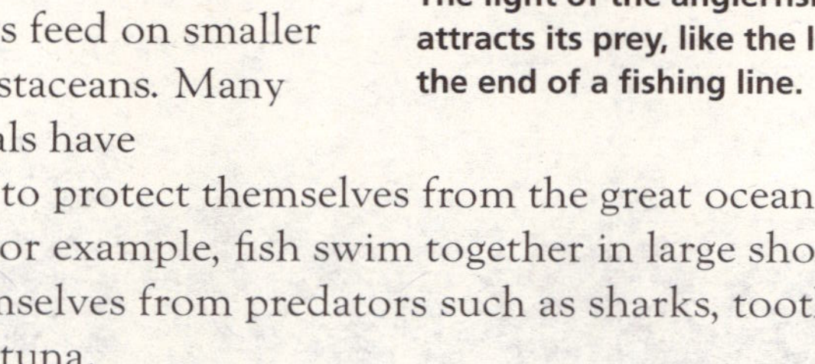

A tiger is at the top of its energy pyramid. It cannot survive without its prey.

# Top of the Chain

A look at the relationship between predators and prey will demonstrate the delicate balance of any ecosystem.

Predators, such as tigers, bears, and sharks, are at the top of their food chains. You might think that this gives them an enormous advantage over their prey. But in fact, all predators are ultimately at the mercy of their prey, because predators cannot survive unless their prey is abundant. The survival of top predators therefore depends upon the success of the very animals they kill.

In many cases this problem creates its own solution. The fewer the prey, the fewer the predators, but when the predators diminish in number, then the prey have their chance to thrive.

However, when the balance shifts because a species is endangered or extinct, then there is no easy solution.

A vole doesn't stand much chance against a swooping snowy owl. But the owl cannot survive unless voles and other rodents thrive.

The polar bear is the most powerful predator in the Arctic. Its only enemies are humans and, rarely, other polar bears. A polar bear's favorite prey is seal. The polar bear is remarkably well adapted to life in one of the coldest places on Earth!

Polar bears swim very well; they have wide forepaws for paddling, and excellent underwater vision. Polar bears are fearsome predators on land, on ice, and in the water.

Most arctic birds migrate south in winter; others, such as the snowy owl, stay. The white feathers of the owl protect it from predators and hide it from its prey.

The polar bear is at the top of the energy pyramid in the Arctic. Its favorite meal is seal.

# Polar Regions

The ecosystems of the Arctic and the Antarctic are among the harshest in the world. Animals that inhabit the polar regions have very special adaptations.

In polar regions, the greatest biological production occurs in the oceans rather than on land. The abundance of fish allows land animals to survive. Some Arctic animals, such as polar bears, seals, arctic foxes, arctic wolves, and caribou, have heavy fur that helps to keep them warm. Polar bears and seals also have thick layers of blubber that insulate them from the cold air and water.

In the Antarctic, penguins have a layer of blubber and thick, waterproof feathers. Penguins are birds that are adapted not to fly but to swim; they can dive very deep and swim very fast, and this makes them dangerous predators for fish!

**A musk ox is much bigger than an arctic wolf, but when a wolf pack works together, it can bring down large prey.**

**Snowy owls normally live in the Arctic. However, if the rodent population drops, they have no choice but to travel south in search of food.**

Whether an animal is predator, prey, or both, it has adaptations that help it to survive. Camouflage, for example, helps hide predator and prey from each other. The teeth of a carnivore, or meat eater, help it to kill and digest its prey. The webbed feet and long legs of a wading bird allow the bird to stand in lakes and streams while searching for meals of insects or fish. Wolves' instinct to hunt together in a pack helps them kill large prey, and wildebeests' instinct to stick together in a herd protects them from predators.

Every ecosystem has different animals that serve as predator and prey, and every ecosystem's animals possess unique adaptations.

Let's take a look at some of the predator–prey relationships in ecosystems around the world.

# Rain Forests

A rain forest is an ecosystem in a tropical location that has dense trees and a very high annual rainfall. Rain forests are among the richest habitats in the world; at least half of the world's plant and animal species live in rain forests.

Animals make their homes in all parts of rain forests, from the forest floor to the tops of the trees. Predators and prey live together and struggle for survival.

Some of the rain forests' most dangerous predators include jaguars, crocodiles, and anacondas. The jaguar's adaptations make it a good climber and swimmer. It may climb a tree and pounce on small prey from above; it may also use its powerful paws to flick fish out of the water. Jaguars have a spotted coat, which camouflages them and hides them from their prey.

**The prey of a jaguar include mammals, fish, reptiles, and birds.**

Some grassland creatures are scavengers, feeding on the kills of other predators. For example, vultures are birds that roam the plains in search of carrion, or dead flesh. Marabou storks are also grassland scavengers. They wait for vultures and other predators to break through the hides of dead animals, and then they feed.

Life is dangerous in the grasslands, and competition for food and water can be fierce. But grassland animals are well adapted to the challenges they face.

**Vultures and other scavengers may seem dirty, but when they clean up dead animals they are doing a service.**

In the African savanna and in grasslands all over the world, predators and prey have adaptations that suit their needs. For example, some grassland predators are solitary creatures, and some work in packs. Hyenas hunting in packs have been known to kill animals larger than deer. Wild dogs also work together to bring down their prey.

Crocodiles are not just well adapted to rain forests; they roam the lakes and rivers of grasslands as well. As hunters, crocodiles do quite well on their own. A crocodile is a solitary animal, using camouflage and stealth to sneak up on unsuspecting prey in the water.

A lot of grassland prey stick together for safety. Wildebeests, for example, graze and migrate in big herds to protect themselves. A wildebeest on the edges of the group is vulnerable, and a wildebeest that gets stuck while crossing water may be in trouble. But group movement protects the herd as a whole.

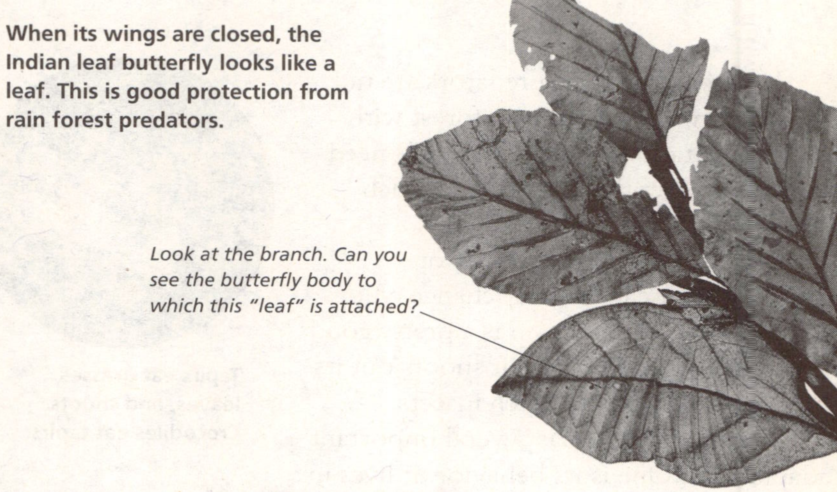
**When its wings are closed, the Indian leaf butterfly looks like a leaf. This is good protection from rain forest predators.**

*Look at the branch. Can you see the butterfly body to which this "leaf" is attached?*

The eyes of a crocodile are raised above its body. It floats through the river with only its eyes above water, almost invisible to any animals standing on the riverbanks. Its enormous, strong jaws and sharp teeth can make short work of a turtle or a tapir that is not paying attention!

The anaconda is the heaviest snake in the world and can grow to be almost thirty feet long. The anaconda coils itself around its prey and squeezes until its prey can no longer breathe. An animal of any size is in trouble if an anaconda catches it sleeping!

**This crocodile may kill one wildebeest, but most of the herd will escape.**

**The tiger centipede is named for its colors, but its poison protects it from predators.**

However, the large predators are not the only animals in the rain forest with clever adaptations. Smaller animals need ways to protect themselves from such fearsome enemies!

The chameleon is a master of camouflage. It can actually change color to hide. And a chameleon is a pretty good predator in its own right; it shoots out its long, sticky tongue to catch insects.

The harpy eagle has several important adaptations. One is its behavior: it lives in the treetops of the rain forest, where it is safe from most predators. Another is its structure: although it is a large bird, it has short, rounded wings. Its small wingspan allows it to fly between the trees in search of prey.

The electric eel, which is actually a fish, can grow to be up to nine feet long. The electric eel is so named because it produces a very strong electrical shock! This makes the electric eel an effective predator and a risky prey.

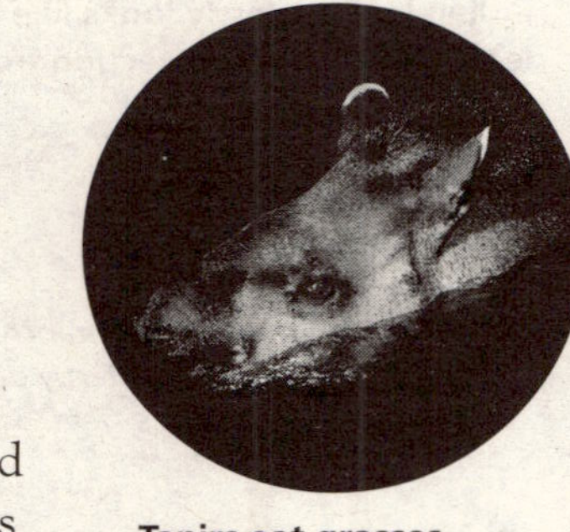

Tapirs eat grasses, leaves, and shoots. Crocodiles eat tapirs.

Lions live in groups called prides. Female lions such as this one do most of the hunting for the pride.

During the dry season, lightning sometimes strikes the savanna and sets the grasses on fire. Many savanna animals, both predator and prey, have adaptations that protect them from these fires. Animals such as gazelles, cheetahs, lions, and leopards can run very fast and escape the flames. Smaller animals may burrow beneath the soil and wait underground until the fires have passed.

The elephant is not a predator; it eats plant matter. Due to its size, it is also rarely prey. Elephants do have one dangerous predator: humans. The African elephant is a threatened species because hunters kill elephants illegally in order to sell their ivory tusks.

Lions are wild animals that live in grassy plains and open savanna. They live in a group, or pride, which includes an average of fifteen members—several generations of lionesses, their cubs, and one or two adult males. Lionesses do most of the hunting. They prey especially on medium- to large-size hoofed animals, such as wildebeest, zebra, impala, gazelle, and antelope. They also prey on baboons and buffalo. Lions are rightfully called the king of beasts.

# Grasslands

A grassland is an ecosystem that primarily has grass or grasslike plant life. Meadows and prairies are both grasslands. The most famous grassland is the African savanna where grazing animals such as wildebeests and zebras are prey for predators such as lions, cheetahs, and hyenas.

The African savanna experiences hot temperatures year-round, and the rainy season lasts only six to eight months. During the dry times, many birds and mammals migrate in search of food. If there is not enough grass for the grazers, then the predators are also affected.

Zebras can run very fast. This adaptation is their best defense against predators such as lions.

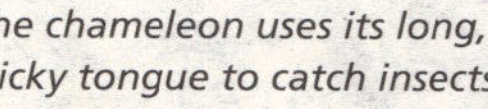

Vampire bats feed only on the blood of other animals. Large amounts of blood are hard to find, so these bats are small. This size adaptation helps the bats survive.

The poison arrow frog is tiny, but this doesn't necessarily mean that it is vulnerable. Its bright colors are a warning to other animals that its skin is poisonous. Animals that ignore the colored warnings may not feel too good once the frog's poison begins working on their muscles and nerves!

Rain forests are among the most diverse ecosystems in the world and are hosts to many kinds of animals with bizarre adaptations. These adaptations suit the animals' dangers and their needs.

These animals are at home in a rain forest habitat. Very few of them would thrive in the next ecosystem we will study: deserts.

A chameleon is an example of an animal that is both predator and prey. It changes color both to trick its prey and to protect itself from predators.

*The chameleon uses its long, sticky tongue to catch insects.*

# Deserts

A desert is a dry, usually sandy ecosystem with temperature extremes and little vegetation. Desert-dwelling predators and prey have one significant thing in common: a need for the desert's most precious commodity, water.

Desert animals have adaptations that help them collect and conserve water. For example, many desert animals are nocturnal, which means they sleep during the day and hunt at night. Others, such as meerkats, are active during the day. Meerkats have excellent vision to spot potential predators. If threatened, meerkats start digging on the ground to make a cloud of dust and distract the aggressor.

**Meerkats stay together to protect themselves from predators. They mostly eat insects.**

Snakes swallow their prey whole. Snakes have strong digestive enzymes that slowly break down their food. minit ip ea feu feugait laorperilit utpat.

**The snake swallows the egg.**

**The snake digests the egg.**

Some of the desert's best predators are snakes. Snakes are cold-blooded, so their bodies have the air or water temperature of their habitat. Snakes can hunt day or night and attack prey by surprise. A few snakes are poisonous. The powerful venom is used to paralyze the prey. A snake's detachable jaw and stretchable body allow it to swallow food whole.

In the desert, plant-eating animals, including insects, get water from the small green plants that grow after rare rainstorms. Meat-eating predators get water from their prey or from dew. All desert animals, whether predator or prey, take advantage of every opportunity to hydrate.

**The caracal is nocturnal. It hunts birds, reptiles, and mammals.**

Science

Science

# Ring of FIRE

by Barbara Fierman

83

| Genre | Comprehension Skill | Text Features | Science Content |
|---|---|---|---|
| Nonfiction | Draw Conclusions | • Captions<br>• Diagrams<br>• Maps<br>• Glossary | Plate Tectonics |

**Scott Foresman Science 6.8**

# What did you learn?

1. What is the Ring of Fire?

2. How is a subduction zone formed?

3. What part of the 1906 earthquake in San Francisco caused the most damage? Why?

4. **Writing** in Science According to the theory of continental drift, the continent Pangaea gradually split into the seven continents on Earth today. Describe the evidence that supports this theory.

5. **Draw Conclusions** Would a volcanologist classify Mount Fuji as an active, dormant, or extinct volcano? Explain.

**Vocabulary**

continental drift
core
crust
fault
lithosphere
mantle
plate boundary
plate tectonics

**Extended Vocabulary**

caldera
cinder cone
epicenter
fissure
magma
magnitude
volcanologists

**Picture Credits**
Every effort has been made to secure permission and provide appropriate credit for photographic material. The publisher deeply regrets any omission and pledges to correct errors called to its attention in subsequent editions.

Photo locators denoted as follows: Top (T), Center (C), Bottom (B), Left (L), Right (R), Background (Bkgd).

Opener: Reuters/Corbis; 4 (B) ©Jim Sugar/Corbis; 11 Reuters/Corbis; 15 (B) Tui De Roy/Minden Pictures; 16 ©Gary Braasch/Corbis; 17 (TR) Philippe Bourseiller /Photo Researchers, Inc., (B) Seiden Allan /PhotoLibrary; 20 (B) PhotoLibrary; 21 (TR) Paul Chesley/Getty Images; 23 Jeremy Bishop/Photo Researchers, Inc.

Scott Foresman/Dorling Kindersley would also like to thank: 15 (TR, CRA) Natural History Museum, London/DK Images.

Unless otherwise acknowledged, all photographs are the copyright © of Dorling Kindersley, a division of Pearson.

ISBN: 0-328-13993-9



2 3 4 5 6 7 8 9 10 V004 13 12 11 10 09 08 07 06 05

# Glossary

**caldera** a large depression formed when a volcanic crater collapses

**cinder cone** a volcano formed from ash and loose bits of rock from an explosive volcanic eruption

**epicenter** the point on Earth's surface that lies directly above the focus of an earthquake

**fissure** a jagged crack in Earth's crust, caused by earthquakes, volcanic activity, and plate movements

**magma** hot liquid rock and gases inside Earth

**magnitude** a measurement of the size of an earthquake based on the energy released and the size of the seismic waves created

**volcanologists** scientists who study volcanoes



# Ring of FIRE

by Barbara Fierman

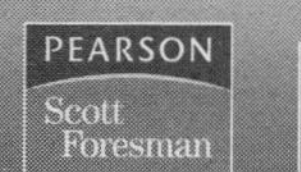

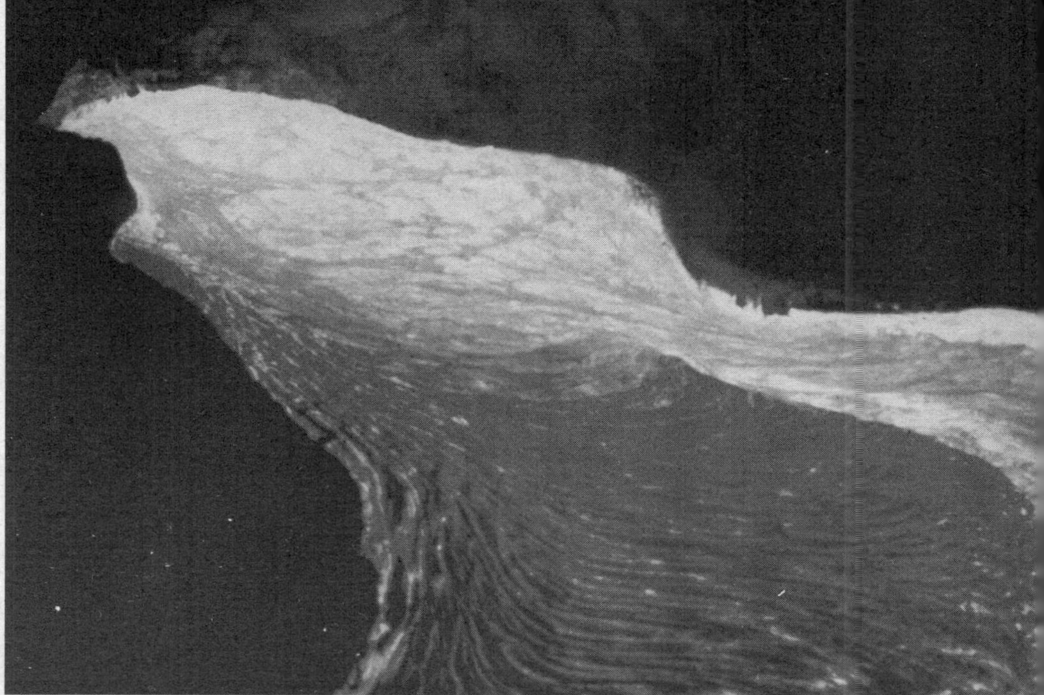

PEARSON Scott Foresman DK

# What You Already Know

The outermost layer of Earth is the crust. The thickness of the crust varies—areas covered by oceans are about five kilometers thick, while areas of dry land can be thirty kilometers thick. The layer below the crust is the mantle. The outer part of the mantle, like the crust, is solid. The inner part is extremely hot, so hot that the rock is partially melted.

The innermost layer of Earth is the core. The core is quite dense as a result of the pressure of the rock above it. The temperature of the core is about 5,000°C, just about the same as that of the Sun.

The crust and the solid part of the mantle make up the lithosphere. The lithosphere is broken into pieces called tectonic plates. These plates are of different shapes and sizes. Most of the lithosphere is actually under the oceans and other bodies of water on Earth.



**This model shows a slice through the Earth.**

# Research

Scientists who specialize in the study of volcanoes are called volcanologists. Volcanologists monitor volcanic and earthquake activity in order to make more accurate predictions and save more lives. Their work involves a variety of research activities. They may climb mountains to search through a lava flow or crawl into craters to collect samples of rock and volcanic gases. By analyzing the gases, they can sometimes predict changes in a volcano's activity.

Many volcanologists work for the U.S. Geological Survey. This government agency maintains five observatories in the United States. The scientists at the location in Hawaii predict, monitor, and study the activity of the Kilauea and Mauna Loa volcanoes. At the site in Washington State, scientists monitor Mount St. Helens and other volcanoes in the Cascade Mountain range. In Alaska, geologists from the agency and the University of Alaska monitor the twenty active volcanoes there and eighty others in the North Pacific.

Volcanologists use special types of equipment and tools in their research. Equipment includes heat suits and gloves to protect them when they observe active volcanoes, and helmets and face masks to protect them from falling rocks, dust, and poisonous gases. They use special thermometers called thermocouples to record the temperature of lava flows.

Volcanologists expect more volcanic and earthquake activity to occur in the Ring of Fire. Hopefully, they will be able to predict it in time to save lives.

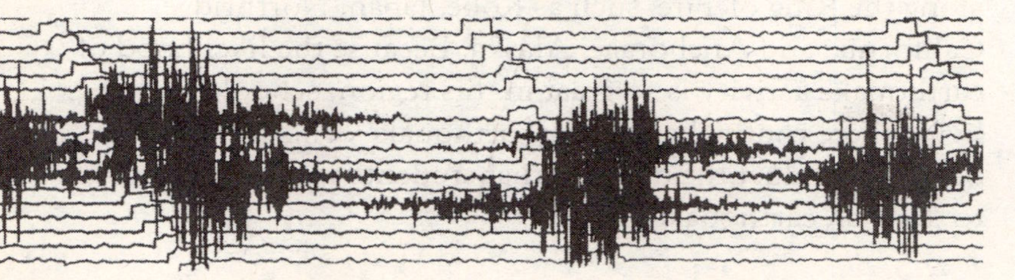

**The zigzag lines recorded on this seismogram indicate the size of an earthquake.**

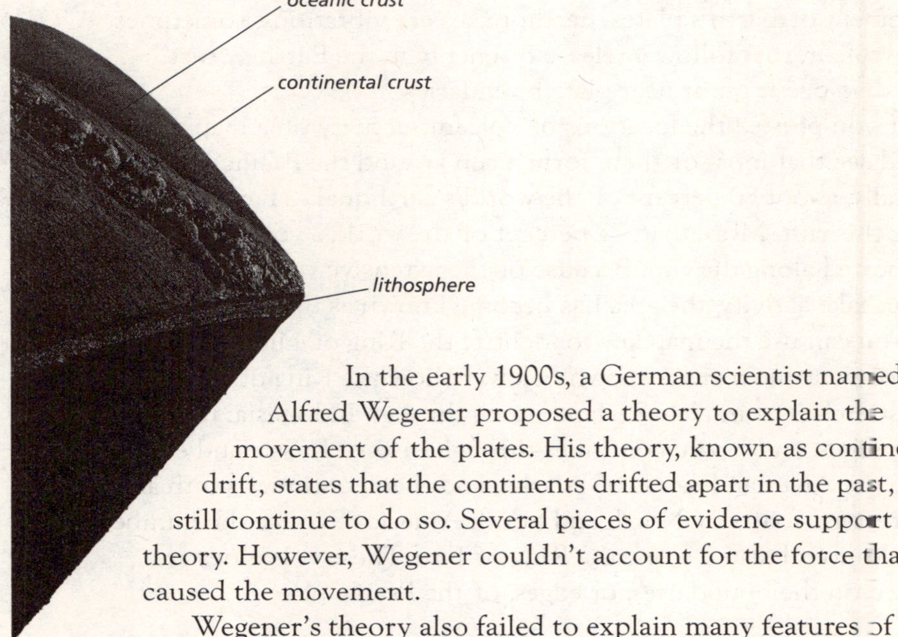


In the early 1900s, a German scientist named Alfred Wegener proposed a theory to explain the movement of the plates. His theory, known as continental drift, states that the continents drifted apart in the past, and still continue to do so. Several pieces of evidence support this theory. However, Wegener couldn't account for the force that caused the movement.

Wegener's theory also failed to explain many features of the Earth's crust. Currently, scientists rely on the theory of plate tectonics to explain the appearance of Earth's features. According to this theory, Earth's lithosphere is composed of about twenty plates floating on a layer of partly melted rock. The theory also explains many of Earth's features, such as how continents break apart, how mountain chains form, how volcanoes erupt, or how oceans change size.

The areas where two plates meet are referred to as plate boundaries. When plates move toward each other, they can rise up and form mountains. When one plate slides below another, faults, or breaks in Earth's crust, may form. This type of movement can cause earthquakes.

# Volcanic Regions

Most volcanoes of the world are found along the boundaries of major plates. The origin of volcanoes is closely related to the movement of Earth's plates. Earthquakes are vibrations, sometimes very violent, that follow a release of energy in the Earth's crust. They also occur on or near plate boundaries.

If you plotted the locations of volcanic activity on a map, you would see that most of them form a rim around the Pacific Ocean. Actually, about 80 percent of the world's earthquakes have occurred along this rim. More than 75 percent of the world's volcanoes are located along the rim. Because of the extensive volcanic and earthquake activity, the area has become known as the Ring of Fire.

You can use the map key to identify the Ring of Fire on the map of volcanic regions shown below. Follow the Ring of Fire as it stretches from New Zealand north through Indonesia, the Philippines, and Japan; continues through eastern Russia and east along the Aleutian Islands of Alaska; and then continues south along the western coasts of North and South America. Notice the number of volcanoes located along the Ring of Fire. These volcanoes are located on the boundaries, or edges, of the Pacific plate.

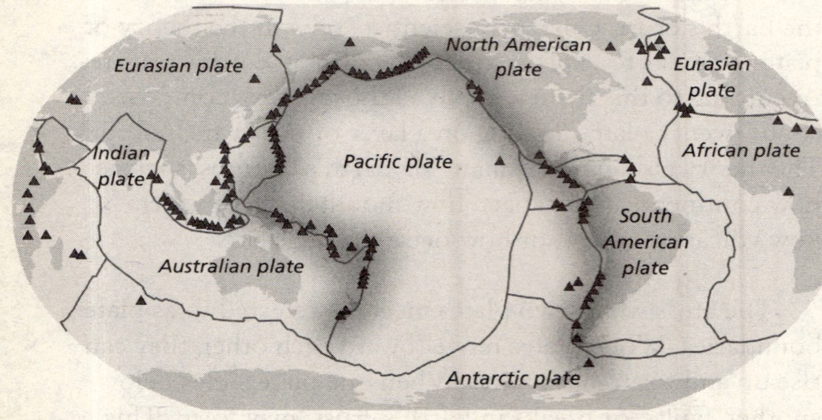


**Map Key:**     **Ring of Fire**     —— plate boundary     ▲ volcano

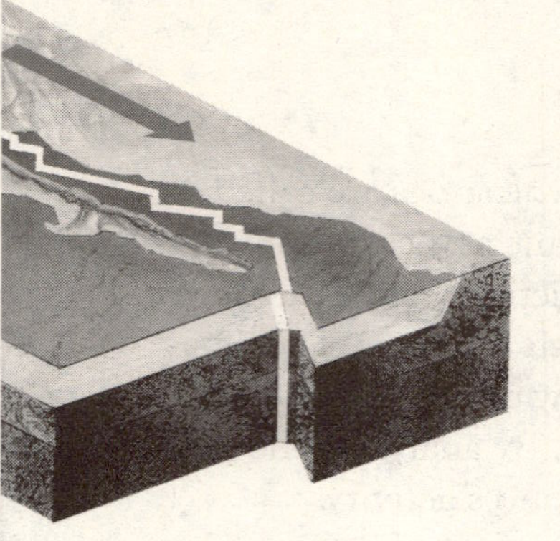

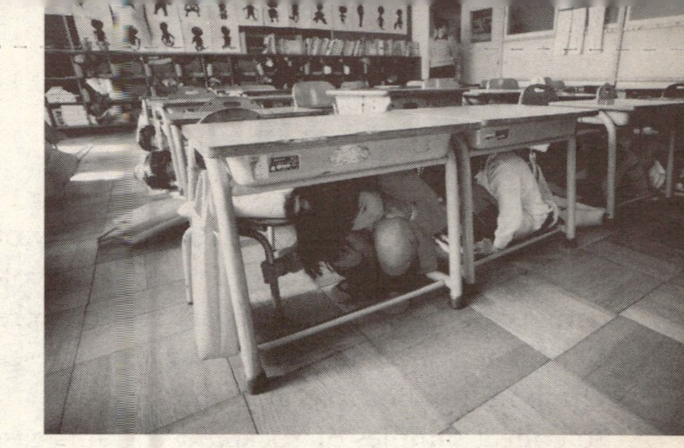
Students in Japan practice regular earthquake drills.

The city of San Francisco is located near the fault line and has been the site of major earthquakes. In 1906 a magnitude 8.3 earthquake, known as the Great San Francisco Earthquake, hit the city in the early morning hours. Buildings crumbled into the streets, gas pipes broke, and the city's main water pipelines broke. Dozens of fires broke out, but without water, firefighters couldn't put them out. The fires raged through the city for three days. In the end, about 90 percent of the total damage was due to fire.

The United States Geological Survey predicted that a moderate-to-large earthquake would hit San Francisco between 1988 and 2018. In October 1989 their prediction proved to be correct when an earthquake shook the city again. This earthquake occurred just before a World Series game was to be played in Candlestick Park. Measuring 7.1 on the Richter scale, the earthquake was responsible for the destruction of 100,000 buildings and the collapse of a section of the San Francisco Bay Bridge.

Other devastating earthquakes have occurred in locations along the Ring of Fire, such as Kobe, Japan; Northridge, California; and Anchorage, Alaska. Because the likelihood of earthquake activity is so great in this region, schoolchildren living there routinely perform earthquake drills in school. Schools conduct the drills so that students will know what to do if an earthquake occurs.

Locations along the Ring of Fire are especially inclined to earthquake activity. The Pacific plate, almost 9,000 miles wide, is the largest tectonic plate. On its eastern boundary, it meets the North American plate. The San Andreas fault is located at the junction of these two plates. The fault is 10 miles deep and stretches north along the coast of California for about 750 miles. About twenty major earthquakes occurred along the San Andreas fault in the twentieth century.

The San Andreas fault is an example of a strike-slip fault. The fault runs vertically through rock. Rock on one side slips and scrapes past the other.

The 1989 earthquake in San Francisco caused buildings to collapse.

Cerro Negro, a volcano in northern Nicaragua, has erupted at least twenty times since 1850.

# Moving Plates

Earth's crust is cracked into about twenty pieces called tectonic plates. Tectonic plates can be classified as continental or oceanic plates. Continental plates are located mainly under continents, and oceanic plates are located mainly under the ocean. Scientists estimate that the plates range from twenty-five to sixty miles in thickness.

Tectonic plates are like rafts of solid rock that float on the mantle beneath them. As the mantle moves, the tectonic plates move too. The moving plates pull away from, collide with, or scrape past each other. Although the plates move very, very slowly, the power of their collisions is great.

When two plates collide, the lighter plate is often forced up over the heavier one. This action can cause cracks in the mantle. Eventually, these cracks create openings that allow molten, or melted, rock to rise up out of Earth's core.

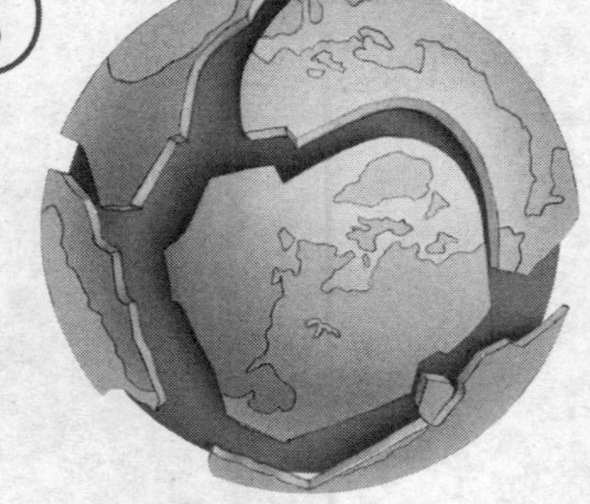

Earth's crust is split into sections called tectonic plates.

Each earthquake has a focus, which is the place where it begins underground. Directly above the focus, on the surface, is its epicenter. Energy moves away from the focus in the form of seismic, or shock, waves. Different types of seismic waves produce the earthquake's initial jolt, shake the ground in all directions, or produce a rolling, wavelike motion.

Seismologists, scientists who study earthquakes, measure seismic waves and determine the magnitude, or size, of an earthquake. They use this information to give each earthquake a number rating on the Richter scale. The scale begins at zero and increases by one number at a time. However, the amount of ground movement is ten times the amount of the previous number. While the Richter scale has no upper limit, the largest earthquakes recorded on the scale have had a magnitude of approximately 8.9.

| Description | Richter Magnitudes | Earthquake Effects | Average Annually |
| --- | --- | --- | --- |
| Micro | Less than 2.0 | Microearthquakes, not felt | About 8,000 per day |
| Very minor | 2.0–2.9 | Generally not felt, but recorded | About 1,000 per day |
| Minor | 3.0–3.9 | Often felt, but rarely cause damage | 49,000 (estimated) |
| Light | 4.0–4.9 | Shaking of indoor items, rattling noises | 6,200 (estimated) |
| Moderate | 5.0–5.9 | Can cause major damage to poorly constructed buildings over small regions | 800 |
| Strong | 6.0–6.9 | Can be destructive in areas up to one hundred miles across | 120 |
| Major | 7.0–7.9 | Can cause serious damage over larger areas | 18 |
| Great | 8.0 or greater | Can cause serious damages in areas hundreds of miles across | 1 |

# Earthquakes

Locations that are likely to have volcanic activity are also likely to have earthquake activity. As tectonic plates slide, scrape, and collide, the movement creates cracks in the crust. These cracks are called faults. Over time, pressure in the crust builds until it can't be contained any longer. Finally, the rock splits along the fault, and an earthquake occurs.

Since most faults exist where plate boundaries collide, most earthquakes happen where two or more plate boundaries meet. However, faults can be located anywhere in the crust. Whenever there is movement along a fault, an earthquake happens. Some faults are close to the surface, while others are deep in the crust. Earthquakes that occur close to the surface are more likely to be felt and to do the most damage. Some earthquakes originate within the upper mantle.

This model of a street illustrates the damage that an earthquake can cause.

The action of tectonic plates results in different types of boundaries between them. Divergent boundaries, such as those of the Mid-Atlantic Ridge, separate from each other. When the plates pull apart, magma, or molten rock, comes up from Earth's inner layers to form a new crust. Convergent boundaries form when two plates meet in a collision, or one slides over the other. Transform fault boundaries form when plates slide along one another. Most volcanoes and earthquakes occur because of the activity at plate boundaries.

Indonesia is located at the boundary of several plates. As a result, more than 125 active volcanoes exist there. An example is Merapi, on the island of Java. Merapi is the most active composite volcano in Indonesia. It has erupted at least sixty-eight times since 1548.

The mountain in the center s Mt. Bromo, one of over 125 active volcanoes in Indonesia.

**Why do plates move?** Scientists have proposed different explanations to answer the question. One explanation is the convection cell theory. It states that streams of magma are pushed upward from deep within Earth and out onto the ocean floor. As the molten rock cools and hardens, it forms new rock and causes the ocean floor to spread. This process pushes the plates.

Another explanation is the plume theory. This theory states that plumes, or huge balls of extremely hot rock, exist in the lower part of the mantle. These plumes rise up into the upper part of the mantle as hot spots. When a plume rises, it can spread out and cover an area a few hundred miles across. A result of this process is volcanic activity.

220 million years ago

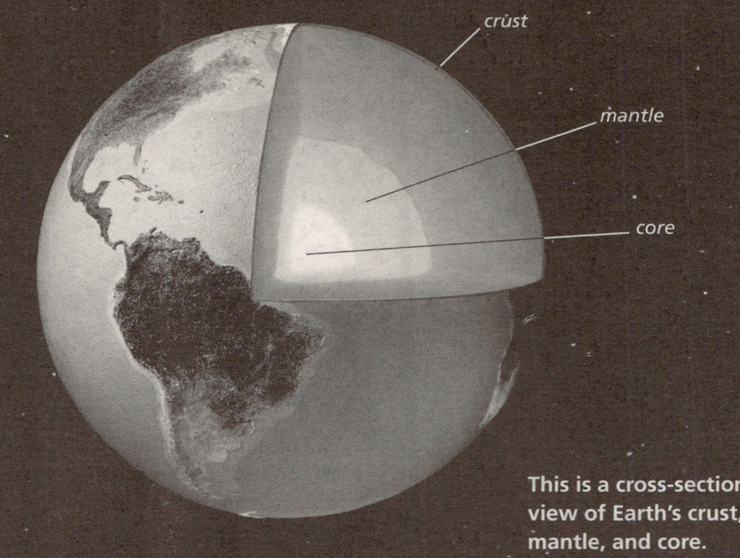


This is a cross-sectional view of Earth's crust, mantle, and core.

Mount Pinatubo, in the Philippines, erupted on June 15, 1991. Three days earlier, a cloud of volcanic ash and gas rose up above the mountain. People in the surrounding area felt the ground tremble and noticed steam spurting from cracks in the rocks. Scientists predicted the eruption and warned people to leave the area. About 300 people were killed, but at least 5,000 lives were saved because of early warning.

Mount Fuji is a composite volcano. Its first eruption occurred at least 3,000 years ago. The most recent eruption was in 1707, when ash and huge pieces of rock were ejected. In 2000, tremors occurred in the area, and in 2003, steam was detected coming from vents on the northeastern side.

A thick coat of ash covered the landscape after Pinatubo erupted.

Mount Fuji, the highest mountain in Japan, has a large, circular crater at the summit.

**92**

Mount St. Helens erupted on May 18, 1980, spewing hot rocks, dust, and gases.

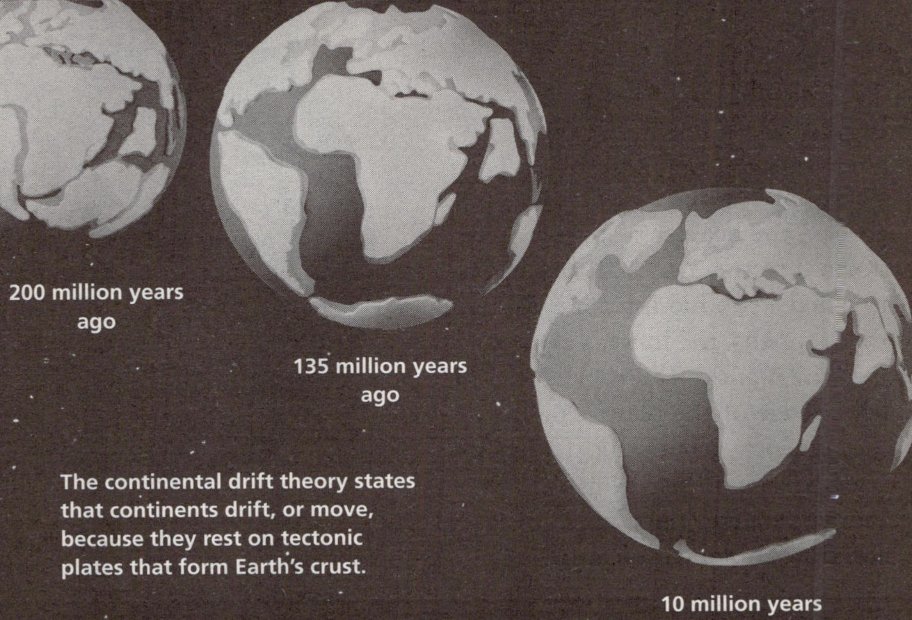



Several famous volcanoes exist around the Ring of Fire. Mount Paricutin, in Mexico, is an example of a cinder cone volcano. Paricutin first erupted in 1943, and the eruption continued for about eight more years. Eruptions of gases and molten lava fell back around the vent and built up the cone to 1,100 feet. The final eruption left a crater shaped like a funnel at the top of the cinder cone. Lava continued to flow out onto the surface surrounding the cone.

Over a period of nine years, Paricutin covered an area of about 100 square miles with ash and destroyed the town of San Juan. During this time, geologists around the world were able to observe Paricutin and study its development.

Mount St. Helens had been inactive for approximately 123 years. In 1978, scientists studying the volcano predicted that it would erupt in the next ten years. In March of 1980, small explosions began, with some ash and smoke coming out of the vent. In April the north side began to bulge out, and in May the devastating eruption occurred. The volcano ejected pieces of rocks, ash, and a cloud of gases. In 1982, the area became Mount St. Helens National Volcanic Monument. Visitors at the site can learn all about volcanoes.

The theory of plate tectonics is based on the theory of continental drift. Proposed by Alfred Wegener in the early 1900s, this theory states that one huge continent, Pangaea, existed on Earth about 200–250 million years ago. After about 100 million years, streams of molten rock in the mantle caused Pangaea to split into pieces. These pieces eventually became the seven continents that exist on Earth today.

Wegener supported his theory with observations about the shape of the Earth's continents. He noticed that the continents fit together like pieces in a puzzle. For example, the eastern edge of South America and the western edge of Africa seemed to fit so perfectly that they could have actually been joined at one time.

Wegener also knew that certain types of rock had been discovered on more than one continent. The discovery of rock formations that extended over the current boundaries of South America and Africa strongly supported the idea that the continents were once joined.

As you read earlier, the movement of plates can cause collisions along boundaries. Sometimes, when two plates collide, the heavier plate is forced down into the mantle, forming what is called a subduction zone. When this happens, the Earth's crust sinks into the mantle. The rock along the lower edge of the plate is melted by molten rock, or magma. The magma rises, forcing its way through the lithosphere and the plate above it, and flows out as a volcano. Since many subduction zones exist in the Ring of Fire, it is a region of intense volcanic activity.

Many hot spots also exist within the Ring of Fire. Scientists believe that the Hawaiian Islands formed over a hot spot. The Pacific plate slid northwest and traveled over the hot spot. Magma rose up through the ocean floor and formed a volcanic island. As the plate continued to move, a magma eruption created another island.

The first islands formed, Kauai and Oahu, have no active volcanoes at this time. Currently the Big Island of Hawaii is above the hot spot. The active volcanoes there are Mauna Loa and Kilauea.

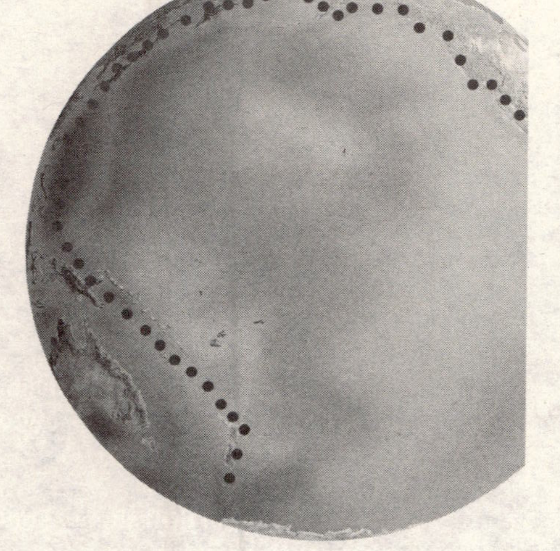
This view of Earth shows the Pacific Ocean. The dots indicate the Ring of Fire.

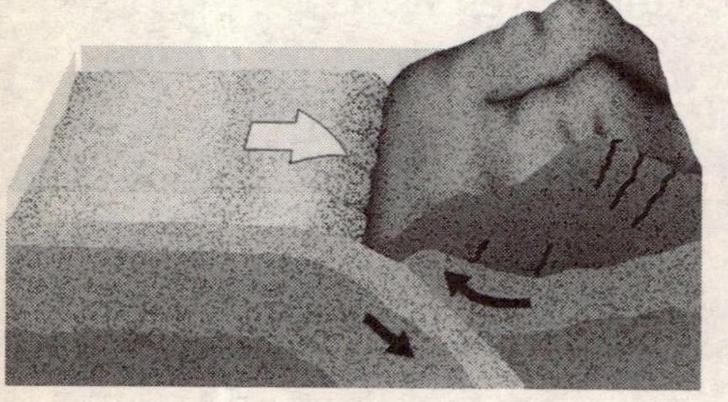
plates colliding

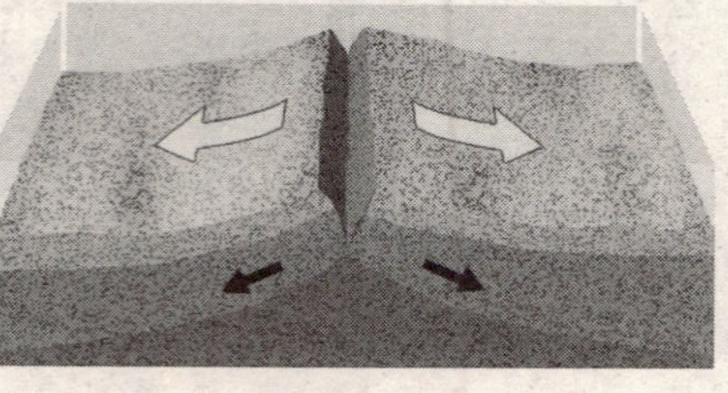
plates moving apart

When an extremely forceful volcanic eruption takes place, it can actually destroy the volcano. The explosion causes the sides of the crater to collapse and form a caldera—a wide bowl-shaped hole more than a kilometer wide. An example is Mount Mazama in southwestern Oregon. When it erupted over 6,000 years ago, it left a caldera more than nine kilometers wide and about two kilometers deep. The caldera that was formed is now known as Crater Lake.

Volcanic eruptions produce different types of lava. One type, *aa*, is lava that cools quickly and hardens into rough chunks of rock. Another type, *pahoehoe*, is thin lava that cools more slowly and hardens into smooth, ropy pieces. Pumice is lava that cools and hardens into a lightweight rock with many air bubbles in it. Pumice can be either *aa* or *pahoehoe*.

aa

pahoehoe

Cerro Azul is a shield volcano located in the Galapagos Islands. The volcano has erupted eight times, sometimes endangering the nesting zones of giant tortoises. The caldera is small in diameter, but very deep.

# Types of Volcanoes

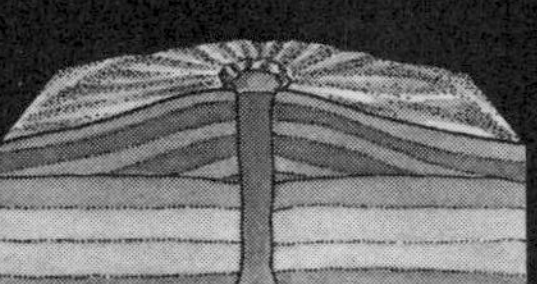
**fissure volcano**

In a fissure volcano, lava erupts from a long crack in Earth's surface. Lava may erupt from several places along the crack.

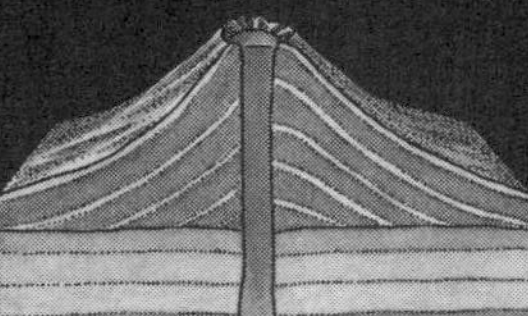
**shield volcano**

Shield volcanoes erupt into broad, flat mounds. Basalt lava pours from many side vents.

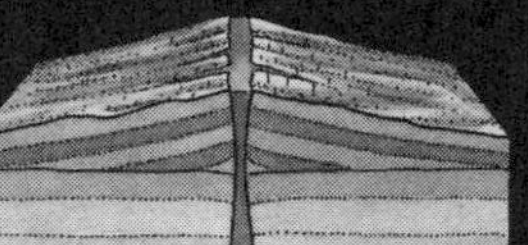
**dome volcano**

Dome volcanoes erupt viscous lava, which slowly builds up over the vent and forms a dome.

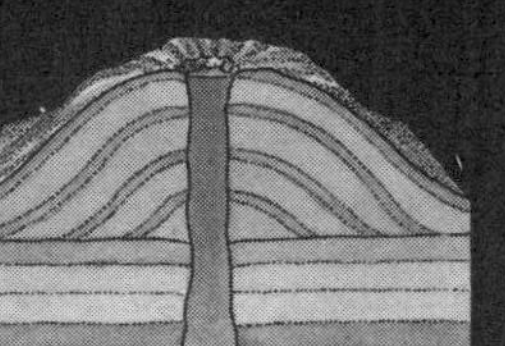
**cinder cone volcano**

Hard fragments of lava, ash, and volcanic gases erupt from cinder cone volcanoes. The volcanic material erupts from a main vent and forms a cone shape.

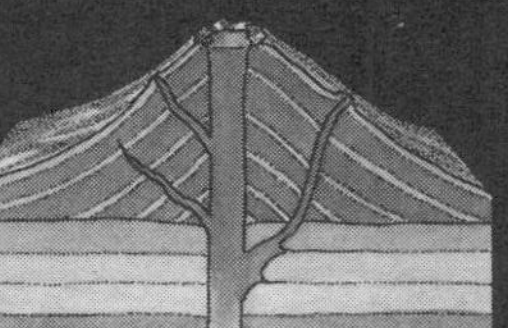
**composite volcano**

These symmetrical volcanoes usually have steep sides and cratered summits.

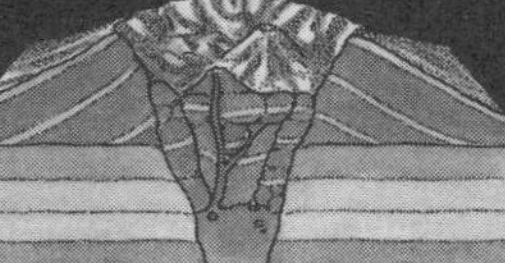
**caldera volcano**

When a volcano is so violent that it collapses in on itself, a caldera, a large bowl shape, is formed.

The Kilauea volcano erupts at a vent known as Puu Oo. Within the cone is a crater enclosing a lava lake. Note the fountains of lava bursting forth from the lake.

# Volcanoes

Volcanoes usually occur in areas where tectonic plates collide. The collision of plates causes Earth's crust to crack. Heat and pressure become so intense that parts of the mantle melt. Molten rock and hot gases are forced out through the cracks in the crust.

Volcanoes are classified as active, dormant, and extinct. An active volcano is one that could erupt at any time, even though it is not necessarily in the process of erupting. There are about 1,500 active volcanoes on Earth, with about fifty in the United States. A dormant volcano is one that has been inactive for a long period of time. Mount Pinatubo is a volcano in the Philippines, an island chain in the western Pacific Ocean. It was dormant for six centuries before it erupted in 1991. The huge eruption covered an area of 4,000 square kilometers with ash. An extinct volcano is one that shows no signs of erupting again.

Although dormant volcanoes are currently inactive, they may still continue to let off steam because of the magma that exists inside them. Dormant volcanoes may have craters, bowl-shaped areas that hold boiling lava. Lava is the name for magma that has erupted. Craters are formed by magma that is expelled through a vent and forms a lava lake. During dormant periods, the lava in the lake cools and hardens over the vent. When pressure builds up, the volcano may erupt again in a huge explosion.

## Explosive Force

The girl in the photo uses a bottle of soda to model the process of a volcanic eruption. She shakes the bottle gently and then shakes it more vigorously. When she opens the bottle, the trapped gas, carbon dioxide, spurts out.

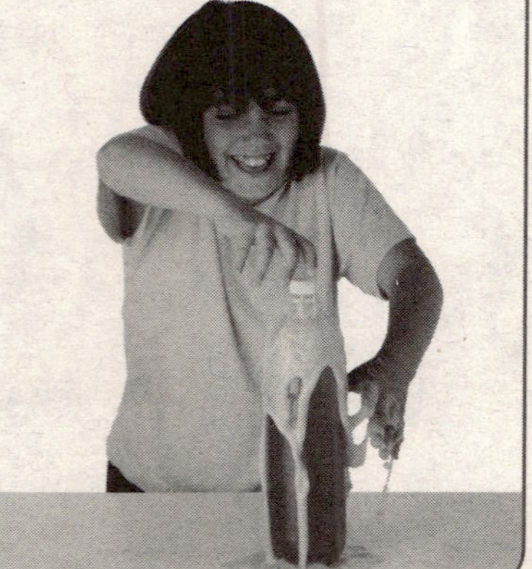

## Inside a Volcano

During a volcanic eruption  magma and hot gases from Earth's mantle flow up. They erupt through a vent, or hole, in the crust. They also may erupt through a vent at the side of the volcano.

Different types of volcanoes produce different types of eruptions. In less-violent eruptions, streams of lava flow gently through vents in the volcano. Runny lava can travel great distances before it solidifies and stops. When the lava is viscous, or thick and sticky, more violent eruptions may take place. Lava fragments, hot rocks, ash, and dust may be shot out over the surrounding area. A layer of ash several feet thick may cover the area. In addition, volcanic ash can be suspended in air for some time.

Science

Science

# Down to Earth

by Jennifer Coates-Conroy

| Genre | Comprehension Skill | Text Features | Science Content |
| --- | --- | --- | --- |
| Nonfiction | Compare and Contrast | • Captions<br>• Labels<br>• Call Outs<br>• Glossary | Rocks and Minerals |

Scott Foresman Science 6.9

PEARSON
Scott Foresman

DK

ISBN 0-328-13996-3

9 780328 139965    90000

scottforesman.com

# What did you learn?

1. Soil began as solid rock. How did it develop into an ecosystem to sustain plant and animal life?

2. Explain the major causes of land erosion.

3. What animals contribute to the formation of topsoil? How?

4. **Writing** in Science Topsoils, rich in humus, are necessary in agriculture. Write to explain in what ways topsoil can be enriched to obtain better crops.

5. **Compare and Contrast** Make a chart to compare and contrast organic farming and non-organic farming.

| Vocabulary | Extended Vocabulary |
| --- | --- |
| crystal | accelerated erosion |
| humus | alkaline |
| igneous rock | carbonic acid |
| metamorphic rock | chemical weathering |
| organic matter | geological erosion |
| rock | landforms |
| sediment | organic farming |
| sedimentary rock | root nodules |

**Picture Credits**
Every effort has been made to secure permission and provide appropriate credit for photographic material.
The publisher deeply regrets any omission and pledges to correct errors called to its attention in subsequent editions.

Photo locators denoted as follows: Top (T), Center (C), Bottom (B), Left (L), Right (R), Background (Bkgd).

3 Getty Images; 7 (T) Claus Meyer/Minden Pictures; 12 (BR) Jacqui Hurst/DK Images.

Unless otherwise acknowledged, all photographs are the copyright © of Dorling Kindersley, a division of Pearson.

ISBN: 0-328-13996-3

# Glossary

| | |
|---|---|
| **accelerated erosion** | the process of soil weathering at a greater rate than normal |
| **alkaline** | with a pH greater than 7 |
| **carbonic acid** | an acid formed by carbon dioxide and water |
| **chemical weathering** | the process in which rocks and minerals undergo chemical changes |
| **geological erosion** | natural erosion |
| **landforms** | all the physical, recognizable, naturally formed features found in land |
| **organic farming** | farming without synthetic fertilizers |
| **root nodules** | abnormal root growth on a plant root system caused by bacteria |





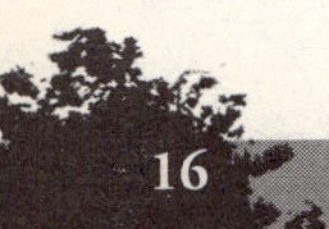

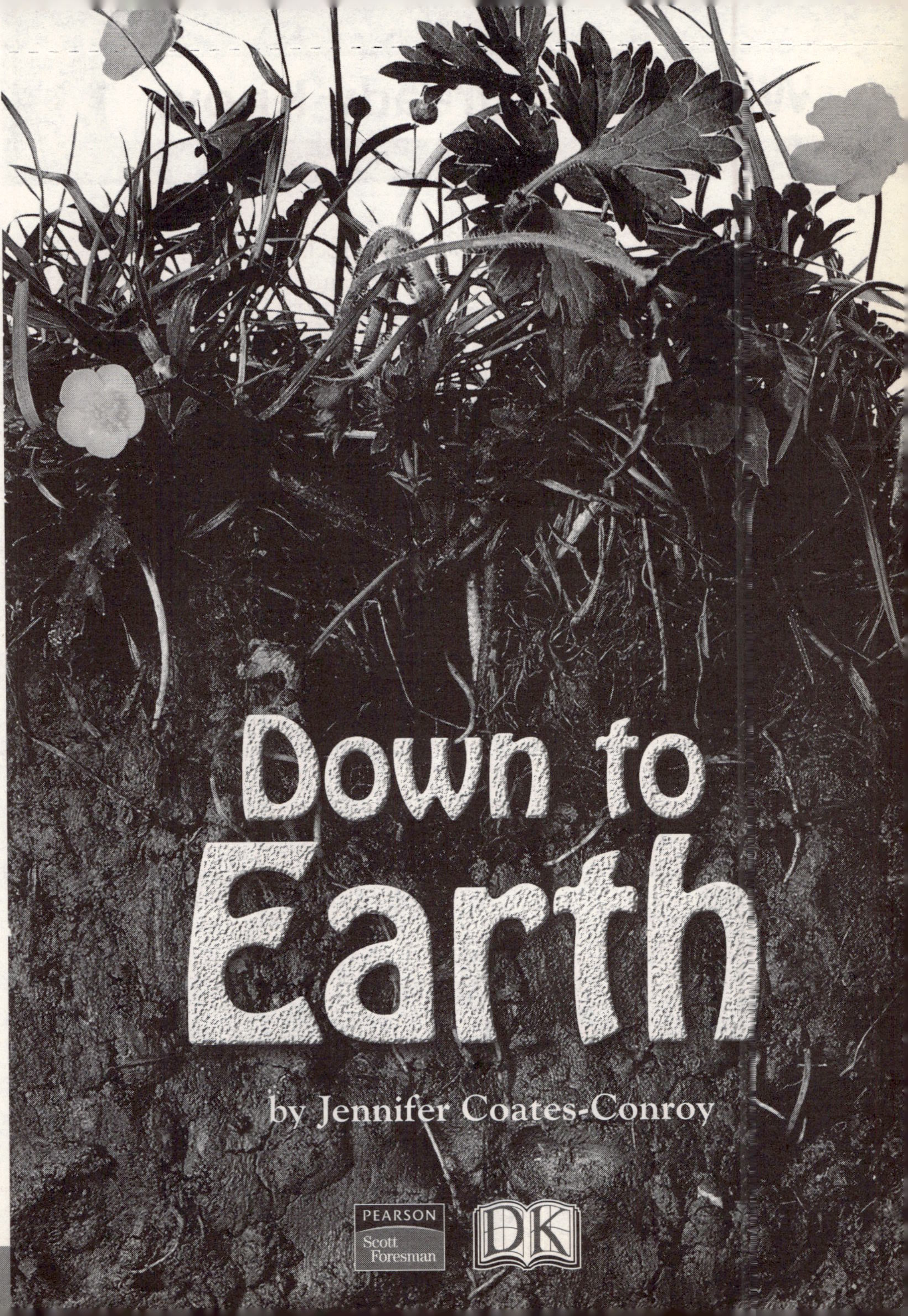

# Down to Earth

by Jennifer Coates-Conroy

PEARSON Scott Foresman DK

# What You Already Know

Our Earth's basic land components are rocks, minerals, and soil. Each has its own unique chemical structure. A rock is a natural, solid material made of many minerals. Types of rocks are constantly changing in a process called the rock cycle. Deep within Earth, newly formed rocks are exposed to heat and pressure. Minerals are naturally occurring solid materials with a definite chemical structure. At Earth's surface, physical and chemical factors change rocks and minerals into soil. This process takes years.

There are more than 4,000 kinds of minerals on Earth. Each mineral is made up of particles that are arranged in a particular way. The distinctive properties of each mineral come from the way it is formed. Minerals are made up of crystals. The particles in a crystal are arranged in a repeating pattern. This pattern determines the shape of the crystals.

Most minerals are found in combinations. When more than two minerals combine into a solid material, a rock is formed. There are three forms of rocks: sedimentary, igneous, and metamorphic.

Years of erosion have exposed the many layers of this rock formation.

Moles have strong, spadelike claws that help them move through soil.

A mole is a mammal that lives most of its life underground. It is usually about five to six inches long and has strong front legs and long claws that it uses to dig tunnels. Moles usually dig their tunnels to a nest about ten feet below the surface and line it with leaves. Moles also dig shallower tunnels in order to find insects and worms. Moles contribute to the recycling process because they eat worms. In a single day a mole can eat about half its weight in worms and insects. If creatures like the mole did not live underground, we would have too many worms. If worms did not live underground, moles and other burrowing mammals would go hungry.

Worms and other small animals eat dead leaves on the ground.

# Animals and Soil

Animals that live underground contribute to the recycling and conservation of soil. Earthworms, for example, make soil conditions more favorable for plant growth. How do they do that? Earthworms eat old, rotten leaves and substances that they find underground. After they eat, they release the vitamins and minerals that are inside these plants into the soil. This makes the soil healthier and allows the growth of new plants. Also, when earthworms dig their underground tunnels, they mix the layers of soil together and let fresh air and water into the soil.

Some rabbits also live underground. The movements of these rabbits provide benefits similar to that provided by earthworms' tunnels.

These holes are rabbit burrows.



Sedimentary rocks, such as limestone, form in layers. These layers often contain sea animal shells and minerals from seawater. Igneous rocks are the result of volcanic eruptions. Most igneous rocks are found below Earth's surface and underwater. Metamorphic rocks are the result of physical and chemical changes in sedimentary and igneous rocks over time. Under high temperatures and constant pressure, limestone can change into marble, and sandstone can become quartzite. In this way, rocks can be cycled in nature.

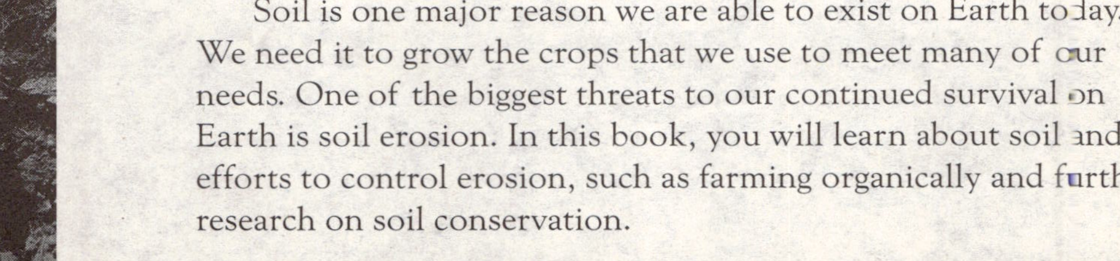
planting a tree to prevent erosion

Some processes in the rock cycle happen quickly, while others may take millions of years. Each rock can tell a story about what happened on Earth at a particular period of time, a year ago or millions of years ago! By studying fossils of animals, plants, and other living organisms, scientists can determine their age, how long ago they lived, their eating habits, and many other characteristics.

Rocks are also part of the formation of soil. The process in which rocks break into smaller and smaller pieces is called weathering. Weathering helps the formation of soil. Soil is composed of organic and inorganic particles. The tiny particles of rock mix with water and air, then blend with the organic decomposed material of living things to make soil.

Soil is one major reason we are able to exist on Earth today. We need it to grow the crops that we use to meet many of our needs. One of the biggest threats to our continued survival on Earth is soil erosion. In this book, you will learn about soil and the efforts to control erosion, such as farming organically and further research on soil conservation.

# Earth's Soil

Soil takes many years to form. Soil begins as solid rock. It is worn by years of rain, wind, and ice, and broken down into smaller and smaller pieces. Eventually it becomes a mix of sand, silt, clay, and organic materials. In time, plants grow in it. With plant and flower growth, other life forms emerge.

There is a vast ecosystem hidden within soil. Every form of plant and animal life on Earth depends on this ecosystem. The living parts of soil are very important. In the world of soil, fungi immobilize and eat tiny worms, and bacteria feed on toxic chemicals.

The living organisms within the soil eventually die, and the decaying process begins. The remains of dead organisms are known as organic matter. One type of organic matter is humus. Humus is what gives soil its richness and dark color. Humus is very important in soil because it contains many nutrients, which living organisms use to grow.

**Soil sustains plant and animal life, both above and below the surface.**

**Some of the small organisms that live in the soil help soil formation by breaking down organic matter.**

# Farming and Soil

For farmland you need more than an abundance of soil and water. In order to produce crops the soil may need fertilizing, because when a plant is harvested, its nutrients do not return to the soil. To replace the lost nutrients, farmers put fertilizers into the soil. To prevent certain nutrients from being depleted, some farmers also plant a different crop in each field every year.

Organic farming—that is, farming with natural fertilizers (animal manure and compost) that do not contain large amounts of man-made chemicals—is growing in popularity. Today, the largest number of organic farms in the United States are located in North Carolina. However, many organic farms are in Europe.

The reason for the growing popularity of organic farms is that the overuse of chemical fertilizers has been proven harmful to people, plants, and animals. Chemical fertilizers can poison the soil, and that poison can accumulate and, in time, seep into rivers and lakes.

Organic farming methods, more than any other method of cultivation, preserve and enhance soil fertility and limit the amount of chemical-based substances in our diet.

**Plant life is sparse in the desert.**

The main feature of a desert is its lack of precipitation. Most deserts are hot and dry, but some deserts are cold and dry. The sparse plant life in a desert indicates that the soil does not contain large amounts of humus. The plants that live successfully in a desert are plants that do not rely heavily on the nutrients found in topsoil. These plants, such as the cactus, are adapted to live on very little water and are able to conserve their nutrients and water to prepare for droughts. The soil in deserts is composed mostly of sand. If you look closely at desert soil, you will see small pieces of broken rock. Sometimes walking on desert sand can feel like walking on solid rock!

On the other hand, where there's an abundance of plant life, the topsoil is rich in minerals. Often this indicates the presence of a natural water source nearby.

**Where there is rich soil, plant life is abundant.**

**Farmers prepare the soil before planting crops.**

People, as well as plants and animals, need soil to live. Without soil, we could not farm. Without farming, we would have no crops. And without food from the crops, we would not survive.

Spring is the beginning of the growing season for many farmers. For many years farmers have used plows and disks to break up soil and prepare crop fields for planting. The mechanical processing of soil is called tilling. Soil is tilled to change its structure and to remove weeds and unwanted crop residues. The main goal is to prepare the soil for planting.

After preparing the soil, farmers plant seeds and use a tractor to apply fertilizer. Fertilizer enriches the soil and feeds the plants, helping them to grow stronger and faster.

Modern farming tools, better growing techniques, and more efficient harvesting and crop processing techniques are very important for today's farmers. But everything starts with good soil.

# How Soil Forms

Soil is formed when rock breaks into tiny pieces near Earth's surface. Organic matter decays and mixes with inorganic material (rock particles, minerals, and water). The compost in a garden is made by the same process—it is a mixture of decayed organic materials. Over time, minerals are often released from the rocks, causing them to erode. This chemical weathering process continually rearranges and builds landforms on Earth's surface. It is constantly transforming rocks into soil.

**Water from oceans and rivers weathers rocks.**

Rain is one of the main causes of chemical weathering. This type of weathering occurs when rainwater mixes with carbon dioxide to form carbonic acid. When carbonic acid comes into contact with certain minerals, they dissolve.

Another form of weathering is physical weathering. Causes of physical weathering include pressure on the Earth's crust and ice-wedging.

**Compost is a mixture of decaying leaves, grass, and manure, which later becomes humus.**

Loam soil is grainy and is a heavy mixture of sand, silt, and clay.

**loam soil**

Chalk soil is chalky and is very fine. When wet, this soil is sticky.

**chalk soil**

Peat soil feels spongy in texture and is dark brown or black in color.

**peat soil**

Silt soil feels powdery. When it is wet, it feels smooth but not sticky. Silt pore sizes are between those of sand and clay.

**silt soil**

Sandy soil feels rough when you rub it. This is because it has sharp edges. Sand doesn't hold many nutrients. Sandy soil is the coarsest of all soil types.

**sandy soil**

Clay soil is smooth when dry and sticky when wet. Soils high in clay content are heavy or coarse. Clay can hold a lot of nutrients, but it doesn't let much air and water through.

**clay soil**

Just as there are different layers of soil, there are different soil types. There are fine soil types and coarse soil types. Fine soil types are the result of greater proportions of clay and silt in the soil. Coarse, sandy soil types are composed mostly of minerals and are considered the skeleton of the soil. The higher the amount of coarse soil, the more permeable a soil is because of the soil's larger air spaces. Scientists describe soil types by how much sand, silt, and clay are present.

# Types of Soil

Soil pH is the measure of how acidic or basic soil is, and it is measured using a pH scale. The pH scale ranks substances on a scale of 0 to 14. Acidic substances have a pH between 0 and 7, and alkaline (basic) substances have a pH between 7 and 14. Seawater, for example, is alkaline and falls in the 7–14 pH range. Pure water is neutral and is a 7 on the pH scale.

The pH of soil is very important because it helps measure the amount of nutrients, such as nitrogen, potassium, and phosphorus, in the soil. Plants need these nutrients in specific amounts in order to grow, thrive, and fight off diseases. When the pH of soil is balanced at a certain level, plants will have the nitrogen and phosphorus they need.

Certain bacteria help maintain the nitrogen level in plants by converting atmospheric nitrogen into a form of nitrogen that plants can use. These bacteria live in root nodules of legumes and function best when the plant they live in is growing in soil of an acceptable pH range. Root nodules rich in nitrogen grow on a plant root system due to the presence of bacteria.

neutral

alkaline

acidic

The pH of soil tells how acidic or basic the soil is. This will help to measure the kind of nutrients in the soil.

Hydrangea flowers are pink when the plant grows in alkaline soil and blue or mauve when it grows in acidic soil.

Erosion in Brazil is due to massive deforestation, which is said to be one of the major man-made causes of land erosion in that country.

Just as rocks are weathered either chemically or physically, soil is threatened by erosion. Erosion is the process of gradually wearing away soil by glaciers, water, waves, or wind. Erosion can be divided into two general categories: geological and accelerated. Although we currently don't know exactly how much land erosion there has been on Earth, we do know some of its causes. Wind and water are the major causes of land erosion. At the same time, we know that trees help prevent the erosion of soil.

Soil erosion wears away our land. The less land there is, the less living space. Currently, about 75 percent of Earth's surface is covered by water. That means that only about 25 percent of Earth, including mountain areas, is above water. To preserve that land, soil conservation and other methods of slowing land deterioration have become important practices.

# Soil Layers

A thin coat of soil covers most of Earth's dry surface. In some places the soil is only a few inches deep. In other places it may be several hundred feet deep. Although the word *dirt* has often been used to refer to the land beneath our feet, the proper word is *soil*.

Although soil may appear to be just soil, thick or thin, you should also realize that there are several layers of soil. These layers are topsoil, subsoil, the lowest layer of soil, and bedrock.

Each soil layer has a different color and composition. The topsoil is the soil at the surface, and it contains small rocks, humus, living things, and inorganic matter. It is darker in color because it is rich in humus. It is lighter in weight, so it can trap air and water. A rich topsoil produces good crops. Water that penetrates this layer carries minerals down to the second layer.

The subsoil is the layer under the topsoil. It is lighter in color and more dense. It is lighter because it contains less organic material. The minerals that are carried from the topsoil are stored here.

The lowest layer of soil, called the "parent" layer, is made up of rocks, gravel, sand, and clay. There is very little organic material in this layer.

The bedrock layer is the base layer. It is solid rock. The construction of buildings starts at this level, so that they have a solid foundation.

Soil covers most of the land on Earth and is made of water, organic matter called **humus, and minerals.**

## Soil Layers

### Topsoil
Topsoil is the top layer of soil that is typically found where vegetation exists. Topsoil contains humus, which is the result of the decaying process in plants and animals.

### Subsoil
Subsoil is the second soil layer, which is lighter in color than topsoil because it has less humus. It also contains fewer spaces in which to trap air and water.

### Lowest Layer
The lowest layer of soil is also called the "parent" layer. It is made of rocks, gravel, sand, and clay. There is no humus in this layer.

### Bedrock
Bedrock is the fourth layer of soil, beneath the parent layer. It is solid rock.

# CAVES

Earth Science

by Lillian Duggan

| Genre | Comprehension Skill | Text Features | Science Content |
| --- | --- | --- | --- |
| Nonfiction | Draw Conclusions | • Captions<br>• Diagram<br>• Glossary | Earth's Surface |

Scott Foresman Science 6.10

PEARSON

Scott Foresman

scottforesman.com

DK

ISBN 0-328-13999-8

90000

9 780328 139996

# What did you learn?

1. Name the acid that can break down limestone.

2. How are animals that live deep inside caves different from most other animals?

3. What is Lascaux Cave famous for?

4. **Writing** in Science  Different types of caves form in different ways. Explain the similarities and differences between the processes of forming two different types of caves. Include details from the book to support your answer.

5. **Draw Conclusions** The water has begun to flow out of a solution cave. What changes will probably take place in the cave next?

## Vocabulary

chemical weathering
deposition
erosion
mechanical weathering
sediment
weathering

## Extended Vocabulary

caves
glaciers
pillar
sinkholes
spelunking
stalactites
stalagmites
water table

**Picture Credits**
Every effort has been made to secure permission and provide appropriate credit for photographic material. The publisher deeply regrets any omission and pledges to correct errors called to its attention in subsequent editions.

Photo locators denoted as follows: Top (T), Center (C), Bottom (B), Left (L), Right (R), Background (Bkgd).

1 Robert Holmes/Corbis; 2 Corbis; 3 Mary Clark/Alamy Images; 5 Tony Waltham Geophotos; 7 Tony Waltham Geophotos; 8 Tom Bean/Corbis; 11 Tony Waltham Geophotos; 14 (TR) Robert Holmes/Corbis, (B) Sisse Brimberg/NGS Image Collection; 15 Stephen Alvarez/NGS Image Collection.

Scott Foresman/Dorling Kindersley would like to thank the Natural History Museum, London/DK Images for the use of photos on pages 12 (TL, CL, BR), 13 (TL, TR).

Unless otherwise acknowledged, all photographs are the copyright © of Dorling Kindersley, a division of Pearson.

ISBN: 0-328-13999-8

# Glossary

| | |
|---|---|
| caves | naturally formed underground cavities |
| glaciers | large masses of ice that move slowly over a land area |
| pillar | a column formed when a stalactite and a stalagmite meet |
| sinkholes | depressions in an area of limestone |
| spelunking | cave exploration |
| stalactites | icicle-shaped calcite deposits that hang from a cave ceiling |
| stalagmites | calcite deposits on a cave floor |
| water table | the top level of a layer of underground soil saturated with water |

PEARSON Scott Foresman    DK

# What You Already Know

The Earth's surface is made up of many types of landforms. These landforms are changing constantly. Some of these changes may happen right before your eyes, but others take place over long periods of time.

The flow of water in rivers changes the Earth's surface. Rivers carry and deposit sediments as they flow. Sediments are solid particles that are moved from one place to another. The movement of sediments causes rivers to shift.

Slow changes to Earth's surface are often caused by weathering, the process of breaking down rock into smaller pieces. Weathering that occurs when forces such as wind, water, or ice break down rock is called mechanical weathering. Chemical weathering is weathering that causes changes to the minerals that make up rock.

**Dust storms destroyed many homes in the 1930s.**

After weathering breaks down rock, the pieces may be carried from one place to another. This movement of soil and sediments from one location to another is called erosion. Dust storms that blew for eight years in the midwest and southern plains of the United States during the 1930s led to severe soil erosion. This area became known as the Dust Bowl.

Great changes have taken place on the Earth's surface. Sediments carried by water are eventually left at a new location. The process of adding sediments to a new place is called deposition. Rivers flowing to the ocean carry sediments and dissolved minerals, including salt.

**Deer Cave at Gunung Mulu National Park in Malaysia is home to millions of bats.**



# Caving

Most caves are fascinating places with amazing natural features. Some people love caves so much that they explore deep inside unknown caves as a hobby. Cave exploration is called spelunking.

Spelunking may be exciting, but it also is dangerous. Cavers must have the proper training. They need to know how to descend into the cave and ascend from it. They also must learn how to use caving equipment. Perhaps the most important part of spelunking is knowing when to stop. When cavers get tired or the cave looks too difficult to pass through, they should return to the surface right away.

**Many young people enjoy caving as a hobby. Caves should always be explored safely.**

# Famous Caves

Caves can be found on almost every continent. Some of the most famous caves are Lascaux Cave in France and the Gunung Mulu caves in Malaysia.

Discovered accidentally in 1940 by four boys, Lascaux Cave is probably the most famous cave in the world. The walls of Lascaux are decorated with hundreds of ancient paintings and engravings of bulls, horses, and deer. Archaeologists believe that the art was created about 15,000 to 13,000 B.C.

Evidence shows that Lascaux Cave was not inhabited, so the reasons for the artwork are a mystery. The people who lived during this period, called the Paleolithic period, were hunters. Perhaps they believed the art would bring them a successful hunt.

Gunung Mulu National Park in Malaysia is home to a cave system composed of some of the world's largest caverns. Lying below a tropical rain forest, the cave system stretches for more than sixty miles. One of the caves at Gunung Mulu, Gua Nasib Bagus—meaning "good luck cave"—contains the Sarawak Chamber. Sarawak, seven hundred meters long, seventy meters high, and three hundred meters across, is the world's single largest cave.

**Lascaux Cave is famous for its Paleolithic cave art. The art is more than 17,000 years old.**



---

Rivers and streams are always changing. Streams combine to form rivers. Rivers erode soil and rock and carry away the sediments, which are deposited in different places according to their weight. Flooding moves huge amounts of sediment to places that normally do not receive them. Overflow water and sediment may move into a floodplain.

Water erosion also causes great changes along coastlines. Waves are made when wind or tectonic activity in Earth's crust transfers energy to ocean water. Waves carry this energy all the way to the coastline, where they may erode rocks or move sand along the shore.

The changes to Earth's surface that you've read about take place above the ground. Next we'll move underground, where weathering and erosion create places of mystery and fascination—caves!

sea cave

# What are caves?

Caves are naturally formed underground cavities, or open spaces. Caves can be found in most parts of the world and can be many different sizes. Some caves extend for many kilometers. Others are barely large enough for a single person to fit inside.

When people see or enter a cave, they are often filled with wonder. What formed it? What is inside? Does anything live in the cave?

Caves might seem like places of mystery, but they are actually geologic features made by natural forces. Most types of caves form very slowly. Some take millions of years to form. Caves may form under the ground with rivers running through them or fantastic natural features.

Many caves may still be undiscovered. The land is changing all the time. Sometimes these changes reveal an entrance to a cave. Other times an entrance can be hidden.

There are several different categories of caves, and each one forms in a different way. The most common caves are called solution caves, or limestone caves. Other types of caves are ice caves, sea caves, lava caves, sandstone caves, and river caves. You'll learn more about the different types of caves later in this book.

Because of their unique form, caves offer protection for humans and animals. People have used caves as shelter for thousands of years. Some animals use caves for shelter part of the time, while others live their entire lives in the darkest parts of caves.

**Gruta do Janelao is located in Brazil. It is known as the "cave of windows."**

**Some bats sleep in caves during the day and hunt at night.**

Deeper inside the cave is the twilight zone. This area receives only dim sunlight and makes a suitable place for some bats, owls, and other birds to live part of the time.

Most of the animals who spend their entire lives in a cave can be found beyond the twilight zone, in the deepest recesses of the cave. Some of these animals are crayfish, salamanders, fish, and insects. Because their habitat is completely dark, these animals cannot use their eyesight. In fact, many of them are blind or have no eyes at all. Instead, they use highly developed senses of smell and touch to find food and detect predators.

Some cave fish are blind but have ridges on the front and sides of their heads that are sensitive to touch. They use these ridges to help them find small water animals to eat.

# Cave Life

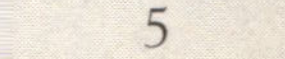

cave spider

You might not think many organisms could live in the darkness of a cave, but caves make ideal homes for animals that are adapted to a cave's unique conditions. Other animals use caves for protection from harsh weather.

The entrance of a cave is often exposed to sunshine, so it makes an ideal place to take shelter. Bears, raccoons, snakes, and mice are some of the animals that seek refuge there. The cave racer snake lives near the cave entrance, where it can take advantage of bats and birds flying in and out. Clinging to the cave wall, it snatches them in midair and eats them.

**Bears often take shelter in caves when they hibernate.**

**Cave fish such as these live in the darkness of caves. They are blind and rely on touch and smell.**

# How do caves form?

As you read, you will discover that most caves are solution caves. These caves, the largest of all types of caves, are formed from limestone, thus the name limestone caves. Limestone is not a hard rock. It contains calcite, and it is found under the surface of the Earth. Because limestone is a soft rock, it dissolves when rainwater flows through it. Streams and rainwater absorb carbon dioxide from the soil and air. The mixture of carbon dioxide and water becomes carbonic acid. Carbonic acid is a weak acid, but it can break down mineral calcite, which is found in limestone.

When a cave first begins to form, rainwater comes in contact with limestone through cracks in the rock. The limestone dissolves along the cracks, opening up passages and forming cavities. Slowly, the passages widen and the cavities form tunnels and chambers. Eventually, these open spaces may connect to form a cave system.

As water drips from the stalactite, it deposits calcite on the floor. The calcite builds up a formation known as a stalagmite. Over time, stalactites and stalagmites may meet and form a pillar.

Other natural features created by calcite deposits include flowstone and cave pearls. Flowstone is solid calcite layered in sheets on the cave walls. Cave pearls are round pebbles of calcite formed in pools of water.

This diagram shows some of the formations that are created when limestone and rainwater mix.

This river seems to disappear into a sinkhole.

An underground river carves a new cave system.

Cave pearls form around grains of sand. The constant motion of the water causes their shape.

# Cave Features

Limestone caves can develop fantastic natural features over time. The groundwater that wore away the limestone to form the cave eventually begins to drain out. Then air enters the cave. When carbonic acid comes in contact with air, the carbon dioxide is released, and the acid breaks down. Therefore, any calcite in the water is released. The water deposits the calcite, which hardens into a rock-like material. This material makes fantastic-looking shapes.

The two most common features formed by calcite deposits are stalactites and stalagmites. Stalactites are long, icicle-shaped deposits that hang from the ceiling. They form when water dripping through the cave roof leaves behind calcite deposits.

Cave systems are made up of different features. For example, a water table is the top level of a layer of underground soil saturated with water. Gradually, the groundwater drains away and the water table drops. This sometimes reveals a horizontal gallery, which is a long, narrow space formed at the water table.

Another example includes sinkholes, which are depressions formed when an area of limestone just below the soil dissolves. They can also form when the roof of a cave just below the surface of the Earth collapses. After the collapse, streams or rivers flow into some sinkholes and continue to flow underground.

Limestone caves form where rivers flow into sinkholes.

Stalactites and stalagmites are common features of limestone caves. They're formed from calcite deposits.

Cave pillars form when stalactites and stalagmites meet.

*This horizontal gallery formed when the water table was higher.*

*Limestone erodes at the surface.*

Although limestone caves are the most common, other types of caves can be found in different environments. First, in very cold places on Earth, ice caves may form under glaciers. Glaciers are large bodies of ice that move slowly downhill. When the ice on the surface of a glacier melts, an ice cave begins to form. The melted water flows into cracks in the glacier and then forms a stream below the surface. As the stream flows, it carves sinkholes, tunnels, and chambers in the ice.

Second, sea caves may form along the coasts of oceans and large lakes. When waves pound against cliffs lining the shore, they erode pieces of rock. Gradually, enough rock may wear away to form a cave.

Meltwater streams erode glaciers to form sinkholes, tunnels, and large chambers within the ice.

Sea caves are formed by wave erosion.

Third, rivers can form caves too. Some rivers flow beside high cliffs. As the water moves through a bend, or turn, it can wear away the cliff rocks and leave gaping holes. Over time, the riverbed drops, leaving behind a cave in the side of the cliff.

Fourth, lava caves, or lava tubes, are formed from lava (melted rock). The lava from an erupting volcano or vent cools on the surface and hardens as it flows, creating a roof. The lava below the roof stays hot and continues to move. After the lava empties out of the tube, the roof remains, leaving a hollow cave.

Fifth, sandstone caves form at the base of sandstone cliffs. They are carved out by rainwater or streams flowing down the cliff. Water loosens the natural cement that holds the sandstone together and washes the sand away. Then a shallow cave is left behind. The Anasazi, an ancient Native American culture, built their homes in huge sandstone caves in the western United States.

Sandstone caves are formed by flowing water eroding sandstone rock.

Earth Science

# Green Homes

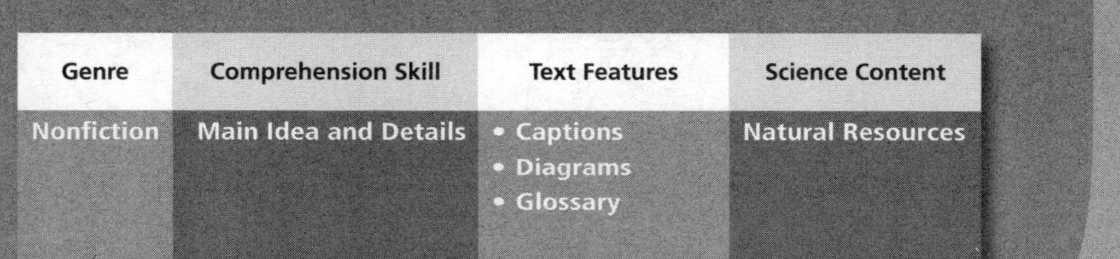

by Charles Miller

| Genre | Comprehension Skill | Text Features | Science Content |
| --- | --- | --- | --- |
| Nonfiction | Main Idea and Details | • Captions<br>• Diagrams<br>• Glossary | Natural Resources |

Scott Foresman Science 6.11

PEARSON
Scott Foresman

DK

scottforesman.com

ISBN 0-328-14002-3

9 780328 140022

90000

# What did you learn?

1. How do eco-friendly building materials help the environment?

2. What are some advantages of a rammed earth wall, such as cob or adobe?

3. Name two kinds of renewable energy that can be used in green homes.

4. **Writing** in Science How are green homes similar to other types of construction and how are they different?

5. **Main Idea and Details** Green homes conserve resources in their design, construction, and daily use. Describe some of the ways that green homes conserve fossil fuels. Include details from the book to support your answer.

| Vocabulary | Extended Vocabulary |
| --- | --- |
| acid precipitation | building materials |
| coal | eco-friendly |
| fossil fuel | heat island |
| geothermal energy | organic garden |
| natural gas | rammed earth home |
| nonrenewable resource | straw bale home |
| petroleum | turf roof |
| renewable resource | |



**Picture Credits**
Every effort has been made to secure permission and provide appropriate credit for photographic material. The publisher deeply regrets any omission and pledges to correct errors called to its attention in subsequent editions.

Photo locators denoted as follows: Top (T), Center (C), Bottom (B), Left (L), Right (R), Background (Bkgd).

Opener: Nicholas Kane/Alamy Images; 1 Gideon Mendel/Corbis; 4 Benedict Luxmoore/Arcaid; 5 (TR) Gideon Mendel/Corbis; 8 Alan Sirulnikoff/Photo Researchers, Inc.; 9 (TR) Mary Ashby/Arcaid; 10 Robert Harding World Imagery/Alamy Images; 12 Eric Draper/AP/Wide World Photos; 13 (T) Nicholas Kane/Alamy Images, (BR) Sam Barcroft/Rex Features, Limited; 15 Martin Bond/Peter Arnold, Inc.; 16 Getty Images; 20 (B) Tony Freeman/PhotoEdit; 23 Bruce Harber/Ecoscene.

Scott Foresman/Dorling Kindersley would also like to thank: 17 (R) Cole Associates/DK Images; 22 (BR) Cole Associates/DK Images.

Unless otherwise acknowledged, all photographs are the copyright © of Dorling Kindersley, a division of Pearson.

ISBN: 0-328-14002-3

# Glossary

| | |
|---|---|
| **building materials** | all the basic materials used in making a building |
| **eco-friendly** | designed to minimize effects on the environment |
| **heat island** | the effect of higher temperatures in cities due to increased absorption of solar energy and fewer plants |
| **organic garden** | a type of garden that does not use harmful, artificial fertilizers or pesticides |
| **rammed earth home** | a building whose walls are made of packed mud, along with sand, straw, or other materials. Examples of rammed earth include cob and adobe |
| **straw bale home** | a house that uses bales of straw instead of lumber as the structural material for walls |
| **turf roof** | a "green" roof consisting of grass or other plants that conserves water and provides insulation to the home |

# Green Homes

by Charles Miller

# What You Already Know

Everything you do—eating, traveling home from school, and even breathing—uses natural resources. Air and water are examples of natural resources that you use directly. Building materials, electricity, and fabric for your clothes are things that are made from natural resources.

Natural processes replace some things, called renewable resources, as they are used. Sunlight, energy from the wind, and water in streams can be renewable resources. Other things, called nonrenewable resources, cannot be replaced as fast as they are used. Nonrenewable resources include fossil fuels, minerals, and water in underground reservoirs.

Fossil fuels are the main source of energy for transportation, heat, and electricity. The process that makes them requires millions of years. As the remains of living organisms slowly decay from heat and pressure below the surface of Earth, they are converted into fossil fuels. This process cannot replenish fossil fuels as quickly as they are used.

The windows in these green homes are positioned to make the best use of the sunlight.

Many of the features of green homes have been used for a long time, such as capturing water for household use or gardening and positioning the windows to make best use of solar energy. Other features rely on new developments, such as solar energy panels and insulating wall materials. As more new materials and techniques for saving energy and resources become available, they will be added to future green homes.

People need electrical energy to light their homes and offices.

# Future Homes

A big part of living greener is just noticing how you use resources. Even a few small changes in how you do everyday things can make a difference.

As people become more aware of the amount of resources and energy used in their daily lives, they can do things to reduce consumption. Saving energy, water, and materials in a home starts with the way it is made. Many home designers and builders have already started to change the way homes are built. If people make green living a priority, homes of the future may look like the model shown below.

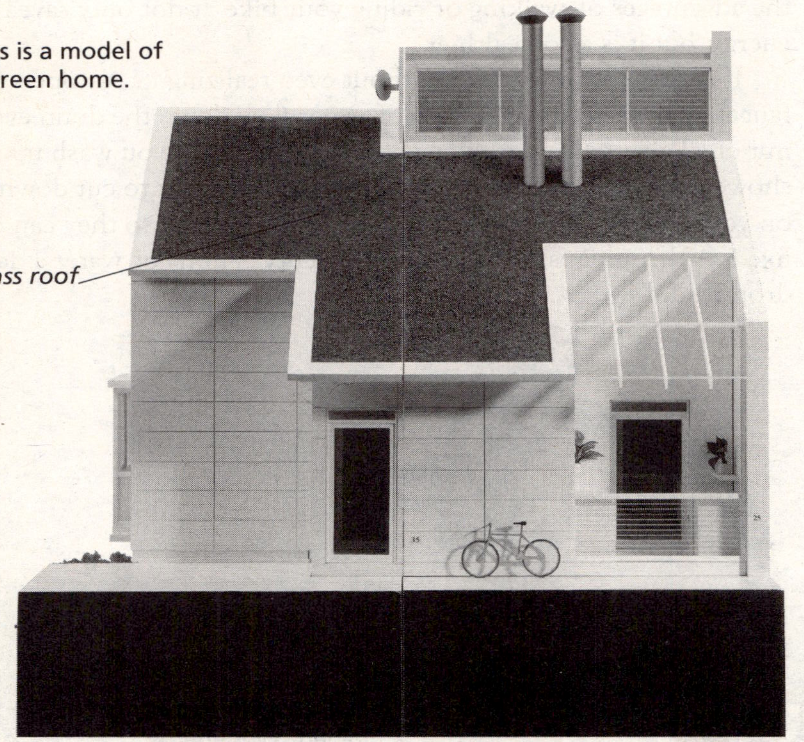

This is a model of a green home.

grass roof





Coal, a solid fossil fuel that is burned for heat and electricity, forms from the remains of plants that lived in swamps millions of years ago. Petroleum is a liquid fossil fuel that is used to make gasoline and other transportation fuels and home heating oil. It forms from the decay of buried remains of marine plants and animals over a very long time. Natural gas, a mixture of gases that can be burned for heat and to generate electricity, is usually found in the same places as coal and petroleum.

Burning fossil fuels contributes to pollution by releasing harmful materials into the atmosphere. These materials, which contain nitrogen and sulfur, combine with water vapor to make acids. The acids fall to the ground in rain and snow, creating acid precipitation, which has harmful effects on plants and animals.

People need energy for transportation, growing food, and heating and lighting homes. However, there are some energy sources that do not consume renewable resources or cause pollution. For example, electricity can be produced by wind turning the blades of large turbines or sunlight falling on solar cells. Some renewable sources of heat energy are used directly. These include sunlight and geothermal energy, the energy from heat inside Earth.

wind turbines

# Green Homes

Everyone needs a home. Along with food, water, and air, shelter is a basic part of human survival. Unlike many animals, people do not have fur or carry a shell for protection. Your home keeps you warm in cold weather and cool in hot weather. It protects you from rain, wind, and snow.

Unfortunately, building a house affects the environment. Some of the effects are easy to see. Before people start building, they remove trees and other plants, change the shape of the land with heavy equipment, and sometimes disrupt natural water flow patterns. Other effects are less obvious—they may actually occur hundreds or thousands of miles away or over time. If you have ever watched a house being built, you know that it takes a lot of materials, such as wood, steel, glass, and concrete. Many of these materials are not renewable and must be shipped from far away.

Even after a house is built, it affects the environment, both local and distant. One of the biggest uses of fossil fuels in the United States is for heating and lighting homes. Some of these fuels, such as natural gas and home heating oil, are consumed in the home to produce heat directly. Others, such as coal, are converted to electricity to provide heat and light far away from the place where they are burned. Most of the energy consumed in the United States comes from nonrenewable fossil fuels.

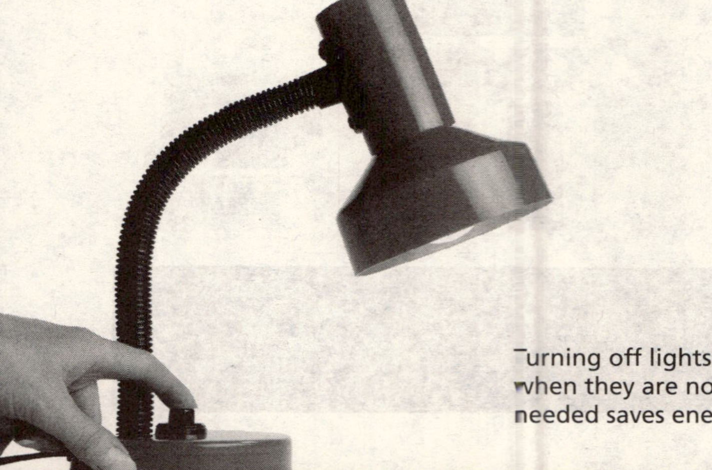

The eco-friendly apartments in the United Kingdom use many of the building techniques described in this book.

Another important way that you can go green in your own home is by reducing wasted energy. Saving electricity helps in two ways: fewer resources are used to make the power, and less pollution is generated. Many of the ways to use electricity are obvious. Turn off lights and appliances when you leave the room. Reduce heat or air-conditioning when no one is at home. The key part of saving energy is remembering not to use it when you don't need it. How do you get from one place to another? Do you have someone drive you everywhere? If so, think about the advantages of walking or riding your bike. It not only saves energy, but it is also healthier.

It is easy to waste water without even realizing it. An open faucet lets two to three gallons of water flow down the drain every minute. Pay attention to how you use water when you wash up, shower, or brush your teeth. You may find chances to cut down on your own water use. Notice any drips and leaks so they can be fixed. A dripping faucet can let out twenty gallons of water a day, drop by drop.

Motion sensors can turn lights off when no one is in the room.

Turning off lights when they are not needed saves energy.

# Going Green

What can you do to live greener if your house is already built or you don't have control over the kind of energy it uses? Everyone can help by using fewer resources and less energy. For example, most communities have a recycling program. Making aluminum products from recycled metal uses only five percent of the energy that is needed to make them from new aluminum. Every time you recycle aluminum, plastic, glass, or paper, you reduce the amount of resources and energy used to make new products. Look for the three-arrow symbol, which means that a material can be recycled.

Look for these symbols—they mean the material can be recycled.

Most communities have a program to recycle materials.

Many builders and architects have begun to look for ways to build houses, apartments, and other buildings that have less impact on the environment. These environment-friendly homes are planned and built to use minimal amounts of nonrenewable resources and to provide heat and light with the smallest possible consumption of fossil fuels.

This cabin is part of a v llage designed to minimize environmental impact.

# Building Materials

Have you ever seen a house being built? Large trucks deliver building materials, which are all the basic materials used in construction. Builders start with the concrete that forms a platform for the building. After building the base, workers frame the house using lumber or steel framing. The frames are usually covered on the outside by bricks or by siding made of aluminum or vinyl plastic, and on the inside by wallboard made of a mineral product called gypsum.

Even a small house requires many tons of building materials, much of it made from nonrenewable resources. Aluminum, gypsum, and the iron used to make steel are mined from the ground. The basic material for vinyl siding comes from petroleum, another resource that is not renewable. Even wood, which is renewable because new trees can be grown, is being used faster than new forests can replace it. An eco-friendly home, one that minimizes environmental effects, uses as many renewable materials as possible.

Although forests produce new trees, so much lumber is used that new forests must be cut every year.

This compost makes good plant food.

Organic gardeners also avoid pesticides and herbicides that are toxic. Pesticides are chemicals that kill unwanted animals, while herbicides kill unwanted plants. Organic farmers solve pest problems by removing the insects by hand, and using less-toxic sprays such as soap and certain natural pesticides that come from plants. This avoids any health hazards that could occur from poisonous chemicals. It also reduces the harm to insects and other animals that are helpful to plants.

The choice of garden furniture is also a concern for a green gardener. While many types of wood come from trees that grow rapidly and are plentiful, others come from forests that are in danger from logging. Furniture for the garden should use woods that are produced in an eco-friendly way. If the wood is treated to protect it from rot, the treatment must be nontoxic to people and pets. An alternative type of garden furniture is made from recycled plastic. This plastic doesn't need preservatives, and it is a better use for the plastic than simply throwing it in a landfill.

Water can be collected from the roof and used in the garden.

# Garden Basics

The ideas behind green living apply in the garden as well as in the house. An organic garden uses only natural fertilizers or pesticides. The plants in an organic garden use compost from the home. Food waste, such as vegetable and fruit peels, tea bags, and eggshells, are mixed with garden wastes, such as pulled weeds and dead garden plants. After these materials are mixed together, bacteria break down the organic material to form a rich, dark soil called compost. This compost is a valuable source of nutrients for garden plants.

Organic gardeners do not use chemical fertilizers or pesticides.

The making of concrete contributes to greenhouse gases in both the production of cement and its delivery by truck.

In addition to consuming resources, many of the materials used in building conventional homes affect the environment in other ways. The production of the cement used in concrete releases large quantities of carbon dioxide, a greenhouse gas. Common building methods produce large amounts of waste as standard-sized materials are cut to fit the space where they are to be used.

Finally, conventional building techniques require a lot of energy. Materials such as metal and plastic are produced by methods that consume large amounts of power in the form of fossil fuels or electricity. Also, trucks that carry the materials used in building a house may come from far away. These trucks consume fuel and produce greenhouse gases as they carry materials to the building site.

Building a typical house uses many tons of nonrenewable resources.

# Back to Basics

Most of the homes built today use wood or steel frames, but there are other ways to design a house. A lot of eco-friendly buildings use techniques that were common before materials were easily transported. In many places, such as the plains of the midwestern United States, there are few trees. Today trucks and railroads deliver lumber and other building materials to these areas. In the past, people built homes with materials from local sources.

One building material that is easy to find in grasslands is straw. The Great Plains settlers used bales of straw, the strong stems of grass and grain plants, as building blocks. In a straw bale home, bundles of straw are stacked to make a well-insulated wall that is covered with some type of protective siding on the outside and with plaster on the inside. Straw is a renewable resource.

The straw bales provide inexpensive and sturdy walls while using no lumber.

The simplest ways of saving water are often some of the best. Taking a shower instead of a bath uses less water. Turning the water off whenever you don't need to have it running will help also. Obey rules in your town regarding watering plants. Don't water plants during the hottest parts of the day, when much of the water will just evaporate into the air.

Many green homes go beyond just reducing water use. They collect their own rainwater through a system of pipes and store it in large water tanks. The water is filtered and purified to be sure that it is safe for home use.

Water can also be saved by reusing it. Water from sinks and showers, known as gray water, can often be used for garden plants. By setting up the plumbing to keep gray water separate from the wasted water from toilets, gray water can replace the fresh water used to water gardens.

Rainwater from the roof collects in a tank. From there it goes to the house or the garden.

# Water Supply

Every home needs a water supply. In many places, water is scarce. It must be piped for miles, or even hundreds of miles, before it reaches the house. Sometimes people use water faster than nature can replace it, making water a nonrenewable resource. Most green homes use water conservation techniques to minimize their impact on the freshwater supply.

One of the best ways to do this is to reduce the amount of water you use. If you have been in a modern public restroom, you may have noticed that the water faucet turns on when you place your hand over the sink and turns off when you move it. Making sure that water is not left running is one way to reduce water use. Many new appliances, such as washers and dishwashers, are designed to use less water than older ones.

Watering on hot days is wasteful because much of the water evaporates before it reaches the lawn.

Another natural building material that is available in most places is mud made by mixing soil and water. Rammed earth homes use mud mixed with other materials and packed tightly. The rammed earth dries to form a strong, waterproof wall. The building in the illustration to the right is made of cob, a mixture of clay, sand, and straw. When ingredients are mixed in the right proportions, the cob dries strong, hard, and waterproof. Adobe is another mixture of clay, sand, and straw. Adobe is used in dry climates, such as the southwestern part of the United States. Adobe is often shaped into blocks and dried in the sun to form a bricklike building block. Cob, adobe, and other forms of rammed earth dry by evaporation of the water and do not require the high temperature kilns, or ovens, used in making clay bricks.

All these natural building materials regulate temperature well. Rammed earth walls are normally thick and absorb heat, protecting the inside of the building from very high or very low temperatures outside.

This cottage is built with cob walls and a thatch roof made of plant materials.

## Eco-friendly Paint

Paints contain solid materials mixed in a liquid. As the paint dries, the liquid evaporates. In many paints, this liquid includes chemicals. These chemicals use nonrenewable resources, and some of them are toxic. Eco-friendly paints are made with nontoxic ingredients and use water as the liquid.

# Green on Top

Take a look at the unique house in the photograph below. The roof stays green as long as it gets sunshine and rain because it is covered with turf. This is a grass covering that protects and insulates the house. Grass, vines, flowers, and even small trees can be used to cover a roof.

Why would you want to grow plants on the roof of your house? One of the best reasons is that turf roofs are good insulators. The layers of soil and plants keep out heat in the summer and cold in the winter. This means that much less energy is required for heating and air-conditioning. A turf roof reduces carbon dioxide from burning fossil fuels. Plus, the plants release oxygen into the atmosphere as they grow.

The roof on this building is made of living grass.

Panels on the roof capture the energy of sunlight and convert it to heat or electricity.

Solar energy can be used in two ways. Some houses have large windows that are placed at the correct angle to use the Sun to heat the home in the winter. This is called passive solar heating. Active solar energy systems either pump water to transfer heat from the Sun into storage or they use panels that convert the solar energy into electricity. This electricity can be used to produce heat and operate appliances, just like the power from the power company.

## Solar-heated Water

When sunlight strikes the black surface, it is converted to heat. Water flows through pipes on the surface, absorbing the heat. The hot water is directed through pipes to provide hot water and heat.

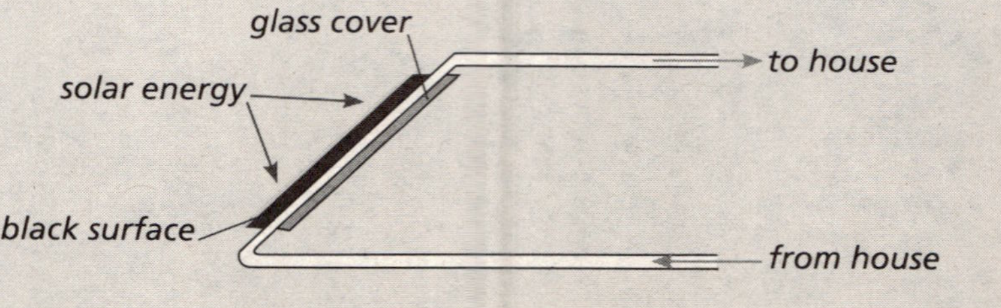

# Energy Sources

Every home needs energy, for heat, lighting, and cooking. But not all homes need to get their energy from burning fossil fuels. Some green homes have their own power plants, which harness the energy of the Sun and the wind. These are renewable resources that don't cause pollution. Solar or wind power can be used directly or converted into electricity to power lights, cooking stoves, and televisions. The wind turbines below are part of a huge wind farm, but some homes use wind turbines also. Sometimes, they produce more electricity than is needed in the home. The extra power can be sold to an electric company.

These turbines generate electricity without making any pollution.

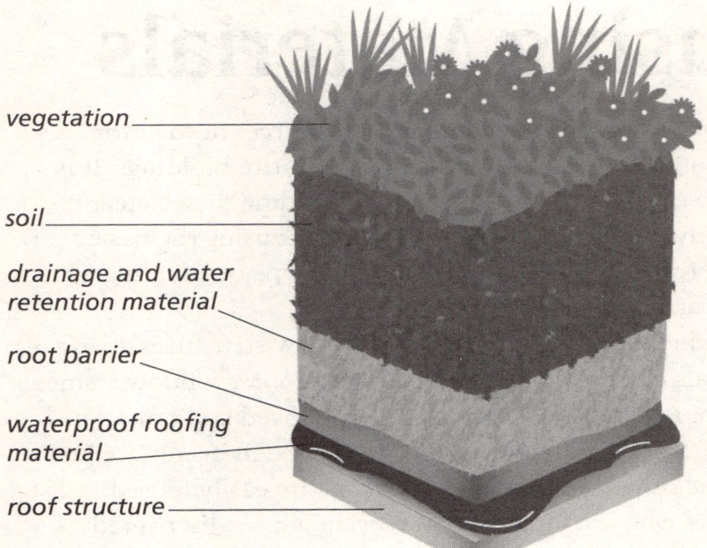


The turf roof is built in layers to provide water to the grass while keeping it out of the house.

If you watch a weather report during the summer, you may notice that cities are usually warmer than the surrounding areas. A region much warmer than its surroundings is called a heat island. The city temperature can be as much as six degrees Celsius warmer than that of the woods or fields around it. What could cause this difference? Look around a city and you see buildings, streets, and parking lots, but very few plants and trees. While plants use the solar energy that reaches them to grow, concrete and asphalt absorb it and release it as heat. Green roofs on houses, as the one shown to the left, and gardens on top of large buildings can reduce the heat island effect.

Turf roofs are useful in other ways. In an open field, most of the rainwater soaks into the ground. If a building covers part of the field, it forces the rain to run off instead of being absorbed. But a turf roof is designed to hold water so that the plants can use it. This reduces the risk of flooding from storm runoff.

# Reusing Materials

One way to reduce the amount of resources needed for construction is to reuse materials or even entire buildings. It is often more efficient to renovate an old building than to tear it down. Many modern homes have been built using the basic structure of an old home or even another type of building, such as a barn.

Even when buildings are replaced by new structures, many of the materials can be reused. For example, doors, window frames, and plumbing fixtures can be carefully removed and reused just as they are. Bricks, siding materials, and wooden beams are just some of the other building materials that are easily reused.

Builders who are interested in recycling have discovered a number of other materials that are normally thrown out. The walls of the building shown below are made of old tires, aluminum cans, and bottles held together by packed earth and concrete. In addition to being constructed of reused materials, this home produces its own electricity, captures solar energy, and recycles water.

This home is built with recycled materials to reduce its impact on the environment.

Many abandoned containers rust away. These make good homes.

There are many kinds of materials that can be reused. Some are almost ready to move into. The homes above are made of cargo containers, steel boxes the size of a truck trailer. These are used to carry cargo on ships, trucks, and railcars. When the containers are no longer needed, they are usually thrown out in junkyards. But they can also be converted into homes.

What do you see in the picture below—an island in a tropical lagoon? Actually, the "island" is a huge raft, floating on recycled plastic drink bottles. Above the plastic bottles is a floor of bamboo poles. The recycled island has a two-bedroom living area, a kitchen, and a garden for vegetables and fruits. Energy comes from the Sun. Five-meter tall mangrove trees provide the island's shade and their roots anchor the island in place in the lagoon.

This island in Mexico was made by humans from recycled materials.

# Solar Power

by Lillian Duggan

| Genre | Comprehension Skill | Text Features | Science Content |
|---|---|---|---|
| Nonfiction | Cause and Effect | • Captions<br>• Diagrams<br>• Glossary | Climate and Weather |

Scott Foresman Science 6.12



ISBN 0-328-14005-8

9 780328 140053

90000

131

# What did you learn?

1. How does sunlight help plants to make food?

2. What are the benefits of solar energy compared with fossil fuels?

3. Why does the International Space Station need solar cells?

4. **Writing** in Science  Flatbed solar panels and photovoltaic cells both harness energy from the Sun, but in different ways. Write to explain the differences in how these two types of panels work. Include details from the book to support your answer.

5. **Cause and Effect** How is energy produced in fusion reactions in the Sun's core?

| Vocabulary | Extended Vocabulary |
| --- | --- |
| air mass | alternative energy sources |
| air pressure | fusion |
| atmosphere | heliostats |
| climate | photon |
| front | photovoltaic |
| humidity | semiconductor |
| meteorologist | solar cell |
| relative humidity | solar collector |
| weather | solar energy |


**Picture Credits**

Every effort has been made to secure permission and provide appropriate credit for photographic material. The publisher deeply regrets any omission and pledges to correct errors called to its attention in subsequent editions.

Photo locators denoted as follows: Top (T), Center (C), Bottom (B), Left (L), Right (R), Background (Bkgd).

Opener: Lester Lefkowitz/Corbis; 1 Getty Images; 2 Tony Craddock/Alamy Images; 4 Getty Images; 10 Otto Rogge/Corbis; 12 David R. Frazier Photolibrary, Inc./Alamy Images; 14 Mike Southern/Eye Ubiquitous/Corbis; 15 Joe Sohm/Alamy Images; 17 ©Kevin Burke/Getty Images;18 Reuters/Corbis; 19 (T) Stringer/David Mariuz/Reuters/Corbis; 20 NASA; 21 (T) NASA; 22 Lester Lefkowitz/Corbis.

Scott Foresman/Dorling Kindersley would also like to thank: 19 (TR) Phil Farrand/DK Images.

Unless otherwise acknowledged, all photographs are the copyright © of Dorling Kindersley, a division of Pearson.

ISBN: 0-328-14005-8

## Glossary

| | |
|---|---|
| **alternative energy sources** | the means of producing energy other than fossil fuels, including wind, water, and solar energy |
| **fusion** | nuclear reaction in which atoms combine and large amounts of energy are released |
| **heliostats** | mirrors in a solar power station that focus sunlight on a boiler |
| **photon** | a particle of light energy |
| **photovoltaic** | able to produce electricity from light energy |
| **semiconductor** | a material that has the ability to conduct electricity in a controlled way |
| **solar cell** | a device that converts solar energy into electricity; also called a photovoltaic cell |
| **solar collector** | a device that focuses sunlight to capture its heat |
| **solar energy** | energy produced by the Sun |

133

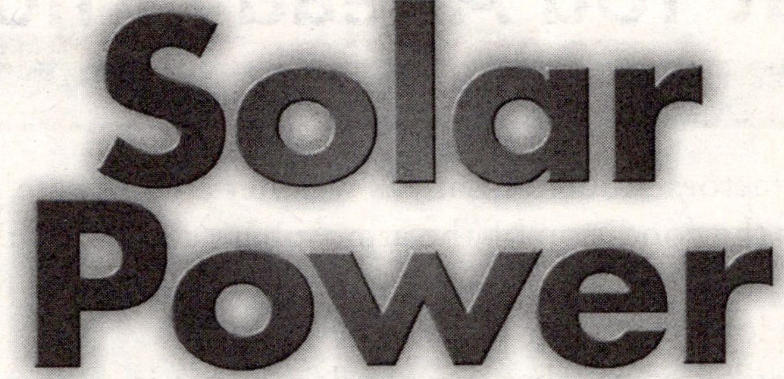

# Solar Power

by Lillian Duggan

PEARSON
Scott Foresman

DK

24

# What You Already Know

Many factors influence Earth's weather and climate. Weather is the condition of the atmosphere at a particular moment. Climate is the pattern of weather that occurs in an area over a long period of time.

The blanket of gas that surrounds a planet is its atmosphere. Earth's atmosphere is composed mainly of nitrogen and oxygen.

The particles that make up the gases in the air are constantly bumping into other matter. The measure of force with which air particles push on matter is air pressure. The different layers of the atmosphere vary in air pressure and temperature.

Differences in air pressure between different areas cause wind. Winds move from areas of high pressure to areas of low pressure.

Water vapor in the air can make it feel damp. Humidity is the amount of water vapor in the air. The amount of water vapor that air can hold depends on its temperature. Relative humidity is the amount of water vapor the air contains compared with the amount it could hold at that temperature.

Because fossil fuels are running out and their use damages the environment, the use of solar power may be a good alternative. Solar cells, troughs, and power towers all offer great promise for providing clean energy to large numbers of users. However, the use of solar energy faces obstacles. Large solar power stations are expensive to build and take up a great deal of space. Also, solar energy cannot be harnessed at night, when heat is needed most, or on cloudy days.

As scientists and engineers work to overcome these hurdles, they're also investigating other energy forms that originate from the Sun. One of these is biomass energy.

Biomass energy is energy produced by organic matter. Wood burning in a fireplace is one example of biomass fuel. The energy from the Sun that is trapped by plants is released when the plants are burned. However, burning plants also produce carbon dioxide, which can be harmful to the environment. Replacement plants must be planted to absorb the released carbon dioxide. Therefore, fast-growing trees such as willows and poplars are ideal for biomass systems. Ethanol is a biomass fuel derived from corn. It is now blended with gasoline sold in some locations in the United States. Mixing ethanol into gasoline reduces consumption of petroleum.

The Sun provides many opportunities for us to use its boundless energy. If we can harness its power in inexpensive and clean ways, the future will be bright!

The solar dish collectors focus sunlight on a central receiver.

# Endless Energy

The Sun has an enormous influence on us.
We depend on the Sun's energy to keep us
warm and to provide us with food.
Many people take advantage of
the Sun's energy, using it to supply
heat and electricity for their
homes. Engineers are developing
the solar car, so that someday
we can drive vehicles
without burning fuel.





Clouds are made up of millions of tiny water droplets that form around small particles in the air. When the water droplets become large enough, precipitation falls from the clouds as rain, snow, sleet, or hail.

Usually precipitation is mild or moderate, but it can also be part of a severe storm. Everyone should know what precautions to take in case of a thunderstorm, tornado, or hurricane.

You may hear your local weather forecaster talk about air masses and fronts. An air mass is a very large body of air that has a similar temperature and humidity throughout. The boundary that forms between air masses is called a front. Weather at a front is often cloudy or stormy. Meteorologists are scientists who study weather. They predict the weather by monitoring the movements of air masses. Although weather can change quickly, the climate of a particular area is usually stable.

Many different factors contribute to the weather. The primary force behind weather, though, is the Sun. In this book, we'll learn how the Sun produces the energy that sustains life, and how we can use its power.

# Energy for Life

Living things on Earth need energy to move and grow. Fortunately, the planet has a tremendous energy source. The Sun is about 93 million miles away from Earth, but it supplies all living things with the energy needed for life.

Plants use sunlight to make their own food. This process is called photosynthesis. In photosynthesis, a chemical reaction between carbon dioxide and water creates glucose and oxygen. Plants use glucose, a type of sugar, for food.

Most plants contain a substance called chlorophyll, which absorbs sunlight. The sunlight provides energy that is necessary for photosynthesis to take place.

**Sunlight stored in these crops will later be transferred to humans.**

**Solar panels on the International Space Station power scientific experiments.**

Solar energy also powers the International Space Station, a scientific laboratory in orbit around the Earth. Almost an acre of solar panels supply power for the six state-of-the-art laboratories in the station. Nations around the world worked together to build the facility.

Solar sails are a new technology to move a spacecraft without an engine. A solar sail is simply a huge sheet of reflective material that is many times thinner than a sheet of paper. Photons, or light particles, strike the sail, pushing it with a tiny amount of force, just as wind pushes a sailboat. Although the force is small, there is no air in space to oppose the sail's movement. The sail accelerates slowly but continuously, until it reaches speeds much higher than those of any rocket. In 2004 Japan successfully launched two solar sails.

**The Hubble Space Telescope has taken thousands of photos of outer space since 1990.**

# Solar Power in Space

Space is an ideal environment in which to use solar cells. Without clouds and other atmospheric conditions, solar cells can easily harness the Sun's energy.

Satellites, space stations, and space probes rely on panels of solar cells to power their communications equipment and scientific instruments. The rover vehicles Spirit and Opportunity, which landed on the surface of Mars in early 2004, used solar energy for their missions.

The Hubble Space Telescope is a large telescope orbiting Earth. It uses solar panels to run its cameras and other scientific equipment.

NASA's Mars rovers get their power from solar cells.

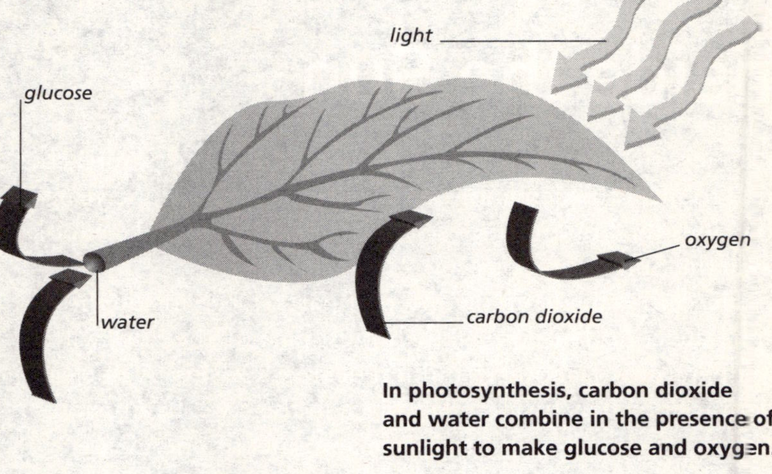



In photosynthesis, carbon dioxide and water combine in the presence of sunlight to make glucose and oxygen.

Animals also rely on the Sun for their energy. Some animals eat plants, which contain stored energy from the Sun. This energy is transferred to the animal. Other animals eat the animals that eat plants. The Sun's energy is then transferred to these animals.

Energy from wood, coal, natural gas, and petroleum is also made indirectly by the Sun. Trees store the Sun's energy in their woody tissue. When the "wood" is burned, the energy is released as heat and light.

Coal, natural gas, and petroleum are all fossil fuels. Fossil fuels were formed over millions of years from plant and animal remains. The Sun's energy was stored in plants and animals. When they died, their remains became buried. Over millions of years, layers of rock pressed down on the remains until they became fossil fuels. Burning these fuels releases the stored energy of the ancient sunlight.

Energy from the Sun even powers the weather. The Sun evaporates water to make clouds which cause rain. It also heats air, causing it to move as wind.

The Sun also keeps the oceans warm and prevents them from freezing. If the oceans were to freeze, the land would be too cold for living things to survive.

# Inside the Sun

In less than one hour, enough energy from the Sun reaches Earth to meet the demands of the entire world for one year. How does the Sun produce so much energy? Let's take a look inside the Sun to find out.

The Sun is made up of different parts. Deep inside the Sun is the core. The core is the hottest part of the Sun, with a temperature of about 15 million degrees Celsius. A nuclear reaction known as fusion takes place in the core. In a fusion reaction, atoms combine and large amounts of energy are released. These reactions are possible only under great heat and pressure.

**Energy made by fusion reactions in the Sun's core travels to the photosphere.**

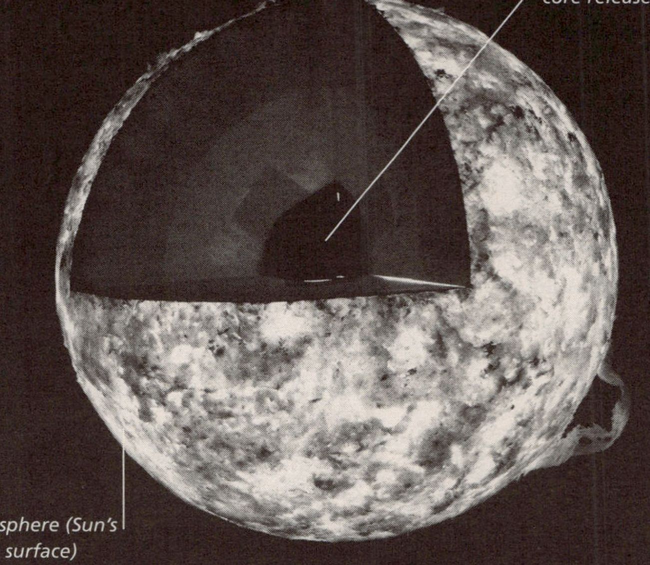


photosphere (Sun's visible surface)

**Nuna II won the World Solar Challenge car race in 2003.**

Like solar cars, solar airplanes have been in development since the 1970s. In 1981, a solar-powered plane called the Solar Challenger flew across the English Channel from Paris to England. The plane, powered by sixteen thousand solar cells on its wings and tail, reached an average speed of fifty miles per hour and an altitude of twelve thousand feet.

Today NASA is taking solar-powered flight to even greater heights. Its solar-powered airplane, Helios, has broken the altitude record for an aircraft not powered by a rocket. Reaching 96,500 feet, Helios almost made its goal of 100,000 feet.

Helios is powered by photovoltaic cells that cover its wings. The cells convert almost 19 percent of the solar energy they receive into electrical energy that powers the plane's motors.

# Traveling Without Fuel

Some day cars may be able to run without ever stopping for fuel. Solar-powered cars use solar cells either to power the car's motor directly or to charge a battery that powers the motor. The first cars that ran totally on solar power were built in the late 1970s and early 1980s. These early vehicles were made mainly by individuals. Today large automobile manufacturers are in on the solar race, literally. These companies and other solar car inventors participate in regular solar car races all over the world.

**NASA hopes to someday use Helios to fly long scientific missions, perhaps even over Mars.**

## Sun to Earth

The energy produced in the Sun's core takes at least thirty thousand years to travel to the Sun's surface. However, this energy takes only 8.3 minutes to reach Earth. Photons follow a random path through the Sun and a straight path to Earth.



The two gases that make up most of the Sun are hydrogen and helium. In the core, hydrogen atoms combine to form helium atoms through fusion reactions. Some of the hydrogen does not get converted into helium. This leftover hydrogen is converted directly into energy.

This energy eventually travels to the Sun's surface in the form of photons. A photon is a particle of light energy. A photon's trip from the core to the surface takes at least thirty thousand years. Along the way the photon encounters many hydrogen atoms, which continuously absorb and release it. When it finally reaches the surface and open space, the photon travels quickly, taking a mere 8.3 minutes to reach Earth.

Photons may have to travel 93 million miles to reach Earth, but they still have tremendous power when they get here. One painful reminder of this power is sunburn. Sunburn happens when skin is overexposed to the Sun. Solar power is usually beneficial to people and Earth, though. We'll now look at some ways we can put this power to use.




139

# Collecting Sunlight

Some people use the Sun as a direct source of energy. Prehistoric cave dwellers, for example, chose caves that faced the Sun so they could take advantage of the Sun's energy to keep their caves warm.

Today our energy needs are much different than they were thousands of years ago. We use energy to run our cars, light and heat our homes and schools, cook our food, power our factories, and even dry our hair. Nearly everything we do requires energy.

For about two hundred years, fossil fuels have been our primary source of energy. However, the supply of fossil fuels is limited. Once they are used up, fossil fuels cannot be replaced. Also, the burning of fossil fuels for energy is damaging to the environment. Most scientists believe it causes environmental hazards, such as acid rain and global warming.

This library in Canada uses glass walls to take advantage of the Sun's energy.

The Solar One power tower operated near Barstow, California, from 1982 until 1988. At the time, Solar One was the world's largest solar power tower plant. It was redesigned as Solar Two in 1996. During its three-year lifetime, Solar Two provided electricity to about ten thousand homes in California.

Compared to solar troughs, power towers are in the early stages of development. Both Solar One and Solar Two were test facilities for power tower technology. Other such facilities have been constructed around the world.

# Solar Power Stations

In some parts of the world solar power stations supply towns and cities with electricity. Although some solar power stations use photovoltaic panels, most are solar trough systems. The world's largest solar trough system is in Kramer Junction, California. It is a huge group of solar trough collectors connected together. The system supplies electricity to 150,000 homes. In addition to Kramer Junction, four other solar trough plants generate power for use in southern California.

Another type of solar collector power station is called a power tower. It consists of a boiler mounted on a tall tower and surrounded by hundreds or even thousands of movable mirrors. The mirrors, also called heliostats, move with the Sun and focus sunlight onto the boiler, which contains either oil or liquid sodium. The liquid in the boiler heats up and travels through a pipe to a power plant. There it heats water to produce steam that powers a turbine, generating electricity.

The heliostats surrounding this solar power tower turn throughout the day to face the Sun.

This simple solar collector is just a disk covered with aluminum foil. It focuses the Sun's energy to toast bread.

As people around the world have become more and more concerned about our use of fossil fuels, they have worked to develop alternative energy sources. Alternative energy sources are other ways of producing energy besides burning fossil fuels. Alternative energy sources are generally renewable, meaning they can be used over and over. Wind, water, and solar energy are alternative energy sources that are clean and renewable. Solar energy is energy produced by the Sun.

Scientists have developed many complex ways to harness the energy of the Sun. However, collecting solar energy can be quite simple. For example, many towers and buildings are purposely built with exterior glass walls. These walls absorb the heat generated by solar energy, which helps save on heating costs. They also provide light for people inside.

A variety of devices called solar collectors have been developed to capture solar energy. Solar collectors would not work without materials that reflect and absorb sunlight. When the Sun's rays shine on an object, the object either absorbs the rays or reflects them. Objects with dark and dull surfaces absorb solar energy, becoming warm. Objects that are shiny and light-colored reflect solar energy away from them, staying cool.

Aluminum foil is a readily available reflective material. You can use aluminum foil to make a solar collector similar to the one above. Such collectors can be used to cook food.



141

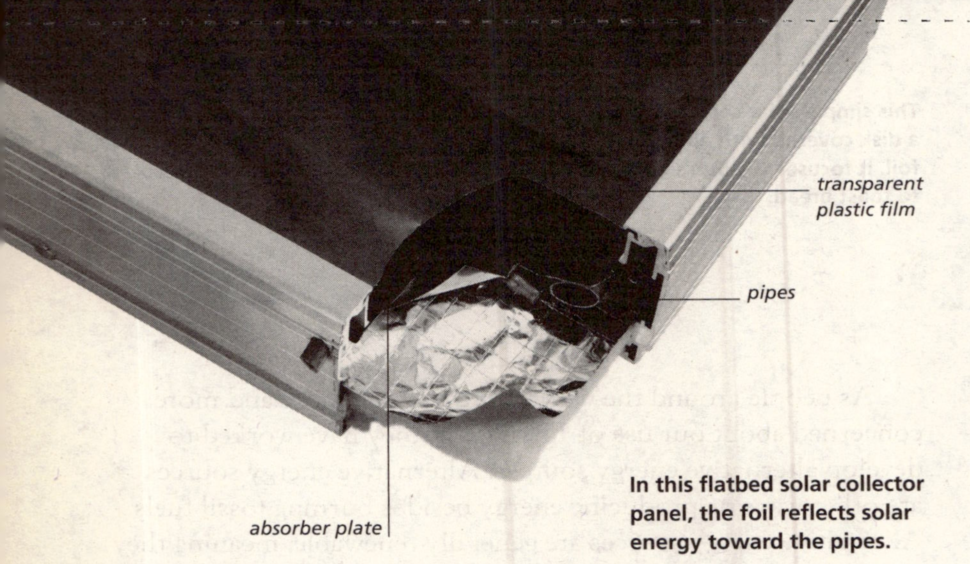



In this flatbed solar collector panel, the foil reflects solar energy toward the pipes.

This house in Nebraska has solar panels on its roof.

The most common solar collectors are flatbed collector panels. These panels consist of a metal box with a glass or plastic cover. Inside the box is a dark absorber plate, a reflective surface, and pipes carrying water or air. The absorber plate collects solar energy, and the reflector transfers the energy to the pipes, which heats the water or air inside. The water or air travels through the pipes to a storage tank. Flatbed collector panels are often mounted on roofs and used to heat homes and other buildings or to heat water.

Concentrating solar collectors collect the Sun's energy over a broad surface and reflect it onto a small area. These collectors reach much higher temperatures than flatbed collectors and may be curved or flat.

Concentrating collectors are sometimes used in large groups to provide energy to run power plants. At central receiving stations, hundreds or thousands of flat collectors transmit solar energy to a single tower, called a solar power tower. The tower is located in the center of the field of collectors.

You don't have to live in a remote village or be a sailor to take advantage of solar cells. Homeowners can buy solar-electric systems and have them installed in their homes. One U.S. university has installed three thousand solar panels on its campus. The panels generate and distribute electricity throughout the campus, saving the school fifty thousand dollars per year in energy costs.

In June 1997 the U.S. government announced its new Million Solar Roofs Initiative (MSRI). MSRI aims to have solar energy systems installed on one million buildings by the year 2010, including thousands of federal government buildings. The systems may be either photovoltaic or flatbed panel systems.

The program has had some success. By the year 2000 more than two thousand federal buildings had solar systems installed. In San Diego, California, the number of photovoltaic energy systems grew from 12 in 1999 to 862 in 2003. MSRI estimates that by the end of 2003 it had helped bring about the installation of 229,000 residential solar systems.

Panels of solar cells are invaluable as power sources in remote areas, where power lines can't reach. The cells are portable and can be used wherever there is sunlight. High in the Himalaya mountains, far from any power lines, Tibetan villages rely on solar panels to provide electricity. Other places may use solar panels to generate electricity to pump water from wells.

Scientists working in isolated places often take portable panels with them to power their equipment. Doctors who travel from village to village in places without electricity use solar panels to run small refrigerators that carry needed medicine.

Some lighthouses are located in areas where there is no power available to run their lights. For this reason, some lighthouses have been converted to solar power. Sailors also use solar cells at sea to power navigational tools.

**This lighthouse is powered by solar cells.**

Trough collectors are the best at concentrating the power of the Sun. Shaped like curved rectangles, trough collectors can concentrate solar energy at thirty to one hundred times its normal intensity. The mirrored surface reflects energy to a pipe that runs along the middle of the trough. The energy heats oil running inside the pipe. The heated oil generates steam that drives an electric generator.

Bowl-shaped concentrating collectors are called solar dishes. The dishes are covered with reflective material. The material reflects sunlight onto a tube in the center of the dish, heating up water in the tube.

**Solar trough collectors in California produce 99 percent of the solar-generated electric power in the United States.**

# Electricity from Sunlight

Some of the concentrating collectors you read about use the Sun's energy to drive power plants that generate electricity. However, solar energy also can be changed directly into electricity by solar cells. Solar cells are also called photovoltaic cells.

Most solar cells are made of silicon, an element found in Earth's crust. Sand on the beach is made up mostly of silicon. Silicon is useful in the development of electronics because it can be made into a semiconductor. A semiconductor has the ability to conduct electricity, but in a controlled way. Semiconductors are used in all sorts of electronic devices, from transistor radios to computers.

Solar cells contain two layers of silicon semiconductors. When photons of light fall upon the silicon, the silicon absorbs some of the photons. When enough solar energy is absorbed, electrons are freed from the silicon. Electrical charges begin to move between the two layers of silicon, producing an electric current.

A solar calculator uses a solar cell to generate power.

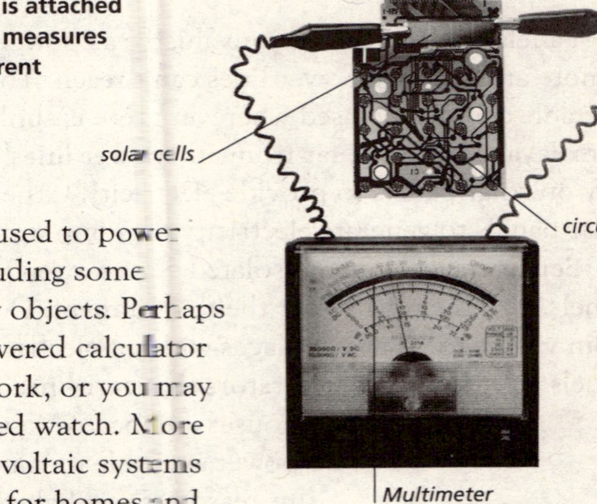

A calculator's solar cell is attached to a multimeter, which measures in volts the electric current generated by the cell.



Solar cells are used to power many devices, including some common, everyday objects. Perhaps you use a solar-powered calculator to do your homework, or you may have a solar-powered watch. More complicated photovoltaic systems generate electricity for homes and communications equipment. Some parking meters and streetlights are powered by solar cells.

A single solar cell is usually less than ten centimeters wide, and generates only about one or two watts of electricity. Because this is not enough power to run most electronic devices, multiple solar cells can be placed onto solar panels. The solar cells are connected on the panels, and their electricity output is combined.

## Solar Panels

Photovoltaic solar panels are made up of many solar cells. The cells are connected to one another, so all the current generated by all the cells is combined. Some solar panels can produce about one hundred watts of electricity per square meter, compared to one or two watts for a single cell.

# Atoms

by Sam Brelsfoard

| Genre | Comprehension Skill | Text Features | Science Content |
|---|---|---|---|
| Nonfiction | Sequence | • Captions<br>• Diagram<br>• Glossary | Matter |

Scott Foresman Science 6.13

PEARSON
Scott Foresman

scottforesman.com

ISBN 0-328-14008-2

90000

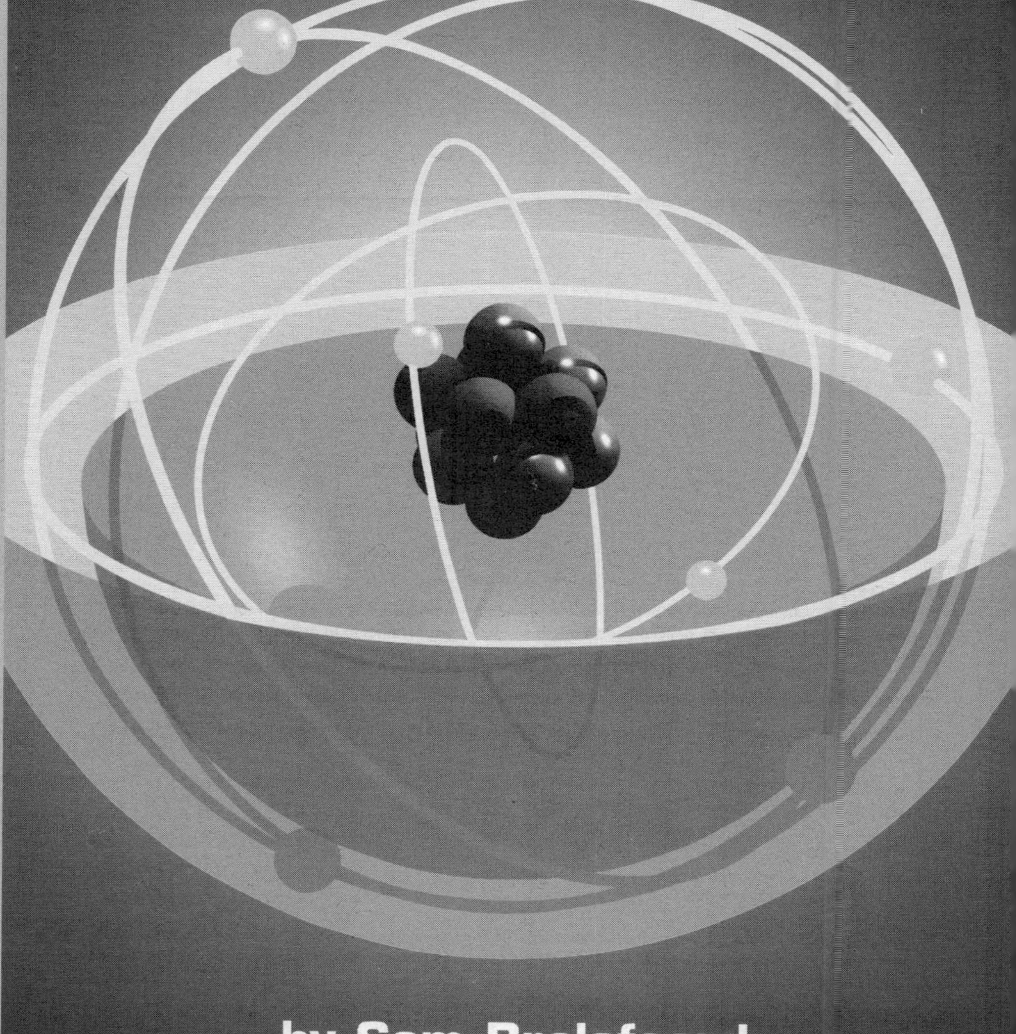

9 780328 140084

# What did you learn?

1. What is the difference between an element and a compound?

2. What three subatomic particles make an atom?

3. Why do hydrogen and oxygen bond together to make water?

4. **Writing** in Science Write a description of the structure of an atom. Use details from this book to support your answer.

5. **Sequence** Describe how an ionic bond might be formed. Use the sequence words *first, then,* and *finally* in your description.

**Vocabulary**

chemical change
chemical property
condensation
density
mass
physical change
physical property
volume
weight

**Extended Vocabulary**

anion
cation
covalent bond
ionic bond
nuclear fission
nucleus
quark
valence shell



**Picture Credits**
Every effort has been made to secure permission and provide appropriate credit for photographic material.
The publisher deeply regrets any omission and pledges to correct errors called to its attention in subsequent editions.

Photo locators denoted as follows: Top (T), Center (C), Bottom (B), Left (L), Right (R), Background (Bkgd).

12 (TR) ©Stevie Grand/Photo Researchers, Inc.; 13 Getty Images; 15 LBNL/Science Source/Photo Researchers, Inc.

Unless otherwise acknowledged, all photographs are the copyright © of Dorling Kindersley, a division of Pearson.

ISBN: 0-328-14008-2

# Glossary

| | |
|---|---|
| **anion** | a negatively charged ion |
| **cation** | a positively charged ion |
| **covalent bond** | a bond in which atoms share electrons |
| **ionic bond** | a bond in which one atom gives an electron to another atom, giving the atoms different charges and causing them to become attracted to each other |
| **nuclear fission** | the process of splitting an atom in two |
| **nucleus** | the center of an atom, which holds the protons and neutrons |
| **quark** | tiny particles that make up neutrons and protons |
| **valence shell** | the outer shell of an atom, around which the valence electrons orbit |

# Atoms

by Sam Brelsfoard

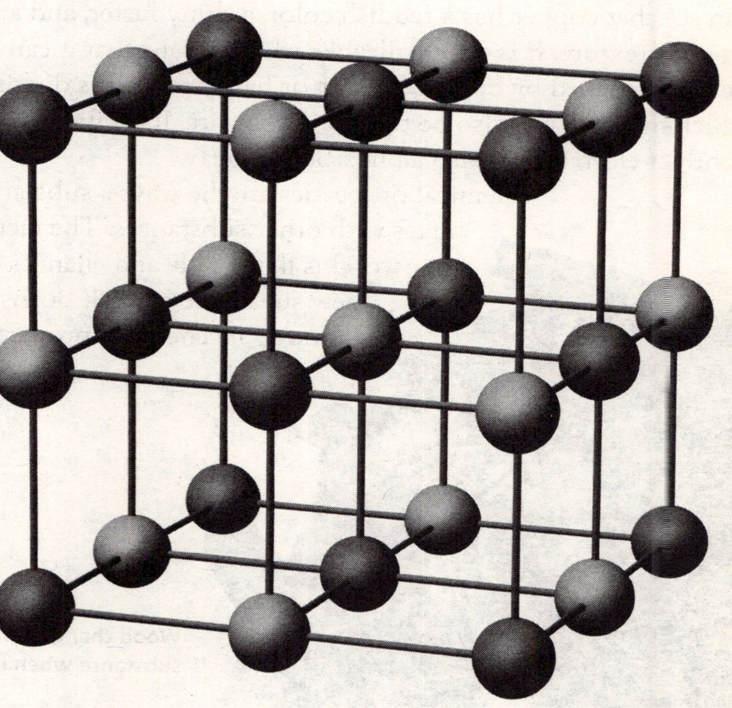

# What You Already Know

Mass, weight, and volume are properties of matter, which can be measured. Using these measurements, you can figure out other properties of matter. In order to determine something's density, divide its mass by its volume. Every element and compound has a unique density, so density can be used to identify materials. For example, if you determine that the density of a cube of metal is 8.96, and you learn that the density of copper is 8.96, you can be certain that you have a cube of copper.

The physical properties of copper help to identify it. You can see that copper has a reddish color, a shiny luster, and a smooth texture. It is also malleable, which means that it can be easily shaped by being pounded or hammered. It is ductile, which means it can also be turned into a wire. Its ability to conduct electricity is also a physical property.

Chemical properties are the ways a substance mixes with other substances. The fact that wood is flammable and changes into a new substance when it burns is one of its chemical properties.

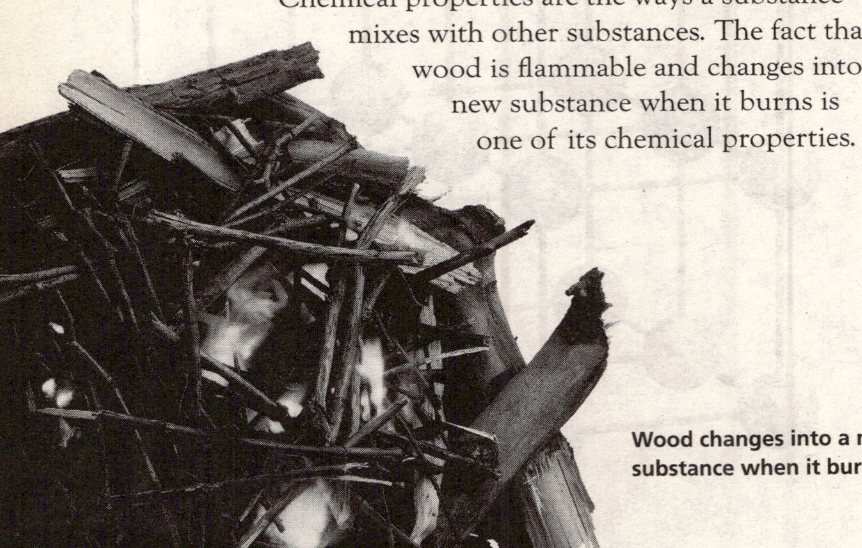

**Wood changes into a new substance when it burns.**

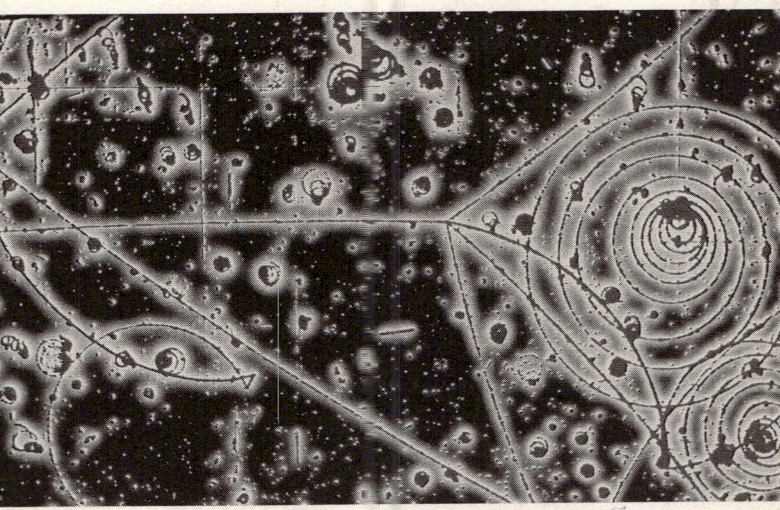

**This computer image shows collisions between particles in a particle accelerator.**

No one has ever seen a quark. How do we know they exist? In the 1960s, scientists were discovering many particles that were similar to protons and neutrons. They began to wonder if there was a more basic particle that had not been discovered yet. They called this undiscovered particle the quark, after a nonsense word in a book by Irish author James Joyce.

The existence of the quark was proven in 1968 by using a particle accelerator. A particle accelerator is a huge ring-shaped machine that measures several kilometers across. Particles travel around the ring at very high speeds and then crash into each other. Scientists used an accelerator to crash a tiny particle into a proton. By observing how the particle behaved as it passed through the proton, they concluded that the proton was not solid. It was made up of several extremely tiny particles. These particles were quarks.

Quarks are the smallest, most basic particles known. But quarks may be made up of ever smaller particles. The more we learn about these tiny bits of matter, the more we learn about how all matter behaves.

# Smaller and Smaller

In the 1800s, it was believed that the atom was the smallest particle. It would take millions of atoms lined up to stretch across the head of a pin. Eventually, protons, neutrons, and electrons were discovered. These particles are about one million times smaller than the smallest atom! It's hard to believe that there could be anything smaller than that, but there is. In the 1960s, scientists discovered an even smaller particle, the quark. Quarks make up neutrons and protons.

Very little is known about quarks. They are always found in groups, and there are six different types, or "flavors." These are called up, down, top, bottom, strange, and charmed. Different combinations of flavors make up different particles. Protons are made of two up quarks and a down quark. Neutrons are made of two down quarks and an up quark.

A neutron consists of three quarks.

Matter can be in any of four states—solid, liquid, gas, or plasma. Matter is made out of tiny particles that move and bump into each other. The energy of the particles and how strongly they are attracted to each other determine the state of matter. Matter can change from one state to another. Temperature can affect the force of attraction between particles. When you heat a substance, its particles will gain energy and move faster. If there is enough heat, the particles can break some of the force of attraction between them.

When water boils, the particles in the water speed up, and the water changes into water vapor, a gas. When the particles cool and slow down again, they start to attract each other and turn back into liquid, or condense. When the particles are cooled further, they attact each other even more and change to a solid.

You know that matter is made up of tiny particles called atoms. In this book, you will learn about even tinier particles that atoms are made of.

Boiling water changes into water vapor.

# Atoms and Elements

An element is a substance that is pure and cannot be broken down into different substances. There are about ninety-four known naturally occurring elements in the universe. There are an additional twenty elements that have been created by humans. Some elements that you may be familiar with are oxygen, carbon, and chlorine.

The smallest particle of an element that still has all the properties of the element is called an atom. A compound is formed when one element is chemically joined to one or more other elements. Table salt, or sodium chloride, is a compound that you are probably familiar with. It is made up of the elements sodium and chlorine.

Quartz is also a compound. It is made up of the elements oxygen and silicon. Gold, on the other hand, is an element. Gold cannot be broken down into a more simple substance.

In order for people around the world to talk and write about elements and compounds in a way that everyone can understand, a code was developed. Using this code, one scientist can write out formulas that another scientist can understand, even if they speak different languages.

In 1939, scientists discovered that it is sometimes possible to split an atom with an unstable nucleus. The best-known radioactive material is uranium. It is one of the easiest elements to split. When uranium atoms are split, they release huge amounts of energy. This process is called nuclear fission.

In order to split an atom, scientists force a neutron through its nucleus. When this happens, the atom splits into two new atoms. In addition to energy, this reaction releases particles that fly off in all directions. Some of these particles are released as radiation. Others strike the nuclei of other uranium atoms, causing them to split. When they split, they also release particles, which split still more nuclei. This is called a chain reaction. The energy that is produced by the chain reaction is in the form of heat. This heat can be used to make steam, which can spin generators to produce electricity.

**Gold is an element. Quartz is a compound of the elements oxygen and silicon.**

Nuclear fission is used to generate electricity in power plants such as this one.

# Splitting Apart

The atoms of some elements are very unstable and break down naturally. Such an atom might have too many protons, neutrons, or both in its nucleus. These protons and neutrons leave the nucleus, producing a type of energy called radiation. Elements that give off radiation are radioactive. Atoms of several elements, such as radium and uranium, are radioactive.

Radiation can destroy cells in the body. But scientists have found many positive uses for radiation. In radiation therapy, tumors are treated with blasts of gamma rays to kill cancer cells.

We must be very careful with radiation because exposure to large doses or even repeated exposure to small doses can be very dangerous. Scientists use instruments called Geiger counters to test whether radiation is at safe levels.

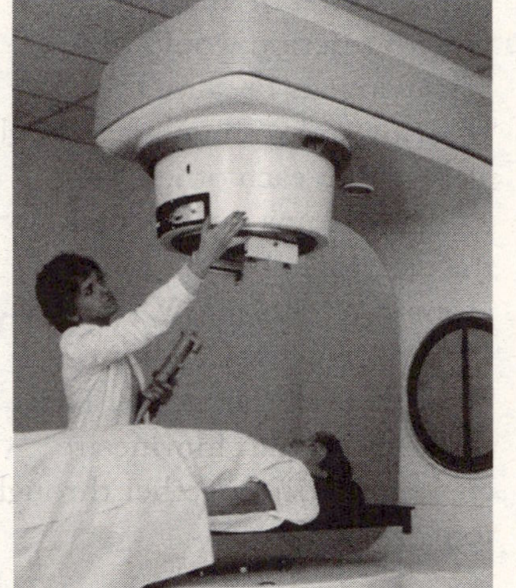

Radiation can be used positively to help combat cancer.

Geiger counters can detect many different types of radiation.

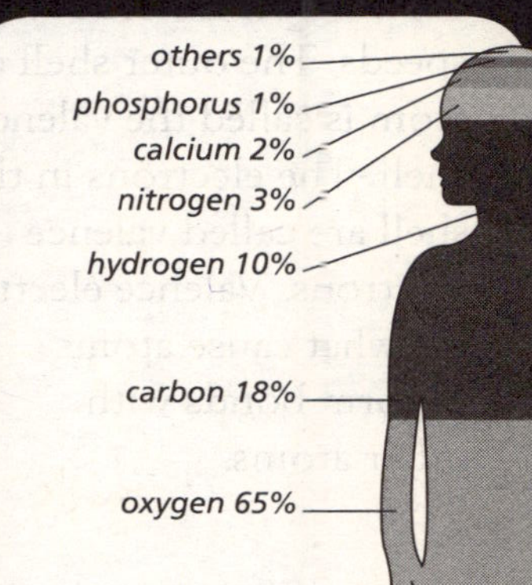

Hydrogen and helium are two of the most basic elements that can be found in space.

In this code each element has a symbol. The symbol for many elements is simply the first one, two, or three letters of their English name. Hydrogen's symbol is H, and helium's symbol is He. Sometimes the symbols come from the Latin name for the element. The symbol for sodium is Na, which stands for "natrium." To write the name of a compound using these symbols, you simply place one symbol next to the other. The symbol for table salt, or sodium chloride, is NaCl.

Everything in the universe is made up of elements. About 65 percent of your body is composed of the element oxygen. The human body contains about fifty different elements. The top six elements that are found in your body make up 99 percent of you. They are oxygen, carbon, hydrogen, nitrogen, calcium, and phosphorus.



## Body Elements

About 99 percent of the tissue of your body is made up of only 6 elements, as listed above.

# Inside the Atom

Atoms are extremely small. But they are made up of even smaller parts, called subatomic particles. The three main types of subatomic particles are electrons, protons, and neutrons. Protons have a positive charge. Neutrons are neutral because they have no charge. Electrons have a negative charge. Protons and neutrons are at the center, or nucleus, of the atom. The number of protons in the nucleus of an atom determines what element that atom is. If an atom has only one proton, then we can be sure that it is a hydrogen atom. If an atom has six protons, then it is a carbon atom.

The electrons are found in layers, called shells, around the nucleus. They move around in the shells, orbiting the nucleus at very high speeds. The outer shell of an atom is called the valence shell. The electrons in this shell are called valence electrons. Valence electrons are what cause atoms to form bonds with other atoms.

If one were to drop sodium into a bucket of chlorine, a violent reaction would occur. This happens because the chlorine and sodium are strongly attracted to each other. The chlorine atoms quickly pick up the electrons that the sodium atoms are releasing. When everything settles, sodium chloride is all that is left. The sodium and the chlorine are chemically tied together through ionic bonds.

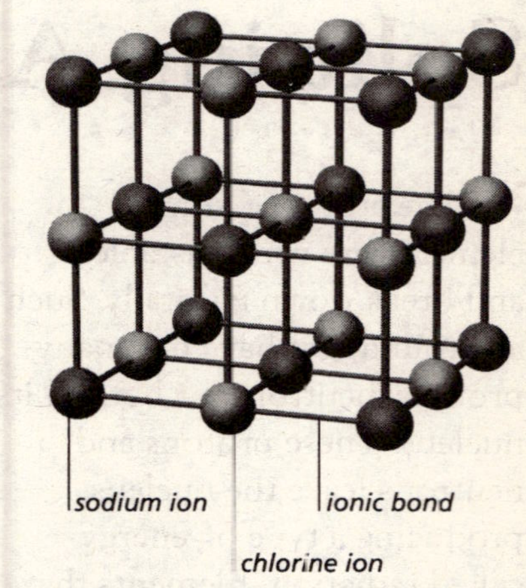


Sodium chloride is made up of positively charged sodium atoms and negatively charged chlorine atoms. They are held together by ionic bonds.

## Carbon

Carbon is found in nature in many different forms, including graphite and diamond. Graphite is soft and diamond is hard. They are different because they have different molecular structures. In graphite the carbon atoms are arranged in sheets and are able to slide over each other. Diamond carbon atoms are arranged in a stiff geometric structure.

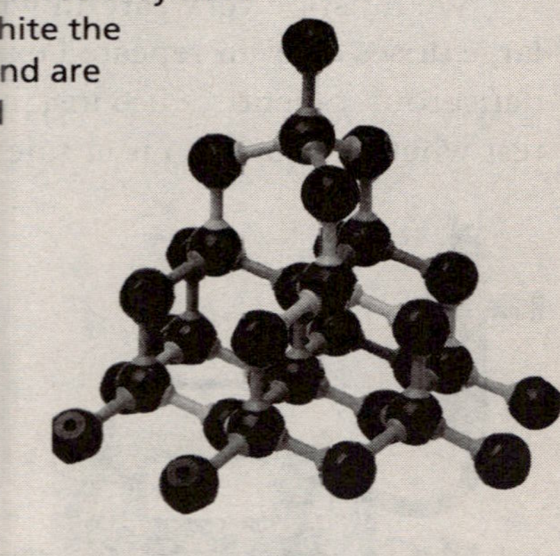

graphite carbon atoms

diamond carbon atoms

# Ionic Bonds

An ionic bond forms when electrons are actually transferred from one atom to another. Sodium and chlorine join with an ionic bond to form table salt. A sodium atom has only one electron in its valence shell. It would need seven additional electrons to fill its shell. It is much easier for sodium to give up one electron than to gain seven. Chlorine has one open space in its valence shell. When sodium and chlorine mix together, the sodium atom gives its extra electron to the chlorine atom.

When the sodium atom gives up an electron, its charge changes. It now has more protons than electrons, giving it a positive charge. The chlorine atom now has more electrons than protons, giving it a negative charge. The different charges of the atoms cause them to stick together, similar to two magnets. This attraction is what causes an ionic bond.

**Salt is a compound that contains ionic bonds between sodium and chlorine atoms.**



# Ions

An ion is an atom with an electrical charge. A neutral atom has an equal number of protons and electrons. The negative charges of the electrons are cancelled out by the positive charges of the protons. This gives the atom no charge. If it loses an electron, it becomes a positive ion, or a cation. The positive protons outnumber the negative electrons. When a neutral atom gains an electron, it becomes a negative ion, also known as an anion. In an anion, there are more negative electrons than positive protons.

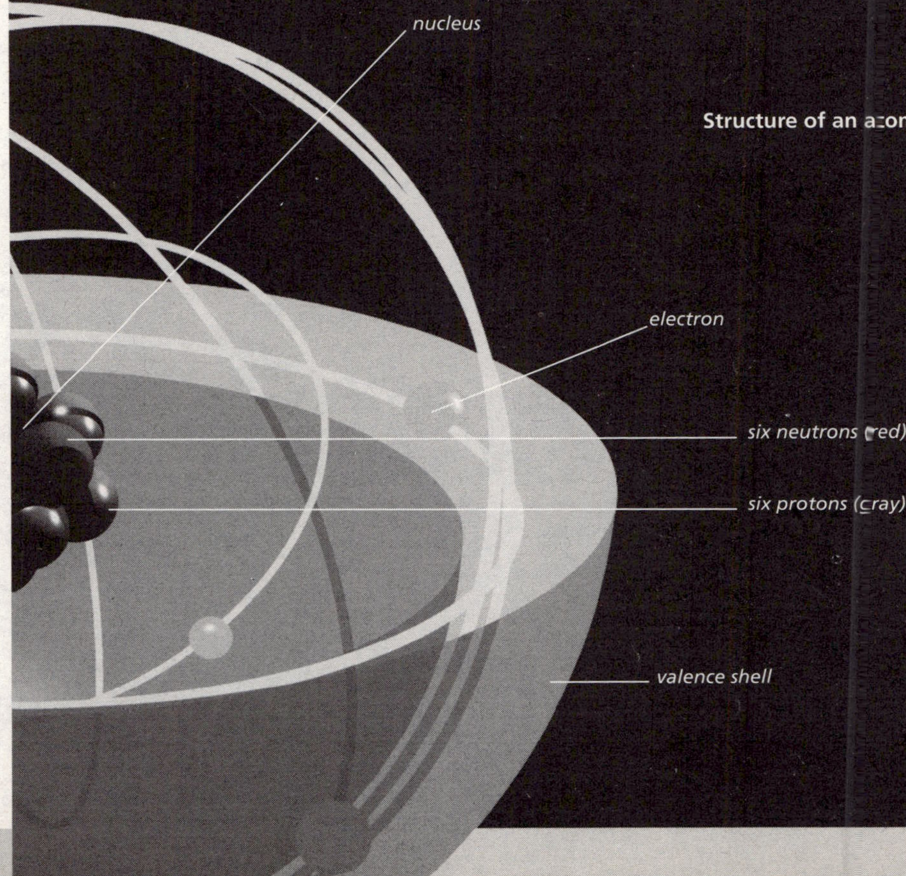


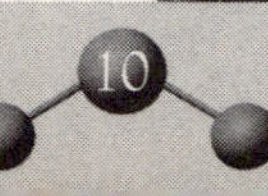

# Joining Together

If the valence shell of an atom is not full of electrons, the atom is unstable. To become stable, an atom can either gain electrons in the valence shell until the shell is completely full or lose them until the shell is completely empty. Atoms do this by joining with other atoms in a process called bonding. Two main types of bonds that atoms can have are covalent bonds and ionic bonds.

## Covalent Bonds

A covalent bond can occur between atoms that need electrons to fill their valence shells. To do this, the atoms share electrons. Oxygen needs eight electrons to fill its outer shell, but it only has six. Hydrogen needs two electrons, but it only has one.

To fill the two empty spaces in its valence shell, oxygen shares the electrons of two hydrogen atoms. The molecule that results is one you are probably familiar with: water.

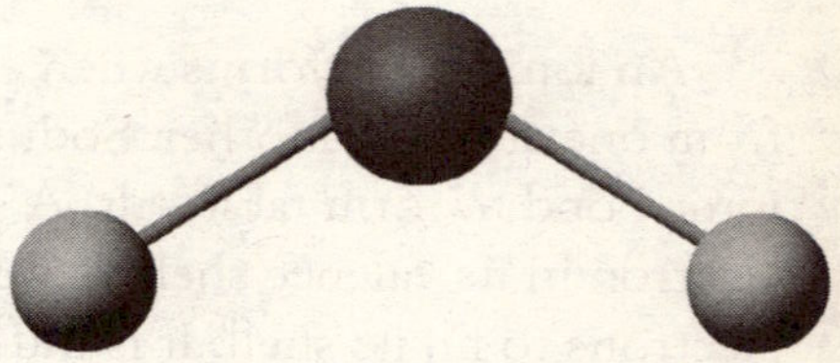

Covalent bonds can take the form of single, double, or triple bonds, depending on the number of electrons shared. Single bonds share one electron, double bonds share two, and triple bonds share three.

Covalent bonds are stronger than most other types of bonds. Covalent bonds are more common between nonmetal atoms.

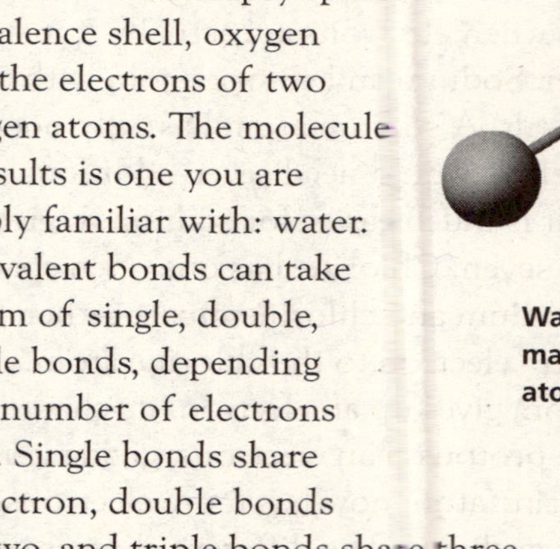

Water, or $H_2O$, is a molecule made from two hydrogen atoms and one oxygen atom.

Water is a simple covalent compound. Two atoms of hydrogen and one of oxygen make a water molecule.

# Acids AND Bases

by Grace Ng

| Genre | Comprehension Skill | Text Features | Science Content |
| --- | --- | --- | --- |
| Nonfiction | Compare and Contrast | • Captions<br>• Diagram<br>• Glossary | Matter |

Scott Foresman Science 6.14

PEARSON
Scott Foresman

DK

scottforesman.com

ISBN 0-328-14011-2

9 780328 140114    90000

# What did you learn?

1. What kind of acids are found inside the body?

2. How are alkalis used in construction?

3. Why is acid rain harmful?

4. **Writing** in Science Write to explain ways in which acids can be useful, and also explain some ways in which acids can be harmful. Give examples.

5. **Compare and Contrast** What are the similarities and differences between acids and bases in terms of their pH?

| Vocabulary | Extended Vocabulary |
| --- | --- |
| compound | acid |
| concentration | alkali |
| element | base |
| mixture | buffer |
| periodic table | corrosive |
| solubility | indicator |
| solute | salt |
| solution | |
| solvent | |



**Picture Credits**
Every effort has been made to secure permission and provide appropriate credit for photographic material. The publisher deeply regrets any omission and pledges to correct errors called to its attention in subsequent editions.

Photo locators denoted as follows: Top (T), Center (C), Bottom (B), Left (L), Right (R), Background (Bkgd).

12 ©James Marshall/Corbis; 18 ©Lester Lefkowitz/Corbis; 19 ©Arthur C. Smith III/Grant Heilman Photography; 21 ©Ted Spiegel/Corbis; 23 Alamy Images.

Unless otherwise acknowledged, all photographs are the copyright © of Dorling Kindersley, a division of Pearson.

ISBN: 0-328-14011-2

# Glossary

**acid**  a substance with a pH lower than seven. Acids react with bases to form salts

**alkali**  a base that has been dissolved in water

**base**  a substance with a pH higher than seven. Bases react with acids to form salts

**buffer**  a substance that makes changing the pH of a solution more difficult

**corrosive**  a characteristic of strong acids or strong bases that can eat away at metals and minerals

**indicator**  a compound that changes color in the presence of an acid or a base

**ion**  an atom or a group of atoms that has an electrical charge

**salt**  a compound that is composed of positive metallic ions and negative nonmetallic ions



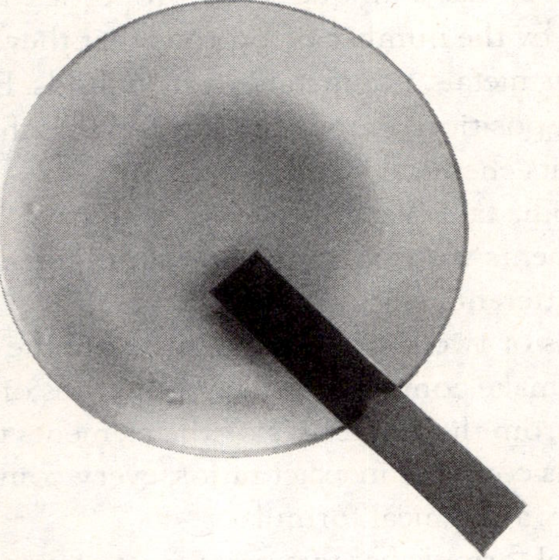

# Acids AND Bases

by Grace Ng

# What You Already Know

All matter is composed of tiny particles called atoms. These particles are difficult to study because they are so small. Over the years scientists have used different models to describe the atom.

Today we use the electron cloud model. At the center of the electron cloud model sits the nucleus. It is composed of protons and neutrons. The electron cloud surrounds the nucleus. It is composed of electrons and a lot of empty space.

Matter can be classified as elements, compounds, or mixtures. An element is a substance composed of only one type of atom. It cannot be separated into simpler substances by physical or chemical means. There are fewer than one hundred different elements found in nature.

Each element has a unique set of properties. Elements are made unique by the number of protons that they have. They can be classified as metals, nonmetals, or metalloids. Every single element has a position on the periodic table. Each one can be identified by its chemical symbol.

The periodic table lists the elements in order by atomic number. Elements with similar chemical properties are grouped together in different areas of the table.

The atoms of two or more elements combine into molecules to make compounds. The properties of compounds are different from the properties of the elements that make them. Because atoms combine in exact ratios, every compound can be represented by a chemical formula.

A chemical formula has two parts: a set of symbols of the elements, and subscripts for the number of atoms for each element. Water, for example, is represented by $H_2O$. It means that a water molecule contains two atoms of hydrogen and one atom of oxygen.

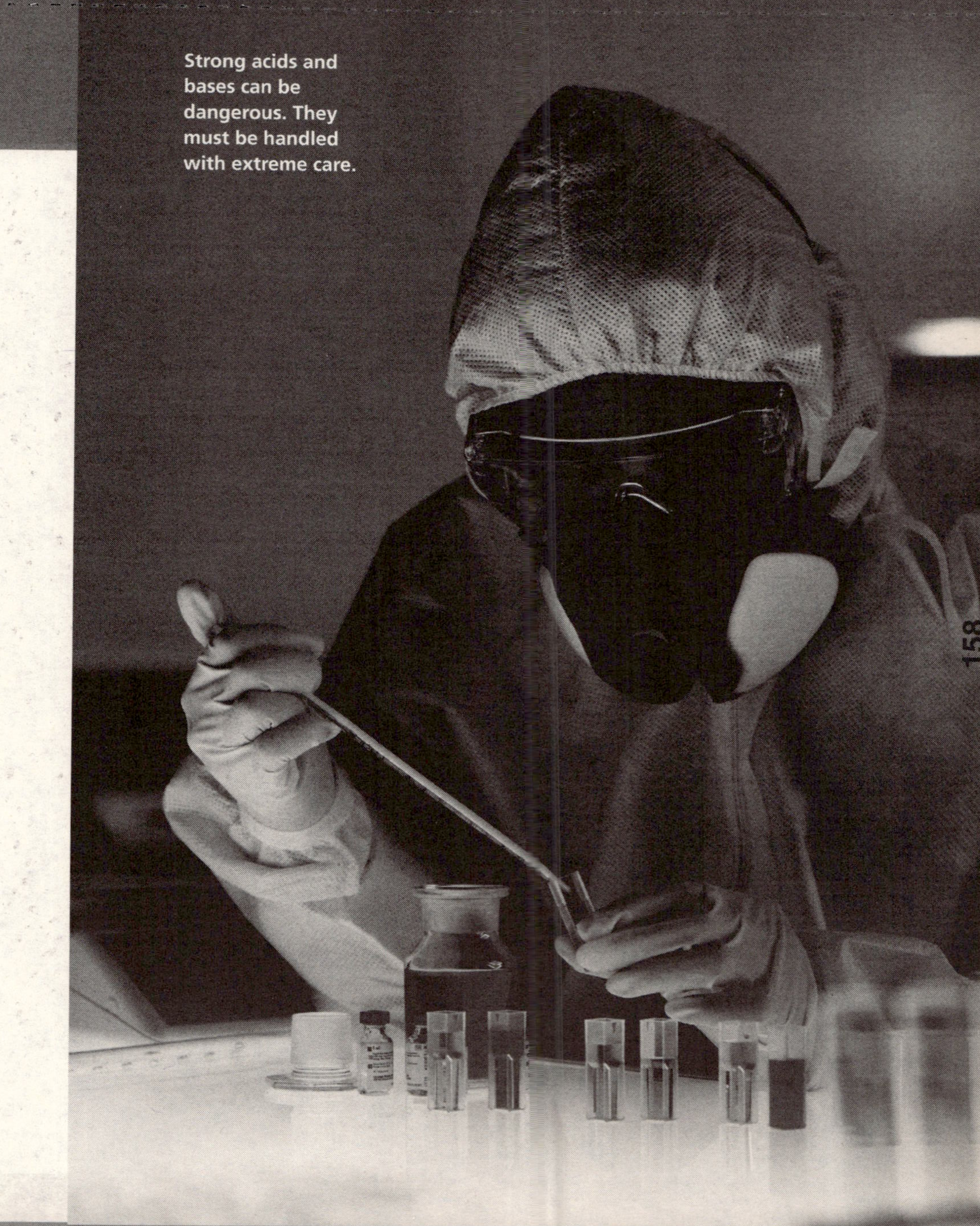

Strong acids and bases can be dangerous. They must be handled with extreme care.

# Living with Acids and Bases

It is important to remember that acids and bases are not always beneficial. Being around some of them may be harmful. For example, sulfuric acid is a very corrosive substance. It can cause blindness and third-degree burns on the skin.

Many products contain chemicals that are dangerous if they are not properly used, stored, and disposed of. Some people just pour these acidic or basic chemicals right down the drain or on the ground outside. Others throw them away with the trash. These are not the proper ways to get rid of acids and bases! Pouring them out like that can contaminate our water, soil, and air. Throwing them away as garbage can start fires or hurt trash collectors. We must find proper locations to dispose of these chemicals.

Acids and bases are everywhere. Many products we use each day contain acids and bases. They keep us clean, give us portable sources of power, and help balance our bodies. While quite useful, they can also be dangerous. Understanding acids and bases helps us use them in safer ways.

### Safety Symbols

If you see this label on a container, it means that the substance is corrosive. It may be a strong acid or a strong base. You must be careful in handling, storing, and disposing of these chemicals.

Substances that form mixtures do not combine in exact ratios. The atoms are also not chemically combined. The substances in mixtures retain their own properties and can easily be separated. Some mixtures that appear the same throughout are called solutions. A solution forms when one substance dissolves into another, such as salt water. The solute is the substance that is dissolved—salt. The solvent is the substance in which the solute is dissolved—water.

The maximum amount of solute that can be dissolved in a solvent is its solubility. Solutions reach a saturation point at this maximum amount. All solutions reach saturation—the point at which no more solute can be dissolved into the solvent.

Compounds can be classified as acids or bases. Acids and bases each have their own properties. There are strong and weak acids. There are also strong and weak bases. Scientists use the pH scale to measure the strength of different acids and bases. Acids and bases are part of our daily life.

Water is a compound. Its elements, oxygen and hydrogen, cannot be separated by physical means.

# What are acids?

Acids are one of the most common types of chemical substances. They are found in many different places. Acids have certain properties. They are sour in taste. Their liquid solutions conduct electrical current. Acids react with bases to form salts and water. They also react with some metals, including aluminum, zinc, iron, and copper. Acids react strongly with these metals to form new compounds. For example, when a hydrochloric acid solution is mixed with zinc metal, it produces hydrogen gas. This gas, which has the chemical symbol $H_2$, is explosive.

Hydrochloric acid is a strong acid. It reacts violently with the metal zinc to produce hydrogen gas.

The acidic water in lakes and rivers can harm or kill fish. Liming, or adding limestone to, this lake can help neutralize the acidic waters.

There are many harmful effects from acid rain. It damages forests and soils. The acidic water damages the leaves of trees, which decreases the amount of nutrients that can be absorbed. As a result, some trees die, and forests grow more slowly. When lakes and streams are filled with acidic waters, fish can be harmed or killed. These rains can remove paint on cars, damage monuments, and weaken buildings. They can also cause heart or lung problems for humans.

What can you do to reduce acid rain? You can start by conserving energy, since electric power generation is the main cause of acid deposition. You can turn off lights, computers, and other appliances when you are not using them. You can use energy-efficient appliances. People can also choose to carpool, use public transportation, use a bicycle, or walk. Although acid rain is a large environmental problem, each person can take steps to help reduce the problem.

# Acid Rain

Acid rain is the term used to describe different ways that acids fall out of the atmosphere. It can actually take the form of acidic rain, fog, or snow. When acidic water flows to the ground, it affects many plants and animals. There is also dry acid deposition, which accounts for half of the acidity that falls from the atmosphere. It occurs when acidic particles are deposited onto buildings, cars, houses, and trees.

Scientists have found that sulfur dioxide and nitrogen oxides are the primary causes of acid rain. Acid rain occurs when these gases react in the atmosphere with water, oxygen, and other chemicals to form acidic compounds. In the United States, about two-thirds of all sulfur dioxide and one-third of all nitrogen oxides come from electric power plants that use fossil fuels such as coal.

Acid rain can damage stone monuments like this one.

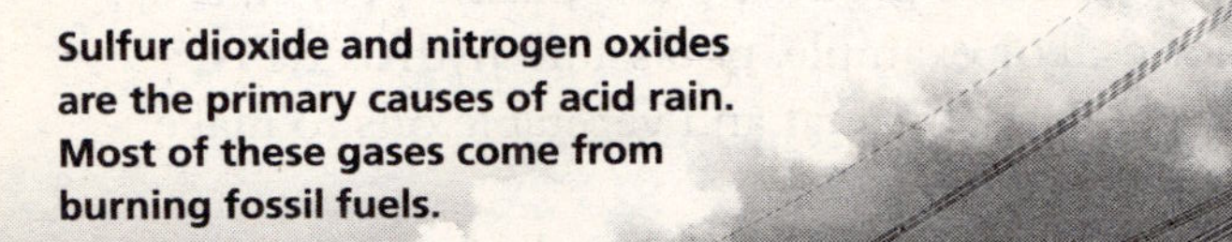

Sulfur dioxide and nitrogen oxides are the primary causes of acid rain. Most of these gases come from burning fossil fuels.

When sulfuric acid is added to sugar, they react to form carbon and water.

There are other physical properties that distinguish acids. Liquid acids tend to be thicker than water. While weaker acids such as orange juice and vinegar are common in our everyday foods, strong acids are corrosive. That means they can eat away at metals and minerals, and they will burn your skin if you touch them. Very strong acids can even eat through metal sheets!

Acids are everywhere. Milk, lemonade, and soda contain acids. Fruits such as oranges, lemons, and grapefruits have citric acids. There are also acids within your body. Your stomach has very strong acids. They are used to break down the foods you eat. Your body cells have weak acids that help keep you healthy. Amino acids help cells make many different things the body needs.

Fruits such as oranges, lemons, and limes have citric acids in them.

# Bases and Alkalis

Bases are one of the most common types of chemical substances. Bases have many industrial and household uses. They react with many common materials. Like acids, strong bases are also corrosive. They can corrode some metals to produce hydrogen gas and metal salts.

Many people think that alkalis and bases are the same thing. While it is true that alkalis and bases are related, they are different in one important way. An alkali is a base that can be dissolved in water.

Both bases and alkalis have specific properties. Unlike acids that taste sour, bases and alkalis are bitter. They are slippery or soapy to the touch. Their liquid solutions conduct electric current. Bases react with acids to make neutral salts. Strong bases and alkalis can cause chemical burns.

Alkalis such as soda ash (sodium carbonate) and caustic soda (sodium chlorite) are used in the production of many industrial products, including glass, paper, cleansers, soaps, and detergents.

**Bleach is a strong alkali. It is a common household cleaner.**

**Ammonia is used as a common household cleaner, but it is also an ingredient in lawn and farm fertilizer.**

Factories use alkalis in manufacturing a wide variety of products. They are used to produce glass, plastics, paper, soap, and dyes for fabrics. For example, potassium hydroxide is combined with boiling animal fat and vegetable oils to make soap. It is also used to make glass.

The fertilizer industry uses alkalis as well. Ammonia is used as a common household cleaner, but it is also an ingredient in lawn and farm fertilizer. The United States produces approximately thirty-five billion pounds of ammonia each year. That is about six pounds of ammonia for every person on Earth. This does not even include the amount of ammonia produced by the rest of the world.

Sodium hydroxide is another very useful alkali salt. It is the most commonly used strong base. Sodium hydroxide is found in cleaners, detergents, and soaps. It is also used to make pulp and paper and to produce chemicals. In the United States, about twenty-four billion pounds of sodium hydroxide is produced in one year.

# Alkali Industry

You may not realize it, but alkalis are used every day. They are used in homes, construction sites, factories, and farms.

At home, many of the common cleaners you use have alkalis as active ingredients. Things that contain alkalis may include drain openers, oven cleaners, and detergents. Construction sites use limestone, which is one of the most common and important alkali products. It is mined throughout the world. Powdered limestone is one of the key components in making cement and concrete. Limestone is used to help build everyday structures.

**Sodium hydroxide is a very useful alkali salt. One application for sodium hydroxide is its use in making pulp and paper.**

**The brass cleaner shown here is a weak alkali. It is used to restore the shine on brass.**

Many strong bases are found in household cleaners such as drain openers, bleach, and ammonia. These bases have grease-cutting properties. Soaps, shampoos, and baking soda contain weak bases. But strong bases and alkalis, such as ammonia, can corrode parts of living things. They are corrosive to mold, mildew, hair, and even skin. Some can also be poisonous if ingested.

Bases are very common. Fresh eggs, cornstarch, and chalk contain bases. The blood in our bodies also contains a base.

Calcium carbonate is a base. It is commonly used as an antacid, to neutralize acids. Calcium carbonate is found in rocks all over the world. It is the main component of seashells.

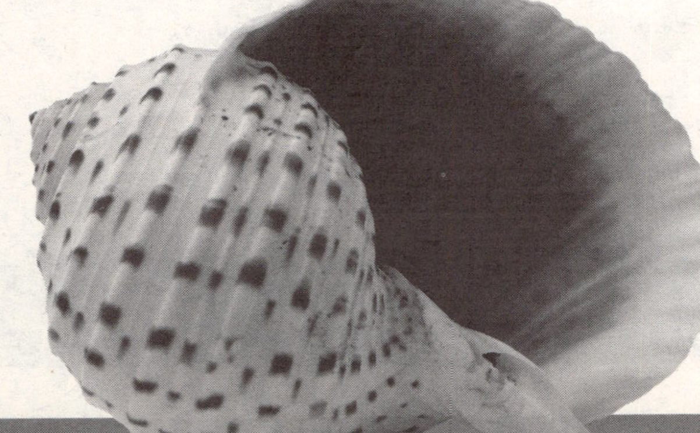

**Calcium carbonate, a base, is the main component of seashells.**

# Measuring pH Levels

Both acids and bases have different strengths. Scientists use the pH scale to describe the strengths of acids and bases. The scale ranges from 0 to 14. Acids have a pH between 0 and 7. As their pH increases, their strength decreases. Bases have a pH between 7 and 14. The strength of a base increases as its pH reaches closer to 14. A substance with a pH of 7 is neither an acid nor a base. It is a neutral substance.

Distilled water is neutral. Most other everyday liquids have a pH that is either a little below or a little above neutral. In a chemistry lab, you will find solutions with a pH below 1 and others with a pH of 14.

In most cases, one type of acid is used in many different ways. For example, nitric acid is used in manufacturing plastics, dyes, fertilizers, and explosives. It is also used to clean metals and in a wide variety of chemical processes to make synthetic fibers, electrical circuit boards, and drugs. The United States produces about nineteen billion pounds of nitric acid annually.

Sulfuric acid is one of the most important industrial acids. It is used to clean metals, help refine petroleum, and manufacture chemicals. It is also present in an automobile's battery. About ninety-six billion pounds of sulfuric acid is produced annually in the United States. That is about sixteen pounds of sulfuric acid for every person on Earth. In North America, about 70 percent of the sulfuric acid produced is used to manufacture fertilizers.

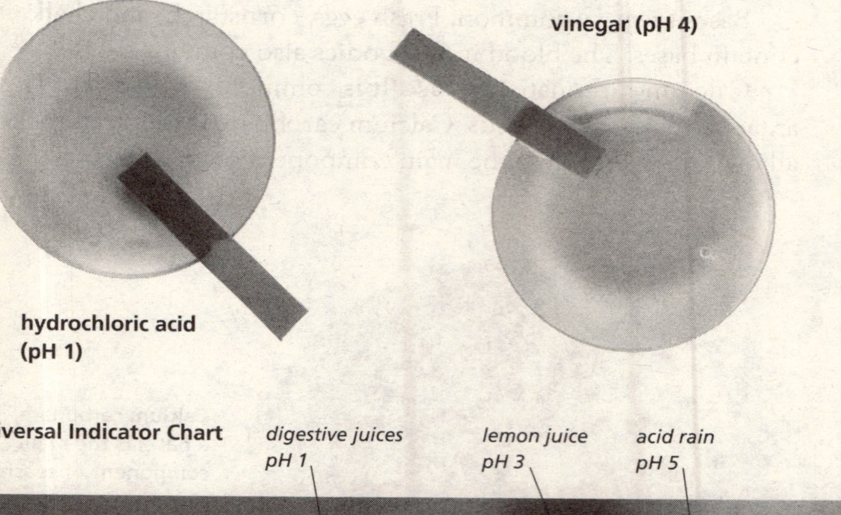


The pH values of different liquids can be tested with universal indicator paper.

Nitric acid has many uses. One of them is to manufacture dyes that can be used in paint.

Nitric acid is also used to make synthetic fibers, such as nylon.

# Acid Industry

Many common items have acids in them. Sodas, citrus fruits, and pickles are all acidic. Acids are also found in many other everyday products.

Acids are used to refine petroleum, manufacture metals, and make plastics. Acids are used in food preservatives, as ingredients in cosmetics, and also as components of insect repellents. Aspirin, a commonly used pain-relieving drug, is a weak acid.

Acids are important components in manufacturing plastics. Many things are made of plastic.

Chemical substances that are strongly acidic or strongly basic are very dangerous because they can burn through materials and your skin.

It is too dangerous to taste or touch substances that are acidic or basic. Because of this, we use indicators to tell whether something is an acid or a base. Indicators are compounds that change color in the presence of an acid or a base. Some indicators change to different colors if they are mixed with an acid or a base. Other indicators will only change colors for an acid or a base, but not for both.

Litmus paper is one of the more popular indicators. It will change into different colors depending on the pH of the liquid it is exposed to. When you dip yellow litmus paper in a neutral substance, there is no color change. A strong acid changes the paper to bright red-pink. A weak acid turns the paper orange. A weak base changes the litmus paper green. A strong base causes the paper to turn violet. The color spectrum of the indicator chart is shown below, with examples of common substances and their pH levels.







165

# Neutralizing Acids

Neutralization of acids and bases is a common process in nature. When an acid reacts with a base, both are neutralized. In many cases, salt and water are produced. A simple experiment can demonstrate this. Fill a glass jar with vinegar (acid). Put a piece of chalk (base) in the vinegar. Observe as the acid and the base are neutralized.

When would you want to neutralize an acid or base? One example is when you want to decrease the acids in your stomach. The stomach has acids that help digest foods. Sometimes the stomach may produce too much acid. This will give you a burning pain in your stomach area. In order to neutralize these acids, you can take antacids, which contain bases.

The metal at the positive terminal pulls the electrons more strongly than the negative terminal repels them. When a wire is used to connect the negative and positive terminals, the electrons travel from the negative terminal through the wire to the positive terminal. This starts a cycle of flowing electrons that will continue until the circuit is broken.

In the simple battery below, the metals copper and zinc are submerged in a solution of sulfuric acid and water. The sulfuric acid reacts with the zinc to release electrons. The electrons are attracted to the copper plate and repelled by the zinc plate. When the plates are connected, the electrons flow through the wire and light the bulb.

When chalk is put into vinegar, the vinegar breaks down the chalk. The reaction produces carbon dioxide gas. The chemical reaction continues until the entire piece of chalk is gone.

This homemade battery uses copper and zinc submerged in sulfuric acid. Electrons flow from zinc to copper through the wire.

# Batteries

One of the most common uses for acids and bases is in batteries. Batteries are a portable supply of electric power. They come in many shapes and sizes. They are made of many types of materials. However, nearly all batteries work in the same way.

Batteries are actually containers of chemicals. Most batteries contain two types of metal and either an acid or a base. In a battery, the acid or base slowly undergoes a special type of chemical change called an electrochemical reaction. Electrons are released in this type of electrochemical reaction.

Batteries have two terminals. Each one is made of a different type of metal. One terminal has a negative charge, and one has a positive charge. The electrons from the acid or base are attracted to the positive terminal and begin to pile up. The negative terminal repels electrons.

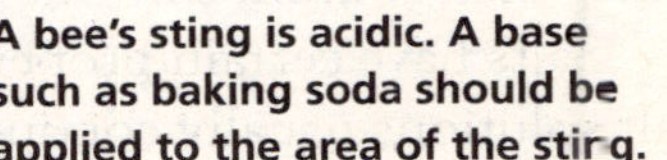



Some watches use alkaline batteries.

Some dry cell batteries use nickel hydroxide and contain an alkali salt.



Cars use batteries that contain a strong acid, lead, and lead oxide.

A wasp's sting is alkaline. An acid such as vinegar should be used to soothe the sting.

A bee's sting is acidic. A base such as baking soda should be applied to the area of the sting.

Neutralizing is important with wasp and bee stings. Wasp stings are alkaline. If a wasp stings you, you should rub some vinegar on the area where you were stung. The vinegar's acid will neutralize the sting. Bee stings are different than wasp stings. Instead of being alkaline, they contain formic acid. You need to neutralize the acidic sting with a base. One way is to make a baking soda and water paste to apply to the area where you got stung.

There are times when we do not want to completely neutralize a substance. We may just want to maintain a specific pH and only neutralize the effects of extra acidity. To do this we use buffers. A buffer is a substance that makes changing the pH of a solution more difficult. We can find many examples of natural buffers of acids and bases. Soil, lakes, and streams sometimes contain natural buffers, such as limestone. The natural buffers help to decrease acid and base levels. Soils can degrade if there is too much acid. Excess acid can harm plants and crops. Lakes and streams can suffer if the pH level drops too much. Certain animals can die if the waters are too acidic. For these reasons, neutralizing any changes in pH levels is important for the environment.

If there is too much acid in your stomach, you may feel some pain. An antacid neutralizes some of the extra acid.

# 12

# Salts

We are all familiar with the table salt that we use in our foods. Its chemical name is sodium chloride. Sodium chloride has the chemical symbol NaCl. There are many chemical compounds other than sodium chloride that can be classified as salts.

Salts have certain properties. They break down in water, and salt solutions usually conduct electrical current. Salts may also react with water.

A salt can be formed in a few ways. One method is for a chemical reaction to take place between an acid and a base. Another method is for a metal to react with a weak acid. Two salts can also react with one another to form two new salts. Finally, a salt may react with an acid to form a different salt and acid.

Salt pans collect seawater. After the seawater is collected, the water is evaporated and the salt crystals remain.



The pH of a salt is not always 7. The pH level depends on the strengths of the original acids and bases that formed the salt. When a strong acid reacts with a strong base, the resulting salt will have a pH of 7. If a weak acid reacts with a strong base, the salt will be basic. When a strong acid reacts with a weak base, the salt will be acidic.

Salts have many uses. Some salts are used to season and preserve foods. Others are used to manufacture soaps, detergents, and toothpaste. Salts are also used to make glass, substances for absorbing moisture, photographic film, soldering materials, and fertilizers.

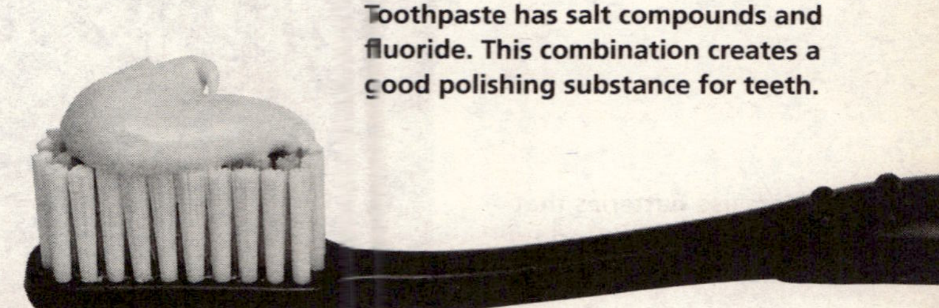

Toothpaste has salt compounds and fluoride. This combination creates a good polishing substance for teeth.

# 13

Physical Science

# ZERO Gravity

by Steve Miller

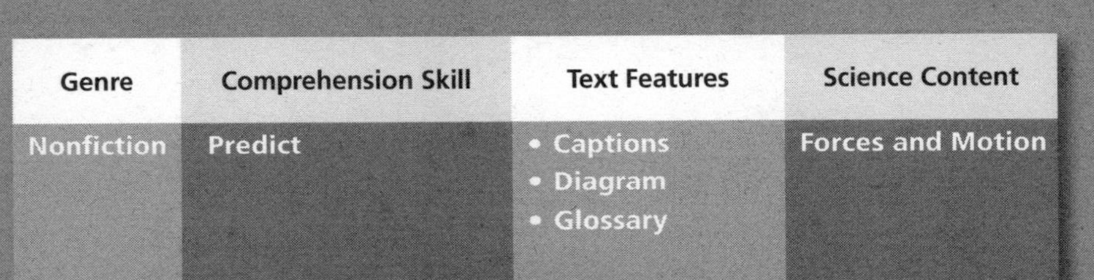



| Genre | Comprehension Skill | Text Features | Science Content |
| --- | --- | --- | --- |
| Nonfiction | Predict | • Captions<br>• Diagram<br>• Glossary | Forces and Motion |

Scott Foresman Science 6.15

PEARSON
Scott Foresman

ISBN 0-328-14014-7

90000

9 780328 140145

scottforesman.com

# What did you learn?

1. How can your weight be different on Earth than on the Moon?

2. What two forces cause ocean tides?

3. Why do astronauts float when they are weightless orbiting the Earth in the space shuttle?

4. **Writing** in Science Gravity cannot be seen or felt even though it affects every object in the universe. Describe some of the ways you know gravity exists. Include details from the book to support your answer.

5. **Predict** Based on your understanding of balance, what do you think will happen if you stand on one foot and then raise your arm and hold it out to one side?

**Vocabulary**

acceleration
force
friction
gravitational force
inertia
momentum
speed
velocity

**Extended Vocabulary**

air resistance
black hole
center of gravity
escape velocity
orbital velocity
terminal velocity
tides
weight

**Picture Credits**
Every effort has been made to secure permission and provide appropriate credit for photographic material.
The publisher deeply regrets any omission and pledges to correct errors called to its attention in subsequent editions.

Photo locators denoted as follows: Top (T), Center (C), Bottom (B), Left (L), Right (R), Background (Bkgd).

Opener: NASA; 1 NASA; 2 Jan Butchofsky-Houser/Corbis; 6 Joe McBride/Corbis; 10 (C) George Bernard/NHPA Limited, (BR) George Bernard/NHPA Limited; 11 (B) NASA; 12  NASA; 14 NASA; 15 (TL, CR) NASA.

Scott Foresman/Dorling Kindersley would also like to thank: 5 (CA) NASA/DK Images; 17 (CA) NASA/DK Images; 18 (CB) NASA/DK Images; 20 NASA/Finley Holiday Films/DK Images.

Unless otherwise acknowledged, all photographs are the copyright © of Dorling Kindersley, a division of Pearson.



ISBN: 0-328-14014-7

# Glossary

| | |
|---|---|
| **air resistance** | the upward pressure exerted by air on a falling object |
| **black hole** | a region of space in which the force of gravity is so great that even light cannot escape |
| **center of gravity** | the point that represents the average location of an object's mass, and below which it can be balanced |
| **escape velocity** | the upward velocity that allows an object to continue moving away from a gravitational pull without additional force |
| **orbital velocity** | the velocity at which the object continues to move around the planet if no additional force is used |
| **terminal velocity** | the velocity at which the air resistance on a falling object balances the force of gravity |
| **tides** | very long waves caused by the gravitational pull of the Moon and the Sun |
| **weight** | the measure of the force of gravity on an object |

# ZERO Gravity

by Steve Miller

# What You Already Know

Every object in the universe, from a pencil on your desk to the most distant star, has forces acting on it. A force is a push or a pull. Some forces act only when objects are touching, but others have effects that extend long distances.

Friction is the force that resists movement of one object past another. For example, when you pick up a pencil, friction prevents it from slipping between your fingers. Friction is a force that only affects objects that are touching. The amount of force depends on the type of surfaces that are in contact. It is easier to pick up a pencil than a wet ice cube because the force of friction is stronger between your finger and the pencil.

Although the balloons seem to float freely in the air, many forces are acting on them.

On an extreme amusement park ride, you can experience many changes in force in several seconds.

There are some places on Earth where you can experience the same effect, but only for a very short time. Remember how a ball thrown up in the air reaches a point at which the upward and downward forces are exactly balanced. You can experience the same thing on a roller coaster. As the roller coaster approaches a peak and starts back down, there is a moment when the forces on your body are balanced. You rise up off the seat and float above the ride. This is a moment of weightlessness—a second or two during which you can ignore the amazing force of gravity.

# Gravity Is Great

Gravity is the force that holds the universe together. It affects everything you do, because without gravity things would not stay where you put them. A tossed ball would just keep moving in the direction of the toss, leaving Earth and heading into space. Of course that statement is too simple, because without gravity there would not even be a planet from which to throw the ball. The universe would consist of randomly moving particles that never pulled together.

It is interesting, though, to think what life would be like without gravity. Shuttle astronauts float from place to place. Even though they are subject to the same forces of gravity as everyone else, they are able to ignore its effects because everything else around them is moving along with them.





When you drop the pencil, it falls to the floor. The force that causes it to fall is gravitational force, the force of attraction between an object and every other object in the universe. Objects do not have to touch one another to experience gravitational force, as when you toss a pencil up in the air. The attraction between the pencil and the Earth causes the pencil to fall.

Forces, such as friction and gravity, cause objects to move. Speed is a measure of how fast an object is moving. Speed is calculated by dividing the distance that the object moves by the time needed to move that distance. If you ride your bicycle 20 kilometers in one hour, your speed is 20 kilometers per hour, or 20 km/h. Velocity is the speed of an object in a particular direction. If you are riding from south to north on your bike, your velocity is 20 km/h north.

When a force acts on a moving object, the velocity of the object can change. Acceleration is the rate at which velocity changes. Acceleration occurs whenever the speed changes, the direction of motion changes, or both speed and direction change. Acceleration is the result of unbalanced forces on an object.

Inertia is the tendency of an object to remain at rest or in constant motion unless a force acts on it. Inertia is the reason that it is hard to pedal your bike when you first start, but it is easier to keep moving once you are going. It takes force to overcome inertia at first, but then the motion continues once you start pedaling. It also takes force to overcome the inertia of a moving object. Momentum is a measure of the force needed to stop a moving object. It is the product of the object's mass and its velocity. Because momentum increases with mass, it is harder to stop a heavier object, such as a baseball, than it is to stop a light object, such as a table tennis ball.

# The Force of Gravity

Inertia means that a moving object will keep moving unless a force acts on it. If you throw a ball upward in the air, it does not keep going upward forever. It falls back toward the ground. What happened to its inertia? A force acted on the ball to change its velocity. As soon as you throw the ball upward, the force of gravity—the attraction between the ball and the Earth—causes the upward velocity to decrease. Eventually, the direction of travel reverses completely and the ball returns to the ground.

Gravity is the force of attraction between any two objects. You usually cannot feel the force of gravity on your body. What you can feel is the force that balances gravity. When you sit on a chair, the chair pushes you upward with a force equal to the downward pull of gravity. If the forces were not balanced, you would move, which is what happens when you sit on a chair that is too weak to push you up, and it breaks causing you to fall to the floor.

The strength of the attraction due to gravitational force depends on the mass of the objects and the distance between them. Weight is the measure of the force of gravity on an object. The object's weight is its mass multiplied by the force of gravity. Gravity pulls with a force of 9.8 newtons for every kilogram of mass. A mass of 40 kg multiplied by 9.8 gives a weight of 392 N.

**The ball eventually falls to the ground due to the attraction between the ball and the Earth.**

**Gas from this blue gas giant star becomes part of the black hole when it gets too close.**

No one can observe a black hole directly because nothing, not even light, escapes from its gravity. We can only observe its effect on other objects.

When an object gets too close to a black hole, the huge gravitational pull of the black hole draws the object in, and the object becomes part of the black hole. Astronomers have found evidence that a black hole may be at the core of some galaxies. These black holes are about the size of our solar system but have a mass equivalent to several billion stars. They are detected by their effect on the motion of the stars in the galaxy. Another way to detect black holes is by observing matter that is accelerated as it passes close to a black hole but does not quite get pulled into it. Like the gravitational slingshot that accelerates a spacecraft, the gravity of the black hole gives these particles enormous energy.

# Black Holes

After the gas has caused the formation of a star, gravity still pulls particles toward its center. Extremely hot reactions in its core give the particles energy that forces them away from the core. Some of these particles and some of their energy escape the star, which is why we can see it.

Sometimes when a very massive star consumes all of its fuel its core collapses, releasing a large amount of energy. The outer parts of the star explode outward, blasting it apart in an explosion bright enough to be detected in distant galaxies. The force of gravity crushes the core causing it to become smaller and smaller. Matter cannot escape this dense mass. Eventually, the mass collapses and becomes a black hole, a region of space in which the force of gravity is so large that even light, which travels at about 300 million kilometers per second, cannot escape.

Matter
that gets too
close to a black hole
disappears completely.

The explosion of a supernova
sends energy and particles
traveling out into space.





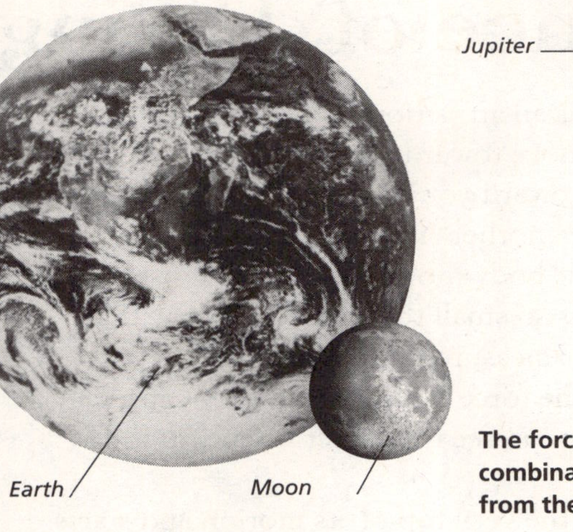



The force of gravity depends on the combination of mass and distance from the center of the planet.

People frequently talk about weight in kilograms, but kilograms measure mass, not weight. Because weight depends on gravity, a person's weight can vary, depending on the gravitational force.

As you can see from the illustration above, the Moon is much smaller than Earth. Since it has much less mass than Earth, its gravity is weaker. The Moon's gravity pulls with a force of only 1.6 newtons for every kilogram of mass. A mass of 40 kg multiplied by 1.6 only gives a weight of 64 N. That means things weigh less on the Moon. This is why astronauts can jump so high on the Moon. Their muscles only have to push about one-sixth the weight when they jump.

Now compare the gravity of Jupiter to that of Earth. Jupiter has more mass than Earth, so its gravity is stronger. It has a pull of 26 newtons for every kilogram of mass. This means that if you were to travel to Jupiter, you would weigh more than twice what you weigh on Earth!

# The Science of Falling

If the force of gravity is an attraction of two objects for one another, why do you move toward the Earth when you fall? Why doesn't Earth move toward you? Believe it or not, you and Earth do move toward one another. You have much less mass than Earth, though, so your body moves most of the distance. The motion of the planet is so small that there is no way that it could ever be detected or measured.

When an object falls, the force exerted by gravity causes its velocity to increase. You can see this effect when you throw a ball upward.

When the ball reaches the very top of its motion and starts to fall, it is barely moving, but by the time it reaches the ground, it is moving very quickly.

These skydivers are experiencing two opposing forces—the pull of gravity and the push of the atmosphere.

The Milky Way looks much like this galaxy, known as NGC 2997.

Distances that are too huge for us to even imagine separate these huge collections of stars from one another. Even so, gravitational forces draw them toward one another. Galaxies travel through space in clusters that have been traveling together for billions of years. Scientists can calculate the mass of galaxies by their gravitational influence on one another.

## Star Formation

Stars begin their existence as clouds of gas floating in space. The force of gravity pulls the gas into blobs that become stars and planets.

This cloud of gas may have formed from the explosion of stars long ago.

Gravity causes some of the gas particles to form clumps.

As the clumps become larger, they attract more gas particles, becoming stars.





176

# A Universal Force

The star that is the Sun's nearest neighbor is so far away that its light takes more than four years to reach us. Even at that distance, stars influence one another through the force of gravity. In space, stars form huge clusters, such as the one shown below. They move as a group, held together by their attraction to one another.

On a clear night, in a dark place, you can see the Milky Way: thousands of stars that are visible as a band of dim light across the sky. Those stars are part of the Milky Way galaxy, a group of billions of stars, including our Sun. The Milky Way galaxy is similar to the one shown to the right. Many galaxies have this kind of pinwheel shape, with stars rotating around their center of mass.

**Each star in this cluster, known as M13, affects all of the others.**

## In a Vacuum

An elephant pushes through the air better than a feather, causing it to fall more quickly. In a vacuum, there is no air resistance to slow falling objects. With no air resistance, an elephant and a feather would fall at exactly the same speed!

Gravity is not the only force that affects falling objects. Moving objects must push through the air. The faster an object moves, the more the air pushes back. Suppose you were riding a bicycle very quickly, the air would feel like a strong wind blowing on you. If you kept speeding up, the force of the air pushing on you would eventually get as strong as the force of your legs pedaling you forward. At this point, you would not be strong enough to push yourself any faster. Air resistance works just the same on falling objects. At a certain speed, the resistance of the air is stronger than the pull of gravity, and a falling object stops accelerating. This speed is called terminal velocity.

An object's terminal velocity depends on its mass and shape. Objects that move through the air easily have high terminal velocities. People can fall no faster than 60 meters per second. Using a parachute, a person's terminal velocity decreases to about 5 meters per second, making it possible to land without getting hurt.

# Balancing Act

Think about balancing on one foot. You feel yourself starting to fall to one side, so you shift your weight to keep from falling. It feels as though most of your weight is at a point in the center of the body.

The point where you feel your weight concentrated is called your center of gravity. All objects have a center of gravity. For an approximately spherical object, such as the Earth or the Moon, it is the center of the sphere.

If an object is supported beneath its center of gravity, it balances. Suppose you are balancing a ruler straight up on the tip of your finger. As the ruler starts to fall to one side, you move your finger in that direction to keep it balanced. As long as you keep your finger under the ruler's center of gravity, it will not fall over.

This gymnast can balance with one foot on a narrow beam by adjusting the position of his body.

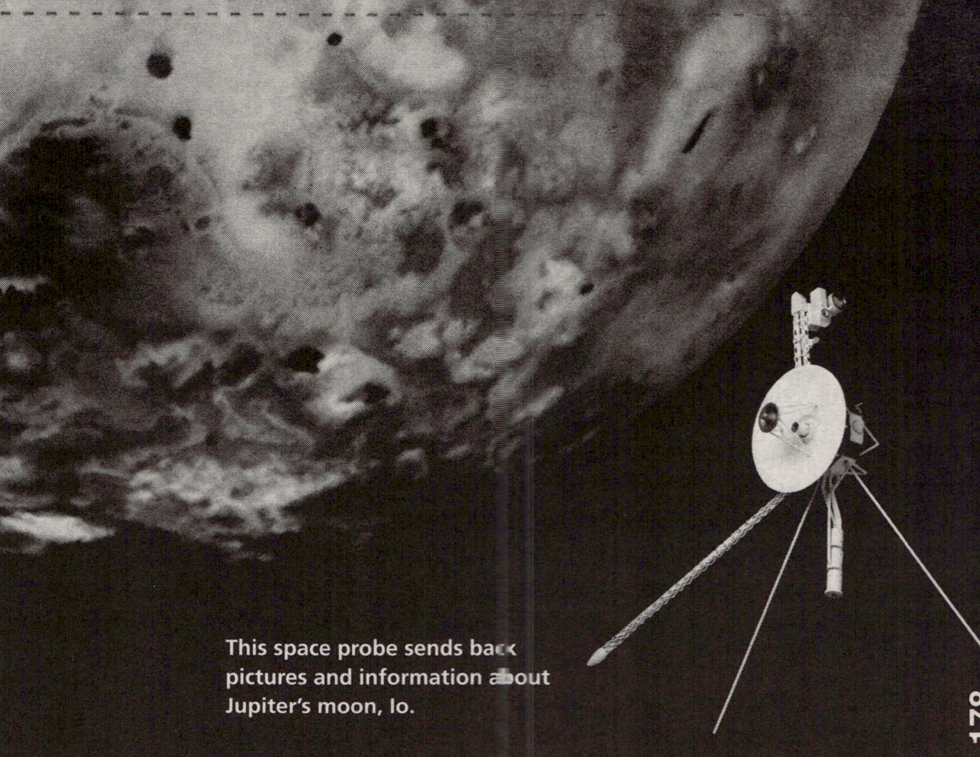

This space probe sends back pictures and information about Jupiter's moon, Io.

Before the middle of the twentieth century, looking through telescopes was the only way to learn about the planets and other objects in the solar system. Since then, space probes that can reach Earth's escape velocity have traveled to the planets and sent back close-up pictures. Probes have even landed on the planet Mars and Saturn's moon, Titan.

The outer planets are very far from Earth, much farther than they appear in the illustration. Probes going to the distant planets need enough force to move away from the Sun, as well as Earth. Gravity helps these probes start moving. The Moon or a planet can be used as a "gravitational slingshot." As the object approaches, it gains momentum due to gravity. Its motion carries it past the planet or the Moon, but the additional momentum adds to its speed, sending it away faster.

# The Solar System

The Sun is the center of a complex system of moving objects known as the solar system. Nine planets orbit the Sun. Most of the planets have their own system of moons—Earth has one moon, while the larger planets, such as Jupiter and Saturn, have dozens of moons. Thousands of smaller objects, called asteroids, also orbit among the planets. Comets orbit so far away that we only see them once in a long while.

This whole system stays together and moves because of gravity. The main gravitational force in our solar system is the pull between the Sun and each object. The mass of the Sun is more than 700 times as much as the rest of the solar system combined. Every other part of the system moves at the orbital velocity that keeps it in place around the Sun.

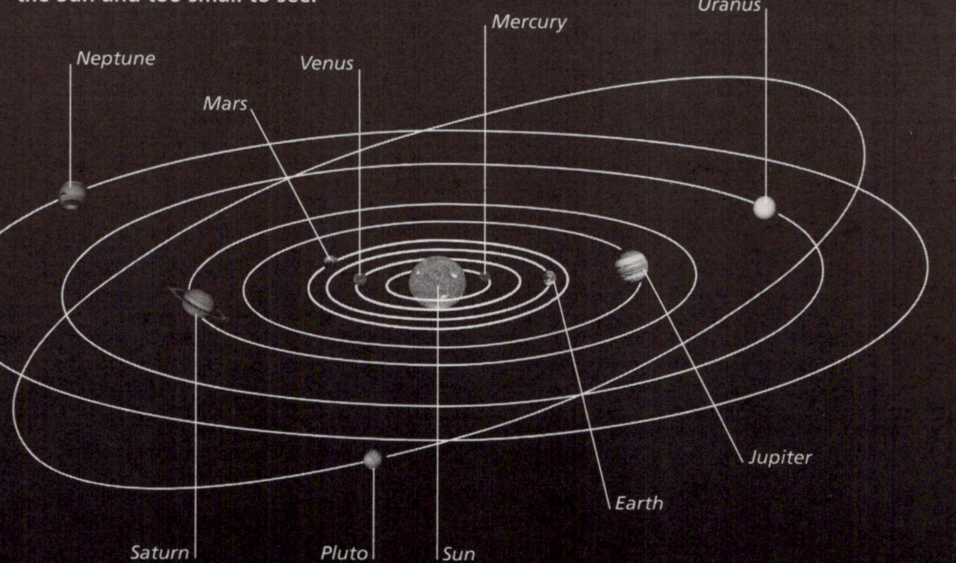



**This model shows the positions of the Sun and planets. If it were true to scale, the planets would be many meters from the Sun and too small to see.**

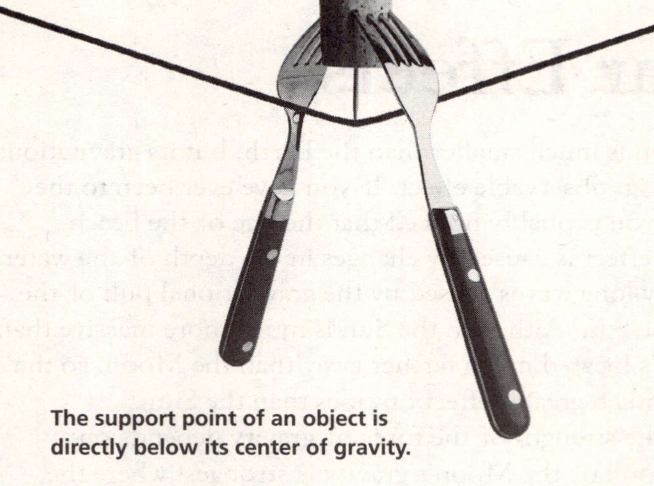

**The support point of an object is directly below its center of gravity.**

The forks, cork, and pin above balance on the string because the center of gravity is in the middle of the cork. If one fork was made of plastic and the other of metal, the center of gravity would shift away from the physical middle of the object—maybe even into the metal fork—and it would not balance on the string. The center of gravity of an object can even be located outside its mass. The center of gravity of a donut, for example, is in its hole.

Where is the center of gravity in your body? That depends on how your mass is arranged. Because the gymnast is balanced on his toes, you know that his center of gravity is located somewhere directly above his left foot. If he moves, his center of gravity will change. If he lifts his right leg higher, his center of gravity will move toward his head. Because the center of gravity is then behind his left foot, he begins to fall backward.

If the center of gravity changes with every movement, how do people keep from falling over? You have organs in your inner ears that detect the pull of gravity. These organs constantly send messages to your brain, which causes your muscles to adjust your center of gravity, maintaining your balance. You can feel these adjustments by standing on one foot and paying attention to how your body moves.

# Lunar Effects

The Moon is much smaller than the Earth, but its gravitational force still has an observable effect. If you have ever been to the ocean shore, you probably noticed that the size of the beach changes. The effect is caused by changes in the depth of the water. Tides are very long waves caused by the gravitational pull of the Moon and the Sun. Although the Sun is much more massive than the Moon, it's located much farther away than the Moon, so the Moon has a much greater effect on tides than the Sun.

Because the strength of the force of gravity depends on distance, the pull of the Moon's gravity is strongest where the surface of Earth is closest to the Moon. Although the solid parts of the surface are tightly connected to one another, the liquid part, such as the oceans, is fluid. The Moon pulls water to one side.

Inertia keeps this weightless astronaut moving forward until she experiences an opposing force.

Astronauts train in water to simulate weightlessness.



Free fall explains how astronauts can float around inside the shuttle. Remember that you cannot feel the force of gravity, only the force that pushes in the opposite direction. The space shuttle is moving at 28,000 kilometers per hour, falling constantly. The people inside it are moving at exactly the same velocity, and so are all the objects inside the shuttle—even the air. Because everything is moving together, there is no force that works against gravity, so the passengers are weightless. They still have exactly the same mass as on the surface of Earth, but if they step on a scale, it will read zero because the scale and the person are moving together with the same velocity.

At high tide, the water fills the whole bay.

Low tide is the best time to hunt for seashells.

# Zero Gravity?

When you watch a film of astronauts in space, they seem to be floating around the cabin, experiencing no pull of gravity. Sometimes you hear the term zero gravity used to describe the effect. Are astronauts in the space shuttle far enough from Earth that they aren't affected by the pull of its gravity? No. In fact the force exerted by gravity at the altitude of the shuttle's orbit is about 90 percent of that at the surface of Earth.

When the space shuttle orbits Earth, it is constantly pulled downward by gravity. However, it is also moving forward at its orbital velocity. This forward inertia tends to push the shuttle in a straight line, away from Earth. If this inertia is perfectly balanced with the pull of gravity, the shuttle is in free fall. It is constantly pulled toward Earth, but it is also constantly pushed away, so its distance from Earth never changes.

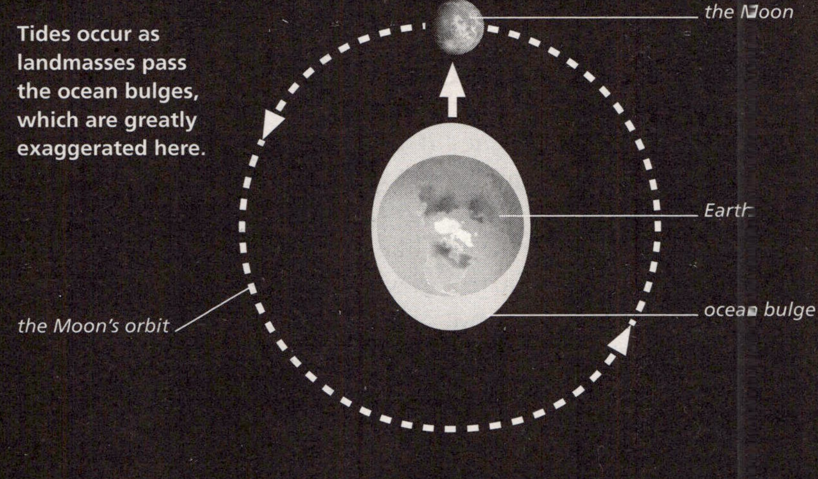

**Because it is moving at orbital velocity, the space shuttle appears to float above Earth.**

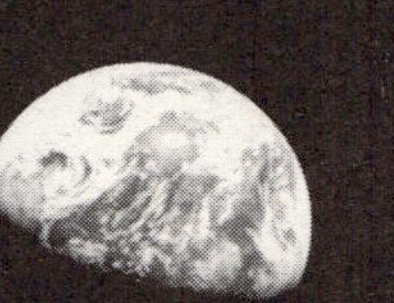


On the other side of the Earth, away from the Moon, there is another bulge of water. This is caused by Earth's movement through space. The oceans get slightly deeper where these two bulges occur. On the sides of Earth where the water is not bulging, the ocean gets slightly shallower. When the ocean gets deeper, water moves up the shore, causing high tide. Where the ocean gets shallower, water moves down the shore, causing low tide. As the Moon moves around the Earth, the bulges move as well. Because of the movement of these bulges, the tide changes from high to low twice a day in the oceans.

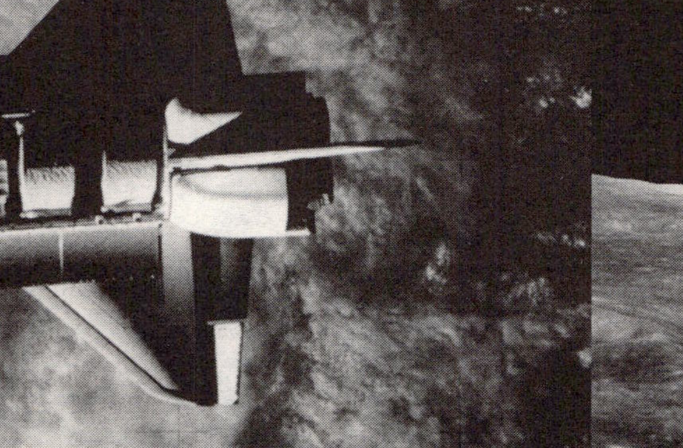

**Even though the Moon is far away, its gravity has a big effect on Earth's oceans.**

# Defying Gravity

When a spacecraft launches, it needs an enormous amount of energy to move from Earth into space. Its upward inertia must be stronger than the force of Earth's gravity pulling it downward. If not, it will fall back to Earth, just like a ball thrown in the air. The speed required to escape Earth's gravity, called escape velocity, is about 11 kilometers per second, or 40,000 kilometers per hour. At this speed, a spacecraft will be able to continue moving away from Earth without any additional force being added. Reaching the escape velocity does not mean that the spacecraft is not affected by Earth's gravity. It means that both gravity and upward acceleration are acting on the spacecraft, but upward acceleration is stronger. Earth's pull decreases the farther a spacecraft travels from the planet. At some point, the pull of another object in the solar system, such as another planet or its moon, becomes stronger than Earth's gravity the closer you move to the other object. The spacecraft is then pulled toward this new object. No matter where the spacecraft travels in the universe, it will always be pulled by some object's gravity.

At a slightly slower speed, a spacecraft does not continue moving away from Earth, but it does not fall either. This is the orbital velocity—the velocity at which the object continues to move around the planet if no additional force is used. The orbital velocity depends how far above the surface of Earth the craft is orbiting. At an altitude of 300 km, a typical orbit for the space shuttle, the orbital velocity is 7.7 km/s, or about 28,000 km/h. It takes a bit longer than 90 minutes for the shuttle to travel all the way around Earth at this speed.

To reach orbital velocity, the space shuttle requires enormous power to propel it upward. The upward force must be stronger than the gravitational pull. As the shuttle accelerates upward, the astronauts are pushed back against their seats with a force that is three times as great as the force of gravity.



**The force of gases leaving the booster rockets pushes the space shuttle upward to overcome the force of Earth's gravity.**

# Levers, Gears, AND Pulleys

by Alma Ransford

| Genre | Comprehension Skill | Text Features | Science Content |
|---|---|---|---|
| Nonfiction | Cause and Effect | • Captions<br>• Diagram<br>• Glossary | Simple Machines |

ISBN 0-328-14017-1

9 780328 140176

90000

Scott Foresman Science 6.16

PEARSON

Scott
Foresman

scottforesman.com

# What did you learn?

1. What are the six simple machines?

2. What are the three components that help differentiate the types of levers?

3. How are gears related to simple machines?

4. **Writing** in Science  Most machines are compound machines that are made up of simple machines. Write to explain how a single simple machine works.

5. Cause and Effect  What would be the effect of using an inclined plane (ramp) to move a heavy load from a lower level to a higher level?



**Picture Credits**
Every effort has been made to secure permission and provide appropriate credit for photographic material.
The publisher deeply regrets any omission and pledges to correct errors called to its attention in subsequent editions.

Photo locators denoted as follows: Top (T), Center (C), Bottom (B), Left (L), Right (R), Background (Bkgd).

Opener: ©Michael Melford/Getty Images; 5 ©Eric Millette/Index Stock Imagery; 7 (BL) Getty Images;
11 (TR) ©Michael Melford/Getty Images.

Unless otherwise acknowledged, all photographs are the copyright © of Dorling Kindersley, a division of Pearson.

ISBN: 0-328-14017-1

# Glossary

**calipers** parts of a bicycle's brake system that squeeze the wheels

**cranks** parts of a bicycle that connect the pedals to the front gears

**interconnected** having parts that are joined together

**intricate** of complicated or very elaborate nature

**modified** changed to improve or simplify

**oscillatory** having a back-and-forth motion

**spur gear** a gear with straight teeth sticking out from its edges





# Levers, Gears, AND Pulleys

by Alma Ransford

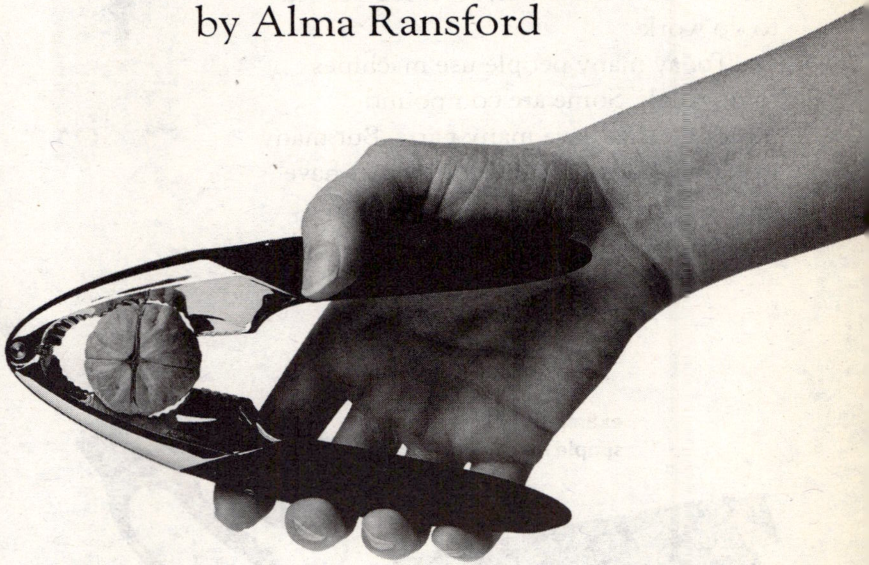

PEARSON Scott Foresman DK

# What You Already Know

The use of force to move an object a certain distance is called work. The formula to express how much work has been done is: work = force × distance. Work is measured in joules. A joule is the amount of work done when one Newton of force is exerted over a distance of one meter. It's important to know how much effort, or applied force, needs to be put into work. Inventors are always trying to find ways to make tasks and work easier. They do this by finding ways to decrease the effort force needed to do work.

Today many people use machines to do work. Some are compound machines that have many parts. But many machines are simple machines that have only one or two moving parts, if any. Knives, scissors, staplers, and doorknobs are all simple machines.

examples of
simple machines

Many compound machines, such as a train, have thousands of parts. Even the biggest of these machines, though, is made up of simple machines. Each simple machine does a different type of job. When simple machines are combined in a compound machine, that machine can perform complex tasks.

Combining the different types of motion that simple machines produce—linear (in a line), rotary (in a circle), and oscillatory (back and forth)—creates an effective compound machine. Engineers and inventors tinker with these elements as they work to develop better compound machines.

Compound machines have been around for a long time. Recently it was discovered that a compound machine must have existed in China about 2,500 years ago. Scientists have discovered that grooves in ancient jade objects are far too intricate, elaborate, and perfectly shaped to have been made by hand or by simple machines. They don't know what the machine that made them looked like, but they do believe that it existed.

lever

A bicycle combines simple machines.

# Combining Machines

It is the combined, or compound, machine that most people think of when they hear the word *machine*. Automobiles, excavators, food processors, elevators, and pencil sharpeners are just a few of the compound machines that you probably see or use on a daily basis. A compound machine is a machine that is made up of two or more simple machines.

A bicycle is a compound machine you probably see every day. The tires, pedals, and handlebars are examples of a wheel and axle. The brakes use levers both where your hands clutch them and as the calipers that squeeze the bike's wheels. The cranks that connect the pedals to the front gears are levers. The gear system on many bikes includes a pulley as well as multiple gears.



Simple machines are very common. Most of them have one movable part. All of them fall into one of the following groups: lever, inclined plane, wedge, screw, wheel and axle, or pulley. Within each of these groups, there are many types. Pulleys can be either fixed or movable. Levers fall into three categories based on the position and role of the fulcrum, load, and effort force.

Machines change the distance over which a force is exerted and the effort force needed to do work. Another important thing for inventors of machines to consider is friction. Inventors try to reduce the amount of energy lost by reducing friction between the moving parts of the machine they are designing.

Understanding simple machines helps you understand compound machines. They may have thousands of parts, but many of those parts are actually simple machines. Wheelbarrows, bicycles, and sailboats are some examples of compound machines made up of many simple machines.

# Simple Machines

Many people think that the word *machine* describes a loud, noisy piece of equipment. In science, a machine is any device that helps people do work.

Machines may require you to use a lot of force. For example, it takes a lot of force to push a wheelbarrow full of soil and rocks, but it is still a lot easier than moving rocks by hand!

A baseball bat is another familiar simple machine. It makes it much easier to hit a baseball or change its direction of motion. Most people can hit a baseball with a bat farther than they can throw one. It still takes some effort force to hit a baseball, but the bat helps people hit the ball with more force than they could without it.

If you push a wheelbarrow up a ramp, you have to push over a greater distance, but your job is easier!

To lift cargo, a block and tackle pulley is used with movable and fixed pulleys.

# Pulleys

A pulley is a grooved wheel with a chain or rope around it. A load is attached to one end of the rope, and effort force is applied to the other end. Pulleys are used to raise flags, sails, and curtains. They open garage doors. Can you think of other uses for pulleys?

Pulleys are either fixed or movable. A fixed pulley will stay in position as its wheel spins. You pull down on one end of a fixed pulley rope to lift up the load on the other end. This changes the direction of the force, but it doesn't lessen the effort force needed. Pulling down on the rope will result in the load moving upward.

A movable pulley is attached to the item being moved. As force is applied to the load, the pulley moves with it. This type of pulley increases force, but the force has to be applied over a greater distance. If the pulley allows you to lift with twice the normal force, you must pull the rope twice as far.

Two or more pulleys can be used together as a system. This is called the block and tackle system. Each pulley reduces the amount of effort required to lift the load. A block and tackle with a lot of pulleys could help lift a heavy load, as shown in the photograph to the right.

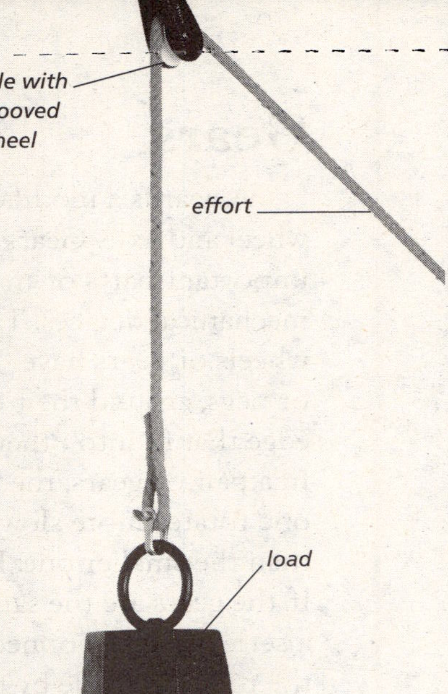




Lombard Street in San Francisco goes up a very steep hill. A series of inclined planes were built back and forth across the slope. This allows cars to travel up and down the hill more easily.

# Inclined Plane

An inclined plane is one type of simple machine. It is also known as a ramp. You probably could not lift a piano one meter above the floor by yourself. But if you used a ramp you could.

Inclined planes are very useful as ramps that help move a load from a low place to a higher place. Moving a load up a ramp takes less effort force than lifting the load straight up. But the load actually has to travel farther as it goes up the ramp than it would if it went straight up. Although it is easier to use the ramp, the same amount of work still gets done. If you multiply the small force and large distance of using the ramp, you get the same number as when you multiply the large force and small distance of lifting the load straight up.

Inclined planes are also used in the construction of roads to make driving on hills easier. Lombard Street in San Francisco is a good example. Engineers used several inclined planes to make it easier for cars to travel on the steep hill.

# The Screw

A screw is one example of a modified inclined plane. It is an inclined plane that is wound around a cylinder to form a spiral with a sharp tip. Its ridges are called threads. Screws are often used to tighten or fasten two objects. The lids of many jars are actually screws. You twist the lid to tighten it. You could push the lid onto the jar, but the screw lets you fasten it securely with much less force. But you have to exert that force over a larger distance.

Nails and screws are both used in construction to fasten wood. It takes a lot of force to drive a nail into a wall. It takes much less force to twist a screw into a wall, but you must exert that force over a larger distance.

A screw is a kind of inclined plane that is wrapped around a cylinder and forms a spiral.

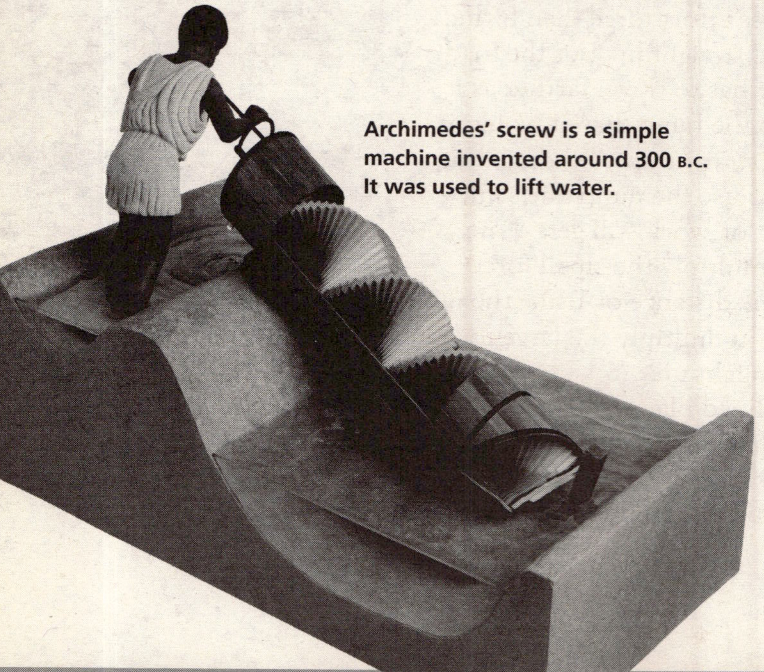

Archimedes' screw is a simple machine invented around 300 B.C. It was used to lift water.

# Gears

A gear is a modified wheel and axle. Gears are important parts of many mechanical devices. The wheels of gears have "teeth," or pegs, around their outer edge that fit into other gears. In a pair of gears, the larger one rotates more slowly than the smaller one. But the larger one moves with greater force. If the gears are the same size, they both turn at the same speed. In a series of interconnected gears, each gear changes the direction of the rotation made by the gear before it.

Spur gears are the most common type of gears. They have straight teeth that stick out from their edges. The gears in bicycles are spur gears connected by a chain.

Often, many individual gears are used at once to make large groups of interconnected gears.



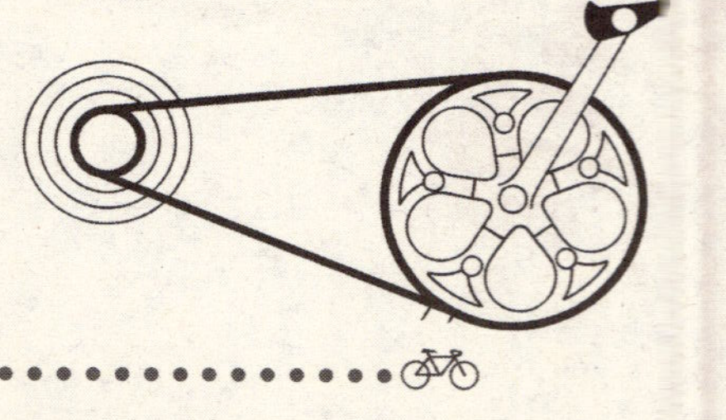

One turn of the small front gear causes less than one turn of the larger rear gear. The bicycle doesn't move very fast, but the pedals can be turned without using much force.

One turn of the large front gear causes several turns of the small rear gear. This makes the bicycle go faster, but requires a lot of force on the pedals.

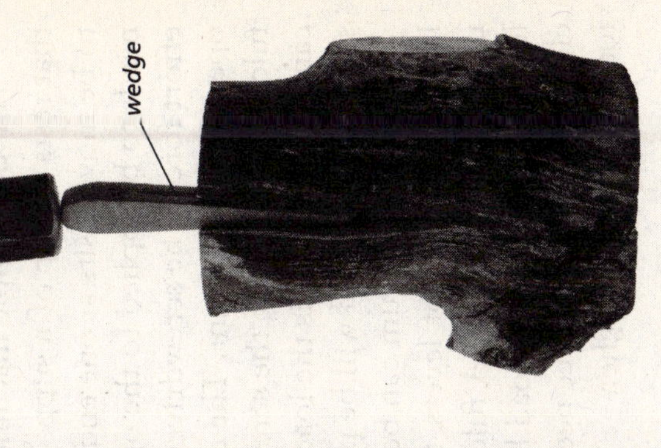


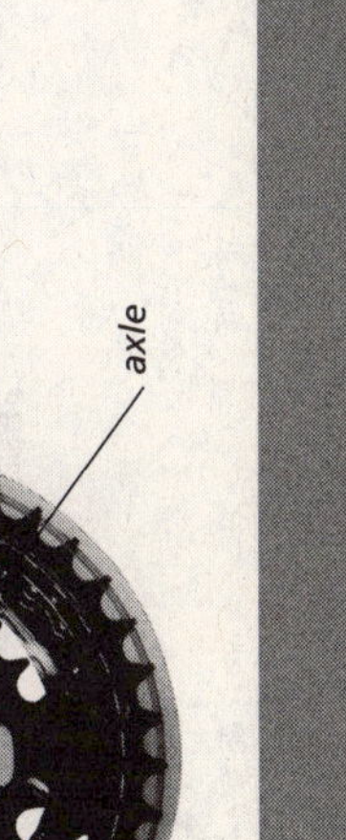
**The hammer supplies the effort force to push this wedge and split the wood.**

**An ax is a wedge, a type of inclined plane.**

# Wheel and Axle

A wheel and axle is another simple machine. It may have been one of the earliest simple machines and has been in use since around 3,600 B.C.

A wheel and axle is really a lever that rotates through a complete, 360° circle. The axle is attached to the center of the wheel. The wheel turns in a larger circle than the axle does. That means the outside of the wheel travels a much greater distance than the axle. The smaller turn of the axle is powerful, though. A wheel and axle can increase force or increase the distance over which a force acts.

When you pedal a bike your foot moves in a large circle, but the axle turns in a small circle. The axle turns with much more force than the pedal turns, but the pedal moves a much longer distance.

# The Wedge

Another variation of the inclined plane is the wedge. It is made up of one or two inclined planes, or sloped surfaces. These sloped surfaces form a point.

Wedges are often used to split materials apart. A force applied to the wider end of the wedge drives the point forward. It focuses the effort force on a narrow area. The slanted sides of the wedge direct some of the force outward, pushing the material apart.

From ax to steak knife, just about all machines that cut use wedges. The longer and thinner a wedge used for cutting is, the less effort is required. Sharp knives are safer and easier to use, since less force needs to be applied to them in order to cut through something. Sharp tools such as chisels and needles are also made of wedges. Snowplows and shovels are other examples of tools using wedges.

# Levers

Another simple machine is the lever. It is made up of a bar that rests on top of a support called a fulcrum. A load, or object to be moved, sits at one end of the lever. To move the load, force needs to be applied to the opposite end. This is applied force, or effort force. The screwdriver below is being used as a lever to open the can of paint. The edge of the paint can is used as a fulcrum. The tip of the screwdriver is under the lid of the paint can. The stuck lid is the load. If a person pushes down on the screwdriver, the lid will be pushed up and off the can.

A lever's fulcrum can be located at any point along the lever. In different types of levers, the load and the fulcrum are located in different positions. A fulcrum that is closer to the load needs less force to move the load but won't lift it as high. A fulcrum closer to the effort force needs more force to be applied, but the load will be lifted higher.

There are three kinds of levers. First-class levers have the fulcrum in the middle, the effort force at one end, and the load at the other end. Second-class levers have the effort force at one end, the fulcrum at the other end, and the load in the middle. A wheelbarrow is a second-class lever. Third-class levers have the fulcrum at one end, the load at the other end, and the effort force in the middle. Hockey sticks, baseball bats, and fishing poles are actually third-class levers. Many common tools use two identical levers that share a fulcrum. Scissors, pliers, nutcrackers, and chopsticks are actually pairs of levers.

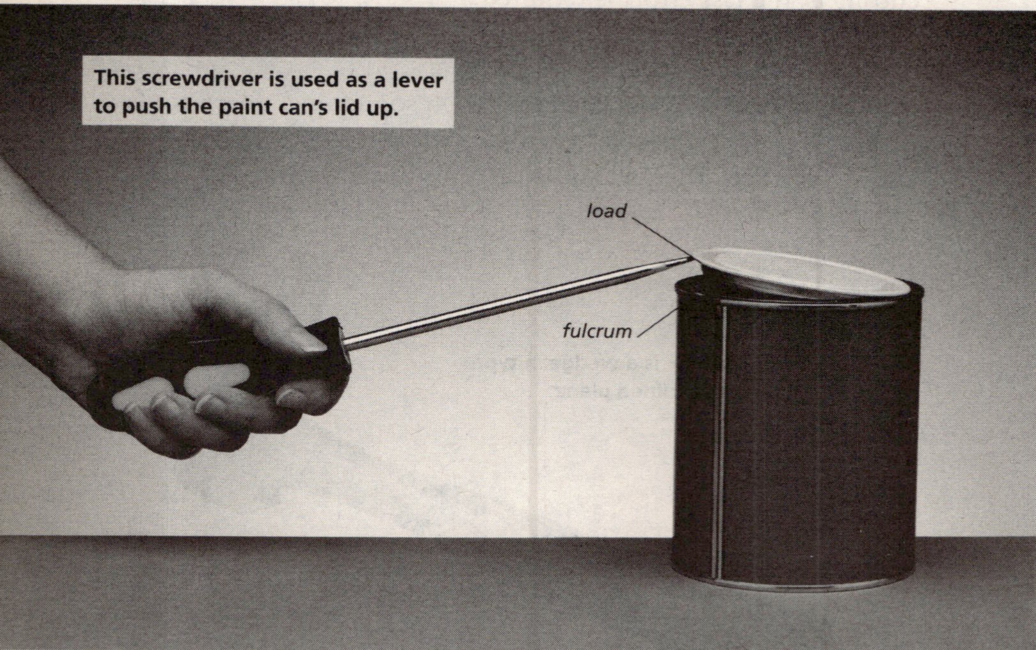


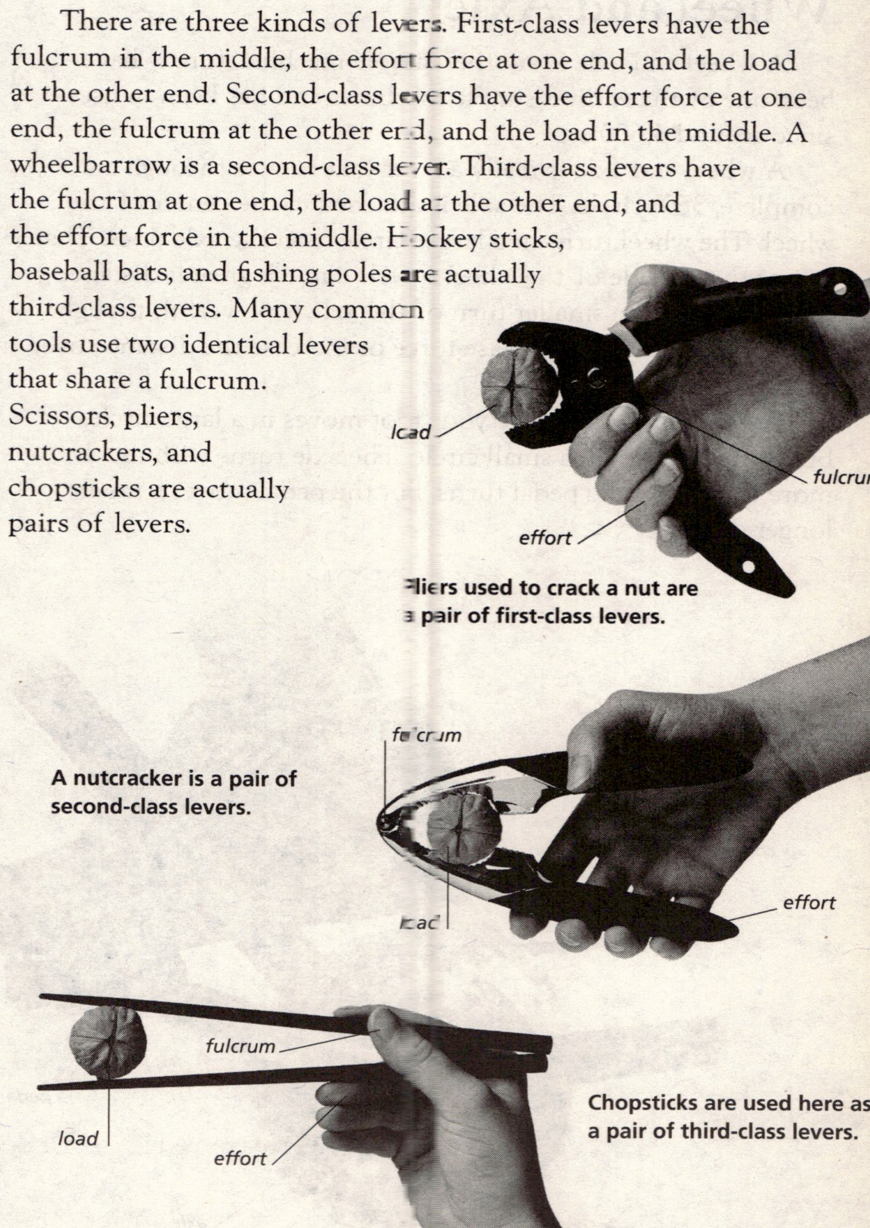




192

Physical Science

# *SPORTS* Champions

by Natalie Goldstein

| Genre | Comprehension Skill | Text Features | Science Content |
|---|---|---|---|
| Nonfiction | Sequence | • Captions<br>• Diagram<br>• Glossary | Forms of Energy |

Scott Foresman Science 6.17

ISBN 0-328-14020-1

9 780328 140206

# What did you learn?

**Vocabulary**

electric circuit
electric current
electric motor
energy
generator
kinetic energy
magnetic domain
potential energy

**Extended Vocabulary**

dehydration
endurance
glucose
lactic acid
marathon
metabolism

1. Describe how an athlete transforms potential energy into kinetic energy.

2. Why does an athlete in an endurance sport require a somewhat different type of diet than an athlete in a power or team sport?

3. In what form does the body store its potential energy?

4. **Writing** in Science Several forces are involved when a batter hits a baseball. Write to explain what these forces are, and how they control the distance the ball travels when hit.

5. **Sequence** Describe the sequence of energy transfers that take place in pole vaulting.



**Picture Credits**
Every effort has been made to secure permission and provide appropriate credit for photographic material.
The publisher deeply regrets any omission and pledges to correct errors called to its attention in subsequent editions.

Photo locators denoted as follows: Top (T), Center (C), Bottom (B), Left (L), Right (R), Background (Bkgd).

Opener: ©Alan Thornton/Getty Images; 5 ©Alan Thornton/Getty Images; 7 (T) ©Rhoda Sidney/PhotoEdit; 11 Reuters/Corbis; 13 ©David Madison/NewSport/Corbis; 15 BSF/NewSport/Corbis.

Unless otherwise acknowledged, all photographs are the copyright © of Dorling Kindersley, a division of Pearson.

ISBN: 0-328-14020-1

# Glossary

| | |
|---|---|
| **dehydration** | excessive loss of liquid from the body |
| **endurance** | activity requiring a large store of energy that can be drawn on over a long period of time |
| **glucose** | a type of sugar that combines with oxygen in cells to produce energy |
| **lactic acid** | a chemical that builds up in muscles due to a lack of oxygen and causes the muscles to ache and work inefficiently |
| **marathon** | a long-distance running race, usually twenty-six miles |
| **metabolism** | the chemical breakdown by the body of food into fuel |

# SPORTS
# Champions

by Natalie Goldstein

# What You Already Know

Energy is the ability to cause change or to do work. There are many forms of energy. An object has mechanical energy when it moves or changes position. Kinetic energy is the mechanical energy of a moving object. Potential energy is mechanical energy due to position. A ball at the top of a hill has potential energy that becomes kinetic energy as it rolls down the hill.

Other forms of energy include chemical, thermal, and nuclear. Energy can change from one form to another. All forms of energy can be used to do work or can be changed into thermal energy. No matter how energy changes, it is never lost; it just changes form.

Electricity, or an electric current, is the flow of an electric charge through a material. Electricity flows easily through some materials, such as copper. These materials are called conductors of electricity. Insulators are materials that hinder the flow of electric current.

Electric current flows through a complete closed path called an electric circuit. An electric circuit must have a source of electric charge and a wire or other material through which the current flows.

When a baseball pitcher throws a ball, it moves forward with a certain amount of momentum. Momentum is a moving object's mass multiplied by its speed. When the batter hits the ball, he or she must overcome this momentum in order to change the direction the ball travels and drive it forward. To do this, the momentum of the bat must be greater than that of the ball. If the bat has more mass than the ball and it travels at a faster speed, it will have more momentum and the ball will fly toward the outfield. If the batter uses a bat that is too light, or swings the bat too slowly, the bat will have less momentum. The ball will not travel as far when hit.

In baseball, kinetic energy from the bat must be transferred to the ball.

In many sports, chemical energy from the athlete's muscles is transformed into kinetic energy that is used to strike a ball. The kinetic energy is transferred to the ball, causing it to move. Soccer players, for example, must kick the ball hard, but also accurately. The speed and angle of the kick determines the speed and direction of the ball. A ball kicked from the ground travels farthest when it is struck at a 45 degree angle. A soccer ball is inflated with air. The more air the ball has, the more energy it will transform into kinetic energy. A soft ball will change shape when struck, absorbing and wasting some of the energy. A fully inflated ball will not bend or deform when struck, so more of the kicker's energy is transformed into kinetic energy by the ball, which travels farther. This is also why a deflated ball does not bounce as high as a fully inflated one.

**When a soccer ball is kicked, energy is transferred from the muscles in the athlete's leg to the ball.**

A magnet has two charged poles. The area around a magnet that attracts other magnets is its magnetic field. The magnetic field is strongest at a magnet's poles. The magnetic domain of a magnet is made up of a large number of atoms that have their magnetic fields pointing in the same direction. When two magnets are brought together, poles with the same charge repel each other, and poles with opposite charges are attracted to each other.

In the 1800s a Danish scientist, Hans Christian Oersted discovered that moving electrical charges cause a magnetic field. All electric charges are surrounded by an electric field. If the charges are moving, they are also surrounded by a magnetic field. This is known as electromagnetism. This knowledge was very useful to create very strong magnets called electromagnets.

An electric motor changes electrical energy into mechanic energy. It consists of a permanent magnet, an electromagnet, and a device that changes the direction of the magnetic field. A generator is a device that changes mechanical energy into electrical energy, and it is made of a permanent magnet and a coil of wire that carries electric current.

The human body uses energy too. Whenever you run, jump, or throw, you are changing one type of energy into another. In order to play any sport, your body must take in, store, and spend energy.

**You use energy when you play sports.**

# Energy for Action

Your body is a machine that needs to get energy and use energy to stay alive. You get the energy you need from the food you eat.

Your body needs energy even when you are still. It uses energy to pump your blood and to maintain breathing. Even when you are asleep, your body uses up some of the energy it got from food.

Energy from food is also used every time you move. If you want to spend recess running around, you know you need to have a healthy lunch. But what about an Olympic runner, who can travel the length of a football field in less than ten seconds? To move the runner's mass such a long distance in such a short amount of time, a great deal of energy must be spent. Athletes get this energy from carefully chosen foods. They train to build strong muscles that are very efficient at changing energy into motion. Years of practice teach athletes to run very efficiently. As much energy as possible is used to drive them forward, and very little is wasted on extra movement.

Although there are many different types of sports, they all require the same basic preparations to achieve top performance. Athletes must eat right, build strong bodies, and master the skills of their sport.

# Transforming Energy

Energy is never used up. It just changes from one form to another. All sports involve energy transformations, and the best athletes know how to get the most out of them. A good example is the pole vault, a sport in which an athlete uses a thin, flexible pole to travel over a very tall obstacle. The pole-vaulter runs quickly toward the obstacle while holding the flexible pole. The running athlete has kinetic energy. As the athlete nears the obstacle, he or she plants one end of the pole in the ground. The athlete's kinetic energy is used to bend the pole, which stores potential energy like a spring. The potential energy of the pole is then transformed into kinetic energy, throwing the athlete high into the air.

The trick to the pole vault is to transfer as much kinetic energy to the pole as possible. To do this, vaulters run with the pole as fast as they can. Then the maximum amount of kinetic energy is stored as potential energy, which is transferred back to the athlete, who rises as high as he can in the air. The speed of the "run-up" and the moment at which the athlete thrusts the pole into the ground is very important.

**The kinetic energy of the running athlete is transformed into elastic energy in the pole.**

Olympic runners change the chemical energy from their food into motion very efficiently.

**1. The athlete plants one end of the pole in the ground and bends the other.**

**2. As the pole straightens, it applies a force to him, lifting him up.**

199

# Stored Energy

Your body needs energy for every function, even thinking. Growing, cell repair, digestion, respiration, and maintaining body temperature are all processes that require energy. This energy comes from the food you eat. But how is food transformed into energy?

Once food is digested and broken down, its chemicals are carried to every body cell. Body cells turn these chemicals into energy by a process called metabolism. During metabolism, chemicals in cells break down components in food and use them to fuel cell functions.

Food contains a type of sugar called glucose, which serves as the fuel for metabolism. The glucose combines with oxygen taken in by the lungs and carried by the blood. Combining glucose and oxygen releases energy. Different foods contain different amounts of usable energy because they contain varying amounts of glucose.

Different activities use up different amounts of the body's stored energy.

Endurance exercise, such as running in a marathon, requires lots of oxygen and a healthy heart to pump oxygen-rich blood to muscle cells.

Energy is released when glucose combines with oxygen. The more energy you need for an activity, the more oxygen your body needs. Endurance activities require lots of oxygen. Anyone who runs a marathon, or a long-distance race, needs healthy lungs to take in lots of oxygen and a healthy heart to distribute it. When you run, your heart beats quickly to provide your muscles with the blood that brings them the oxygen they need.

But if the muscles work too hard, the lungs can't supply oxygen fast enough. This causes a chemical called lactic acid to build up. Too much lactic acid can cause muscles to ache and work inefficiently.

# Muscle Power

Your body's muscles are not 100 percent efficient at turning stored energy into kinetic energy. As fuel is used, some energy is lost as heat. At one time or another you have probably tired yourself out and begun to sweat. Sweat is the body's way of getting rid of excess heat.

Your body must maintain a constant internal temperature. The heat generated by burning fuel for exercise is released through your skin as sweat. Evaporation of sweat on your skin cools your body and helps it maintain its normal temperature.

Losing too much liquid through sweat is harmful. In extreme circumstances, dehydration, or loss of body fluids, may even be deadly. Losing only 2 percent of your body fluids can have serious effects on your health and athletic performance. Because your body needs to maintain a certain amount of liquid, it's important to drink plenty of water when you exercise.

Replacing your body's lost fluids is extremely important when you exercise.

Different foods contain different amounts of energy. Fruits contain lots of natural sugars, which give you energy.

In the same way, different activities demand different amounts of stored energy from your body. Eating right and maintaining a healthy body weight means balancing your energy intake with the energy you burn during different activities.

Glucose that is not needed for energy is stored in the body. This adds body weight. It is important that the amount of energy you take in from food is balanced by the amount of energy you use. Too much food energy causes weight gain, but too little can cause you to become sick.

Fruits are an excellent and healthy source of energy.

# Eating to Win

In many major sports competitions, the difference between winning and losing can be a few thousandths of a second. When the margin of success is so slim, every aspect of an athlete's training must be fine-tuned, including the athlete's diet.

Different sports require different diets, because different foods provide the athlete with different types of energy. A long-distance cyclist needs endurance, which requires a large store of energy that can be drawn on over a long period of time. A weight lifter, shown on the next page, needs a short but enormous burst of intense energy.

Endurance athletes require more energy-rich carbohydrates in their diets. Athletes engaged in power sports, such as weight lifting, need diets rich in proteins, which build muscle.

Different diets and types of exercise affect the development of specific muscle fibers. Fast-twitch fibers are activated during short bursts of intense activity, such as platform diving, volleyball, or gymnastics. Fast-twitch fibers quickly burn up the energy stored in muscles. However, this energy is replenished fairly quickly.

Slow-twitch fibers are used during long-term, moderately intense activity, such as long-distance cycling or cross-country skiing. Slow-twitch fibers use stored energy slowly. Athletes in endurance sports have more slow-twitch fibers in their muscles.

A balanced diet contains the right proportion of food from each food group.

A long-distance cyclist needs a lot of stored energy. Carbohydrates are a good source of long-term energy.

Foods with lots of protein help a weight lifter get an intense burst of energy.

# The SCIENCE of Cooking

by Sarah Bright

| Genre | Comprehension Skill | Text Features | Science Content |
| --- | --- | --- | --- |
| Nonfiction | Compare and Contrast | • Captions<br>• Diagram<br>• Glossary | Light and Heat |

**Scott Foresman Science 6.18**

PEARSON
Scott Foresman

scottforesman.com

ISBN 0-328-14023-6

9 780328 140237

90000

ISBN 0-328-14023-6

# What did you learn?

**Vocabulary**

conduction
conductor
convection
heat
insulator
radiation
reflection
refraction
thermal energy

**Extended Vocabulary**

braise
denaturing
fluid
immersed
Maillard reactions
porous
salmonella

1. What are the three types of heat transfer used in cooking?

2. In general, what kinds of materials are good conductors?

3. What is happening when you boil water?

4. **Writing** in Science Most ways of cooking use a combination of methods of heat transfer. What single way of cooking is most important in your household? What methods does it use?

5. **Compare and Contrast** Compare two different methods of cooking that use different forms of heat transfer. What are the advantages and disadvantages of each of these methods?




**Picture Credits**
Every effort has been made to secure permission and provide appropriate credit for photographic material.
The publisher deeply regrets any omission and pledges to correct errors called to its attention in subsequent editions.

Photo locators denoted as follows: Top (T), Center (C), Bottom (B), Left (L), Right (R), Background (Bkgd).

1 Getty Images; 5 Ghislain & Marie David de Lossy/Getty Images; 12 (BL) Corbis; 14 (BR) Getty Images; 15 ©Ramon Manent/Corbis.

Unless otherwise acknowledged, all photographs are the copyright © of Dorling Kindersley, a division of Pearson.

ISBN: 0-328-14023-6

# Glossary

| | |
|---|---|
| **braise** | to cook in a closed pot over low heat using fat or oil |
| **denaturing** | changing the chemical structure of a protein |
| **fluid** | a substance that lacks a definite shape such as a liquid or a gas |
| **immersed** | completely surrounded by a fluid |
| **Maillard reactions** | a series of chemical reactions through which food is browned |
| **porous** | full of small holes |
| **salmonella** | a type of bacteria that can cause infections of the digestive system |



# The SCIENCE of Cooking

by Sarah Bright

The particles that make up matter are always in motion. They have kinetic and potential energy. The total kinetic and potential energy in a substance is called thermal energy.

Thermal energy determines how warm a substance feels. Warm liquids have more thermal energy than cool ones. The particles in warm water move more quickly, and with more kinetic energy, than those in cold water. Thermal energy can move from one substance to another. This is known as heat. Heat will always move from something that is warmer to something that is cooler. Conduction, convection, and radiation are the three ways thermal energy can be transferred. If two objects touch, the transfer of thermal energy is called conduction. Energy gets passed from particle to particle. The transfer of thermal energy by liquid or gas is called convection. This results in a stream of fluid called a convection current. If thermal energy is transferred by waves, either through matter or space, it is called radiation.

A material can be either an insulator or a conductor. An insulator does not transmit heat easily. Liquids and gases are usually good insulators because their particles are farther apart. Other materials, especially metals, are conductors. They transmit heat easily. Have you touched a cold car door on a winter day, or a metal spoon in a hot bowl of soup? You know that metal conducts heat very well.

Waves of solar radiation hit Earth every day. Some radiation is absorbed and warms Earth. Reflection occurs when radiation travels back into space.



# Cooking Science

**Bread is baked in an oven using convection currents. It is one of many foods that have been cooked in much the same way for thousands of years.**

There are three main ways to cook food: radiation, convection, and conduction. Often cooking uses more than one method. A pressure cooker cooks food using boiling water and hot steam. It uses conduction and convection. Steaming uses convection, while baking uses convection and sometimes conduction. Grilling uses radiation and convection, while microwaving uses radiation exclusively.

Food science helps us to discover and understand the chemical changes food goes through when it is being prepared or cooked. The more we understand the chemical processes we call cooking, the more we will benefit from the foods that sustain us.

# Temperatures

Some foods cook more quickly than others do. This can depend on the kind of liquid used for cooking. Every substance has a particular boiling point. For example, oil has a very high boiling point; it is higher than that of water. Oil is used in deep-frying, which is a very quick way to cook a potato. It takes longer to boil the potato in water. You can even deep-fry ice cream! The ice cream is covered with batter or breadcrumbs. The crust cooks so quickly that the ice cream doesn't melt.

Jams and other foods with lots of sugar have high boiling points. These types of foods can be heated on a stove, but if they reach their boiling point, their chemical composition changes so much that you may end up with a gooey mess.

Oil has a higher boiling point than water.

Water boils at 100°C.

Sound waves are compression waves; they travel through matter. Light travels as a transverse wave. It can travel through empty space, and can travel through or be absorbed by matter. Light travels slowest through solids, faster through liquids, and fastest through gases. It also changes speed when it moves from one direction to another. This is known as refraction.

Understanding the science of heat transfer helps you learn how to cook foods properly. Depending on the method we use, food can taste better, cook faster, and retain more of its nutritional value. In this book you will learn about heat sources, cooking methods, and chemical interactions that occur when preparing food.

Metal frying pans are good conductors of heat.

# Heat and Cooking

Some raw foods are good for us. But much of the food we eat should be cooked. Food often tastes better and is more easily digested when it is cooked correctly. Bacteria called salmonella, which can cause infections in the digestive system, sometimes grow inside raw eggs and meat. Cooking food kills these and other harmful bacteria.

Cooking involves the transfer of thermal energy. Thermal energy can be transferred by conduction, convection, and radiation. Thermal energy that moves from one substance to another is called heat. Heat can cause chemical reactions in foods.

In 1912 a French chemist named Louis Camille Maillard discovered that all foods go through a browning process at temperatures above 154°C (310°F). This process, known as the Maillard reactions, is a series of chemical reactions between sugars and proteins that produces a brown color and a taste that most people enjoy.

Sugar undergoes a chemical change when it is heated above 154°C. It breaks down and changes from a solid to a thick brown liquid you probably know as caramel.

Increasing heat also makes it easier to mix things. Tea and coffee are examples of mixtures that are much easier to make with hot water than with cold water.

This woman is demonstrating an early cooking method using a clay oven.

Eggs can be prepared using different methods of cooking. Whatever the method, cooking an egg will change the egg's form. Natural proteins in raw eggs exist in individual units. They are wound up in very tiny coils. The coils are held tightly by bonds within the molecules. When the protein is heated, some of the bonds within the individual molecules are broken. The broken bonds cause the protein to unwind, leaving the bonds exposed and sticking out. This process is called denaturing. Then the exposed bonds of the egg proteins come together, forming a solid material. This is why an egg turns solid white when it is cooked.

Hard-boiling is one way to cook an egg. Both the white and the yolk harden in the shell as they are cooked.

# Hard or Soft?

Many foods expand when heated and contract when cooled. Think about cookies. Bakers often shape cookies into small balls and then place them on a baking sheet. While they are in the oven, the cookies spread and become flatter as they cook. Other foods change from a soft state to a hard state. When you toast a slice of bread, it becomes hard. Bread contains carbohydrates, which are chemicals made up of carbon, hydrogen, and oxygen. When bread is toasted, the carbohydrates break down into black carbon and water. The carbon gives the bread a dark color and a crunchy texture. The water escapes into the air.

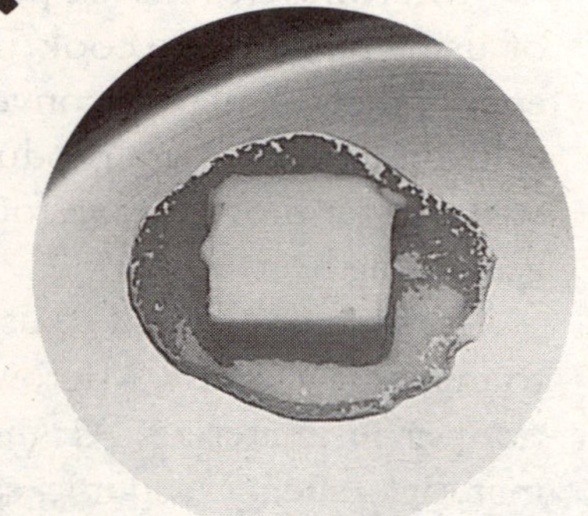

Butter changes from hard to soft as it melts.

Bread changes from soft to hard as it toasts.

People have been cooking since the discovery of fire more than 500,000 years ago. Early humans cooked over an open fire; it was the only heat source available to them. Over the years people have sought to prepare safe, good-tasting food faster and more conveniently. To do this, people had to learn how to use heat. Today slow cookers, or crockpots, work for people who want food to cook over a long period of time, while microwaves cook food very quickly.

**Today barbecuing is a good way to cook food. Is it really that different from how our ancestors cooked their food thousands of years ago?**

# Cooking With Conduction

One method of cooking is by conduction. Conduction occurs when a piece of matter that is hot comes in direct contact with matter that is cooler. Thermal energy naturally moves from hot matter toward matter that is less hot. In order to cook by conduction, food has to come in contact with a hot surface. Frying and braising are common methods of cooking using conduction. When you fry, food comes in contact with the pan, which is in direct contact with the heat source. When you braise, food is cooked slowly in a closed pot using fat or oil.

**Stir-frying is a form of conduction cooking that brings food into direct contact with a heat source in order to cook it quickly.**

Microwave ovens are perhaps the best-known example of using radiation to cook. They are more efficient users of energy than regular or conventional ovens. Invisible waves called microwaves are produced by the oven. When they strike water molecules in food, the molecules vibrate, generating heat.

It is recommended to use only containers specially made to microwave foods. Microwave-safe containers are made of nonporous materials. Air molecules trapped in some materials, such as ceramic, can get very hot.

**Barbecuing absorbs infrared radiation given off by the hot coals.**

# Heat Radiation

Radiation is yet another method used in cooking. Radiation is energy traveling as electromagnetic waves. When you feel sunlight on your skin, you are experiencing radiation. Your food does not have to be in contact with a hot surface or surrounded by a fluid when using radiation. A microwave oven cooks by radiation. In grilling and barbecuing, foods absorb the infrared radiation given off by the hot coals.

Unlike other methods of heating and cooking, radiation can occur in empty space. It does not rely on matter to transfer energy. This explains how the Sun's heat can reach Earth. To test this you can use radiation from the Sun to make sun tea. The energy from the Sun's rays warms the water by radiation. The tea is brewed without boiling water.

**Microwaving cooks food faster than other cooking methods.**

Some materials are poor conductors of heat. Glass, wood, plastic, and water do not conduct heat well. Suppose you are stirring a pot of boiling water with a wooden spoon. Wood is a poor conductor, so the thermal energy from the water does not travel up the spoon, and your hand does not get too hot. But metals are excellent conductors. Metal pots and pans transfer heat to food easily.

Food scientists test different types of cooking utensils and cookware to see which work best in recipes. In fact, on the back of a muffin mix, you will often see different instructions for cooking times and temperatures when using different types of pans.

**Since wooden skewers are poor conductors, you can use them to handle hot food without getting burned.**

## The Best Radiator

Each of the jars on the right is filled with hot water. After a few minutes, the thermometer shows that the water in the black jar cools down more quickly than the one covered with foil. Why? Because the black jar loses heat from radiation, while the foil-covered jar absorbs radiation.

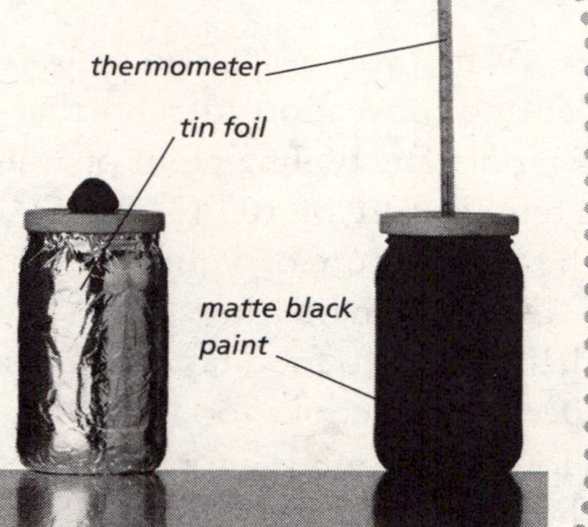


## Which melts first?

Find a metal spoon, a plastic spoon, a wooden spoon, and a straw. Stand them in a cup. Stick a frozen pea to the end of each one with an equal amount of butter, which acts as a sort of glue. Pour warm water into the cup and see which pea falls off first. This will tell you which instrument conducted heat the fastest to melt the butter.

# Convection Currents

Convection is the transfer of thermal energy by a moving fluid, such as air or water. The circular patterns created by this movement are called convection currents. When a fluid gets hot it has less density. It will rise above cooler fluids. A cooler fluid is heavier and sinks below the warmer fluid, taking its place. This means that there is a continuous, moving current of rising and falling fluids, which cook the food. To cook by convection, food needs to be immersed in fluid. Boiling is an example of convection cooking; stewing and deep-frying are other methods. Special convection ovens use fans to circulate hot air and cook food faster.

Soup is simmered rather than boiled. Simmering requires a lower temperature than boiling.

## Circulation

Convection currents occur because heated oil becomes lighter and rises to the top of the bowl. As the oil cools it sinks to the bottom, creating continuous currents, or circulation. The blue food coloring in the bowl shows the circulation taking place.

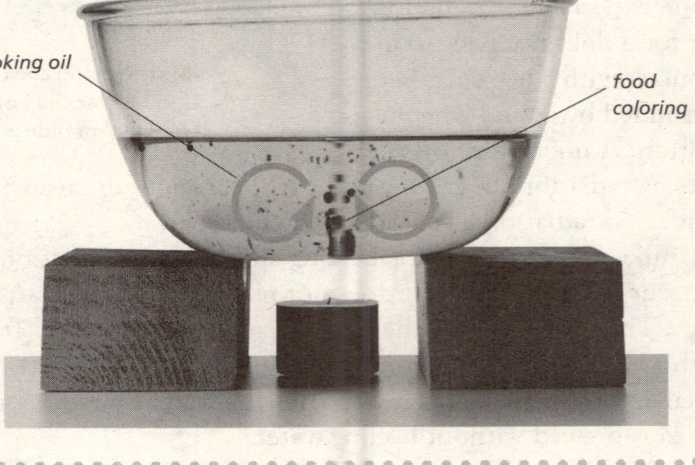

When you heat a pan of water until it boils, you are causing convection currents that distribute heat throughout the pot. The boiling point of water occurs when it reaches a temperature of 100°C (212°F). Under normal pressure, the temperature of liquid water never rises above 100°C (212°F), no matter how much heat is applied. Boiling can deliver heat to food faster than any other cooking method. Deep-frying cooks food in much the same way as boiling. Hot oil surrounds a food. Water that is at the surface of the food turns to gas in the presence of the hot oil. As the water vapor leaves the food, oil from the outside gets in.

Space and Technology

# Many Moons

by Steve Miller





| Genre | Comprehension Skill | Text Features | Science Content |
| --- | --- | --- | --- |
| Nonfiction | Main Idea and Details | • Captions<br>• Charts<br>• Diagrams<br>• Glossary | Earth and Space |

**Scott Foresman Science 6.19**

PEARSON
Scott Foresman

DK

ISBN 0-328-14026-0

9 780328 140268

90000

scottforesman.com

# What did you learn?

1. Why do the features on the face of the Moon always look the same?

2. How do irregular satellites differ from other moons?

3. Why do astronomers know very little about Pluto's moon, Charon?

4. **Writing** in Science Several of the moons in the Solar System are larger than the planet Pluto, and Ganymede is larger than Mercury. What distinguishes a moon from a planet?

5. **Main Idea and Details** Ancient astronomers knew of only one moon, but today astronomers know of at least 140 moons. Advances in technology such as telescopes and spacecraft have helped people find many moons. List some details from the book that support this idea.

**Vocabulary**

lunar eclipse
orbit
revolve
rotate
solar eclipse

**Extended Vocabulary**

crater
Galilean satellites
irregular satellite
satellite
waning
waxing


**Picture Credits**
Every effort has been made to secure permission and provide appropriate credit for photographic material. The publisher deeply regrets any omission and pledges to correct errors called to its attention in subsequent editions.

Photo locators denoted as follows: Top (T), Center (C), Bottom (B), Left (L), Right (R), Background (Bkgd).

6 (C) Brand X Pictures; 8 (CR) ©Anglo-Australian Observatory/DK Images, (B) Brand X Pictures; 9 (T) SPL/Photo Researchers, Inc.; 12 (BL) Corbis, (BR) ESA/©Galaxy Picture Library; 14 (BR) NASA; 15 (B) STScI/©Galaxy Picture Library.

Scott Foresman/Dorling Kindersley would also like to thank: Opener: NASA/DK Images; 1 NASA/Jet Propulsion Lab (JPL)/DK Images; 2 NASA/DK Images; 7 (BR) NASA/DK Images; 8 (CR) NASA/DK Images; 10 NASA/Finley Holiday Films/DK Images; 11 (CRA) NASA/Finley Holiday Films/DK Images, (BR) NASA/Jet Propulsion Lab (JPL)/DK Images; 12 (TL, CLA) NASA/Jet Propulsion Lab (JPL)/DK Images; 13 (TR, BR) NASA/Jet Propulsion Lab (JPL)/DK Images; 14 (TL) NASA/Jet Propulsion Lab (JPL)/DK Images.

Unless otherwise acknowledged, all photographs are the copyright © of Dorling Kindersley, a division of Pearson.

ISBN: 0-328-14026-0

# Glossary

| | |
|---|---|
| **crater** | a hole on the surface of a moon or planet caused by a collision with another object |
| **Galilean satellites** | the four largest moons of Jupiter, discovered by Galileo in 1610 |
| **irregular satellite** | a moon that revolves around a planet in the opposite direction of the planet's rotation |
| **satellite** | a smaller body that revolves in an orbit around a planet |
| **waning** | gradually becoming smaller |
| **waxing** | gradually growing larger |



# Many Moons

by Steve Miller

# What You Already Know

Our Sun is a star. It is similar to the other stars in the sky; but it is much closer, so it seems bigger and brighter. The Sun is made of plasma. It is so hot that it glows, sending energy outward in every direction. Some of this energy, which is produced by reactions deep inside the Sun, reaches Earth and provides heat and light that plants need for making food.

An orbit is the path that one object follows when it moves around another. Earth and the Moon move together in an orbit around the Sun. At the same time, the Moon moves in an orbit around Earth. When one object moves around another, we say that it revolves. Earth revolves around the Sun while the Moon revolves around Earth. Each of these bodies also rotates, or spins, on its axis.

As Earth rotates, the Sun and the Moon appear to move across the sky. The Sun seems to rise in the east and set in the west because of the rotation of Earth, causing day and night. Nighttime is the period when the Sun is visible on the other side of the planet.

At different times, different portions of the Moon's lighted half can be seen from Earth. These are called phases of the Moon.

the Sun

# Pluto's Moon

Pluto, the most distant known planet from the Sun, has one moon, Charon. Charon revolves around Pluto every 6.4 days, which is the same amount of time taken by Pluto to spin around its axis. That means that Pluto always keeps the same face toward Charon. Pluto's diameter is 2,300 km, about two-thirds the size of Earth's moon, and Charon's diameter is 1,200 km. Pluto and Charon are often considered to be a double planet system, revolving around each other. Astronomers think that the system may have started when two small planets collided billions of years ago.

Because Charon is so far away, very little is known about it. The photograph below, taken by the camera on the Hubble Space Telescope, is the best image of Charon that is available. No other moons are known to revolve around Pluto, although it is possible that very small moons exist that cannot be detected from Earth.

artist's impression of Charon

Charon

Pluto

Pluto and Charon can be viewed as two planets orbiting one another.

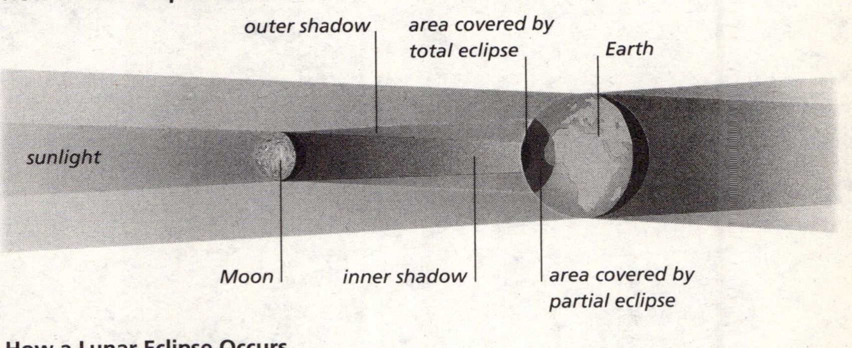

The smooth areas on Triton appear to be frozen lakes and a polar cap of frozen nitrogen and methane.

# Neptune's Moons

Neptune has at least thirteen moons, but only one is larger than 400 km in diameter. That moon, Triton, is a bit smaller than Earth's moon. It revolves around Neptune in the opposite direction to Neptune's rotation. This makes it the only large irregular satellite in the solar system and means that Triton was probably not always a moon of Neptune. Triton has many smooth regions, which may be frozen lakes that formed when water mixed with other materials that flowed from beneath the surface. At Triton's south pole there is an ice cap made of frozen nitrogen and methane, both of which are gases at Earth's temperatures.

The rest of Neptune's moons are much smaller, from about 28 km to 400 km in diameter. About half of them have orbits that are close to Neptune, revolving in the direction of Neptune's rotation. The rest are much farther away and are irregular satellites.

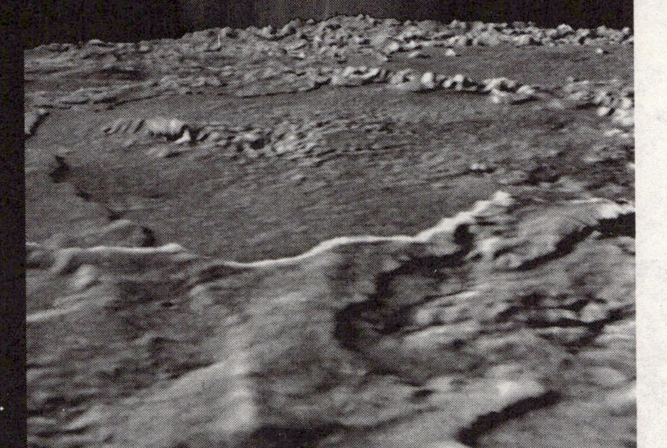

Neptune reflects the distant Sun's light dimly as it moves along Triton's horizon.



A New Moon appears completely dark. A Waxing Moon gradually grows larger until it becomes a Full Moon. A Full Moon appears fully lighted. A Waning Moon gradually becomes smaller until it becomes a New Moon again. The Moon cannot usually be seen during a New Moon. Sometimes the Sun, the Moon, and Earth are arranged in a straight line, with the Moon in the middle. When this happens, the Moon blocks the light of the Sun, making a solar eclipse. A different type of eclipse occurs when the three bodies line up with Earth in the middle. Then, Earth blocks sunlight from reaching the Moon. When Earth's shadow falls on the Moon, a lunar eclipse occurs.

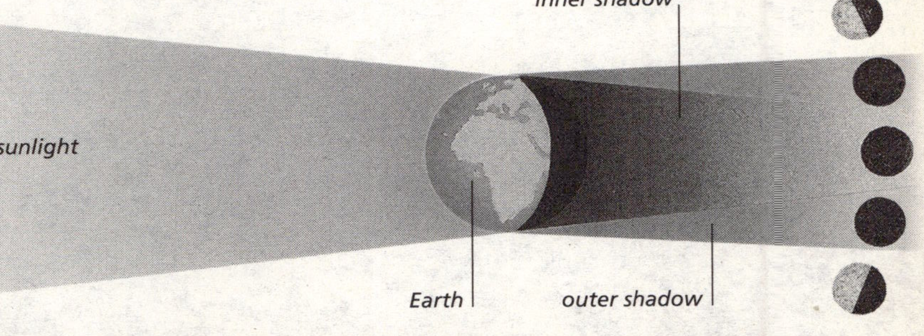

**How a Solar Eclipse Occurs**



**How a Lunar Eclipse Occurs**

# Many Moons

All but two of the planets in the solar system have at least one satellite, a smaller body that moves in an orbit around a planet. Earth's one natural satellite is the Moon, but satellites around the other planets are also known as moons. Only Mercury and Venus have no moons at all.

This illustration does not show the real scale of the distances between planets. If Earth were the size of a marble, the Sun would be more than 100 meters away. That's farther than the length of a football field!

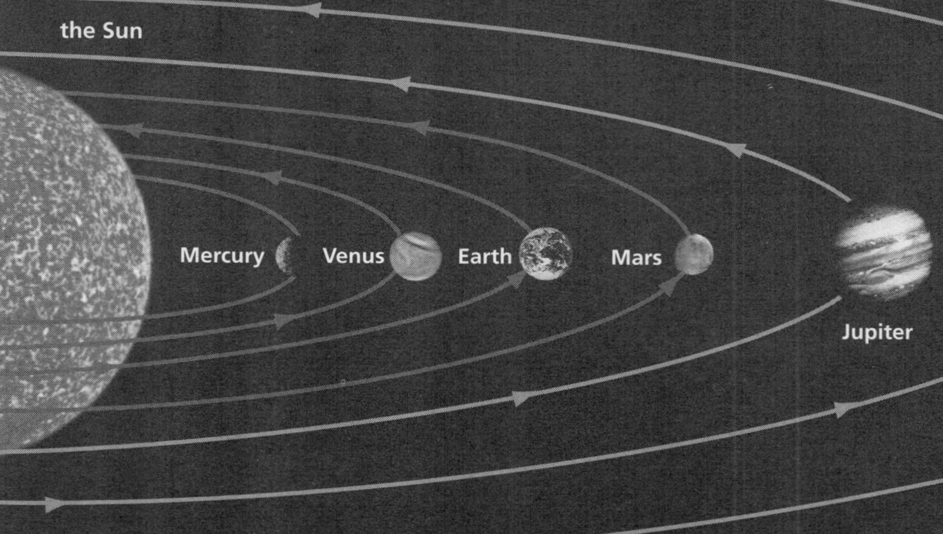


# Uranus' Moons



Uranus has at least twenty-seven moons but only five of them are large enough to detect using telescopes on Earth. These range from 470 km to 1,580 km in diameter. Titania is the largest, and Stephano the smallest. Most of the moons' names are the names of characters from plays by William Shakespeare. Even the large moons cannot be studied from Earth because they appear as tiny points of light. Most of what we know about them came from photographs sent back to Earth from the *Voyager 2* spacecraft, which passed Uranus in 1986.

The large moons of Uranus all have craters and large cracks on their surface. One theory about how the cracks formed is that long ago, when the moons were cooling, water under the surface froze and expanded. Miranda has a wide variety of surface features, including huge mountains, deep trenches, steep cliffs, and craters. Although Miranda's diameter is only 470 km, it has cliffs that are 20 km high No one has proposed a theory that can completely explain the strange appearance of Miranda.

Like the other Uranian moons, Ariel is covered with large cracks.

# Saturn's Moons

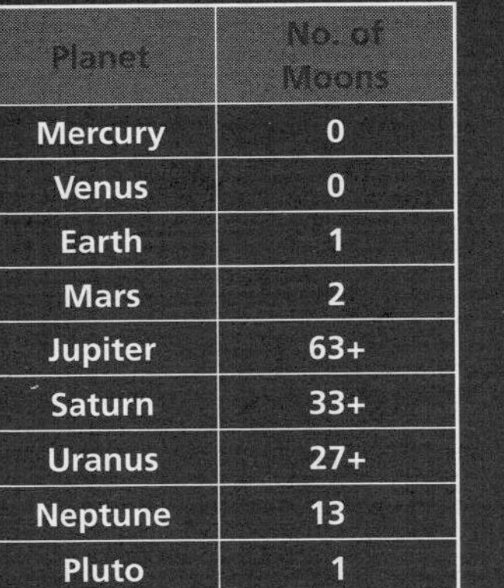

Like Earth's moon, Dione is covered with craters formed by collisions with large rocks.

Enceladus has large smooth areas, apparently caused by layers of ice.

The impact that caused this crater probably came close to destroying Mimas.

Saturn has more than thirty known moons. One of them, Titan, is almost as large as Ganymede, with a diameter of 5,150 km. Titan is the only moon in the solar system with an atmosphere. But Titan could not support life because its temperature is −180° Celsius. Made mostly of nitrogen, Titan's atmosphere is thicker than that of Earth. It may also have lakes and oceans of ethane, a chemical found in natural gas on Earth, which is a liquid at Titan's very low temperature.

Saturn has six more large moons—Mimas, Enceladus, Tethys, Dione, Rhea, and Iapetus—whose sizes range from 418 km to 1,530 km. These moons are believed to have formed at the same time as the planet. All of these moons are covered with craters, but each has its own characteristics. In addition to these seven moons, Saturn has many small moons whose diameters range from about 7 km to about 220 km. Many of these moons are irregular satellites and may be captured asteroids.

| Planet | No. of Moons |
| --- | --- |
| Mercury | 0 |
| Venus | 0 |
| Earth | 1 |
| Mars | 2 |
| Jupiter | 63+ |
| Saturn | 33+ |
| Uranus | 27+ |
| Neptune | 13 |
| Pluto | 1 |

**This table shows the number of moons known when this book was written.**

Ancient astronomers only knew one satellite—our own Moon. In 1610 the Italian scientist Galileo Galilei turned a telescope toward Jupiter and discovered four points of light that he described as "small stars." After observing them for several weeks, Galileo determined they were moving around the planet. These four moving objects, which he named Io, Europa, Ganymede, and Calisto, are now known as the Galilean satellites. The largest, Ganymede, is actually larger than the planets Mercury and Pluto.

As larger telescopes were built, many more moons were discovered. Since 1970 the *Viking, Voyager,* and *Galileo* spacecrafts have carried telescopes and cameras into space and have discovered many more moons. Astronomers now know of at least 140 moons in our solar system.

# Earth's Moon

The Moon is the most visible thing in the sky other than the Sun. That is because the Moon is closer to Earth than any of the planets. The diameter of the Moon is about one-fourth that of Earth. Most of the other moons in the solar system are much smaller when compared to the size of the planet they revolve around.

The Moon takes 27.3 days to complete one revolution around Earth. It also rotates on its axis in the same amount of time. Because of this, the same side of the Moon always faces Earth. It is sometimes called the "near side" of the Moon.

The Moon's appearance changes during each month. Depending on its position, different parts of it reflect sunlight in a repeating pattern called phases of the Moon.

The Sun always lights one-half of the Moon. The phase depends on how much of the lighted part is visible from Earth.

New Moon

Crescent Moon

Quarter Moon

Gibbous Moon

Full Moon

Unlike Io, Europa has a smooth appearance. Its tallest hills are only about 1 km high and there are very few craters. Photographs from the *Galileo* spacecraft have provided evidence that most of Europa is covered with ice that moves like a glacier, filling and eroding craters. In addition, there may be an ocean of liquid water below its crust.

Ganymede is the largest moon in the solar system. It is larger than the planets Pluto and Mercury. Its surface is covered with craters, and it has large dark areas that are much older than other parts of the surface. These may be old continents that have moved apart in the same way that continents move on Earth.

Callisto is almost as large as Ganymede, but it looks very different. Callisto is covered with craters and there is no evidence of movement of its crust. Its surface is very old compared to that of the other Galilean satellites.

The dark areas of Ganymede are older than the light areas.

Europa's shiny, smooth appearance is due to ice on the surface.

Io's surface is constantly changed by volcanic eruptions that send plumes of gas more than 100 km above its surface.

The mass of the giant planet Jupiter affects its moons, such as Io and Europa, shown here.

# Jupiter's Moons

Jupiter is the largest planet, and it has the largest known family of satellites—at least sixty-three of them. The largest and best known of Jupiter's moons are the four Galilean satellites: Io, Europa, Ganymede, and Callisto. Scientists think that these moons were formed at the same time as Jupiter. The other moons are very small, ranging from about 10 km to 26 km in diameter. Many of the smaller moons are irregular satellites, which means that they move in the direction opposite to the planet's rotation. Most of these irregular satellites move in orbits far from Jupiter. The main theory of their origin is that they are asteroids captured and sometimes broken up by Jupiter's strong gravity.

Of all the Galilean satellites, Io is the closest to Jupiter, although there are at least five small moons inside Io's orbit. Jupiter's gravitational pull causes the surface of Io to bulge out. Huge volcanoes cover the surface and their eruptions constantly change its features, giving it a splotchy appearance.

The near side of the Moon is the face that we always see.

The darker areas are caused by different amounts of light reflecting in the Moon's craters.

The phases come from the positions of Earth, the Sun, and the Moon. When the Moon is on the side of Earth opposite the Sun, the part of the Moon that we see reflects the sunlight and we see a Full Moon. When the Moon and the Sun are on the same side of Earth, sunlight falls on the part of the Moon that we can't see, causing a New Moon. In between these extremes, the Moon seems to grow larger and smaller, which is called waxing and waning.

The dark and light parts of the Moon are caused by a combination of impacts with other objects and ancient volcanoes. Large rocks, attracted toward the surface by the force of gravity, hit the Moon and caused large holes, or craters. Billions of years ago, some of the large craters were partly filled by lava from volcanoes. The Moon has no atmosphere, nor light of its own. The moonlight that we see is caused by the reflection of sunlight from the surface. Different surface characteristics of these features reflect light differently, creating the light and dark areas of the Moon's surface.

Impacts and ancient volcanoes are the causes of the irregular surface of the Moon.

# Moon Landings

Earth and the Moon are the only places in the solar system that people have set foot on. The longest trip ever taken by humans started on Earth, landed on the Moon, and returned to Earth. The first lunar landing occurred in 1969, when two astronauts walked on the Moon's surface. Because the Moon has no atmosphere, the astronauts had to wear spacesuits. It also means that their footprints may last many thousands of years because there is no erosion or wind to disturb them.

Humans have made a total of six trips to the Moon. The astronauts who made these trips brought back hundreds of kilograms of rock and dust from its surface. This material has helped scientists learn about the Moon's composition and its history.

footprint on the Moon

This flag has a frame to hold it out because there is no atmosphere and, therefore, no wind on the Moon.

# Mars' Moons

The two moons of Mars, Phobos and Deimos, were first observed in 1877. They are not spherical in shape and are rather small. Phobos is about 28 km by 20 km, and Deimos is about 16 km by 12 km. Phobos is an unusual moon because it orbits Mars in less than eight hours, which is a much shorter period than a day on Mars. Because of this, Phobos rises and sets about three times every day. Gravity on Phobos is one thousand times less than on Earth.

Because Phobos and Deimos are so small and so far away, very little was known about them until the *Viking* spacecraft passed close to them and sent pictures back to Earth. Astronomers believe that Phobos and Deimos may have been asteroids captured by the gravity of Mars. Asteroids are rocks, smaller than planets, that orbit the Sun. Many asteroids orbit in a belt between Mars and Jupiter.

Phobos and Mars

Deimos

Space and Technology

# Following the Stars

by Patricia Walsh

223

| Genre | Comprehension Skill | Text Features | Science Content |
| --- | --- | --- | --- |
| Nonfiction | Draw Conclusions | • Captions<br>• Charts<br>• Diagrams<br>• Glossary | Stars and Solar System |

Scott Foresman Science 6.20

PEARSON

Scott Foresman

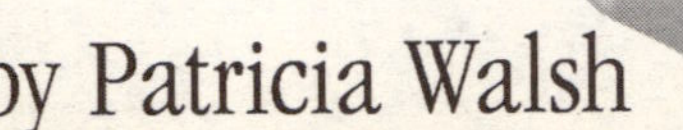

ISBN 0-328-14029-5

9 780328 140299

90000

scottforesman.com

# What did you learn?

**1.** How did early sailors navigate before they learned to navigate by the stars?

**2.** What other name is given to the North Star? In which constellation will you find it?

**3.** What do the letters GPS stand for and how is GPS used?

**4.** **Writing** in Science  Navigators used the cross-staff in the 1500s to determine the ship's latitude. Explain the advantages and disadvantages of their use.

**5.** Draw Conclusions  Today GPS is used by navigators to pinpoint the position of their ships with accuracy. Why is it still important to know how to follow the stars?

**Vocabulary**

astronomical unit
constellation
galaxy
light-year
magnitude
nuclear fusion
solar system
star

**Extended Vocabulary**

altitude
astrolabe
celestial navigation
celestial sphere
horizon
latitude
navigator

**Picture Credits**
Every effort has been made to secure permission and provide appropriate credit for photographic material.
The publisher deeply regrets any omission and pledges to correct errors called to its attention in subsequent editions.

Photo locators denoted as follows: Top (T), Center (C), Bottom (B), Left (L), Right (R), Background (Bkgd).

Opener: National Maritime Museum, London /DK Images;  2 (CA) ©Anglo-Australian Observatory/DK Images;
4 ©Jerry Schad/Photo Researchers, Inc.;  5 (C) ©John Prior Images/Alamy Images;  6 ©Erich Lessing/Art Resource, NY;
8 National Maritime Museum/DK Images; 9 ©Ronald Sheridan/Ancient Art & Architecture Collection Ltd.;
15 ©Philippe Psalia/Photo Researchers, Inc.

Unless otherwise acknowledged, all photographs are the copyright © of Dorling Kindersley, a division of Pearson.

ISBN: 0-328-14029-5

# Following the Stars

by Patricia Walsh

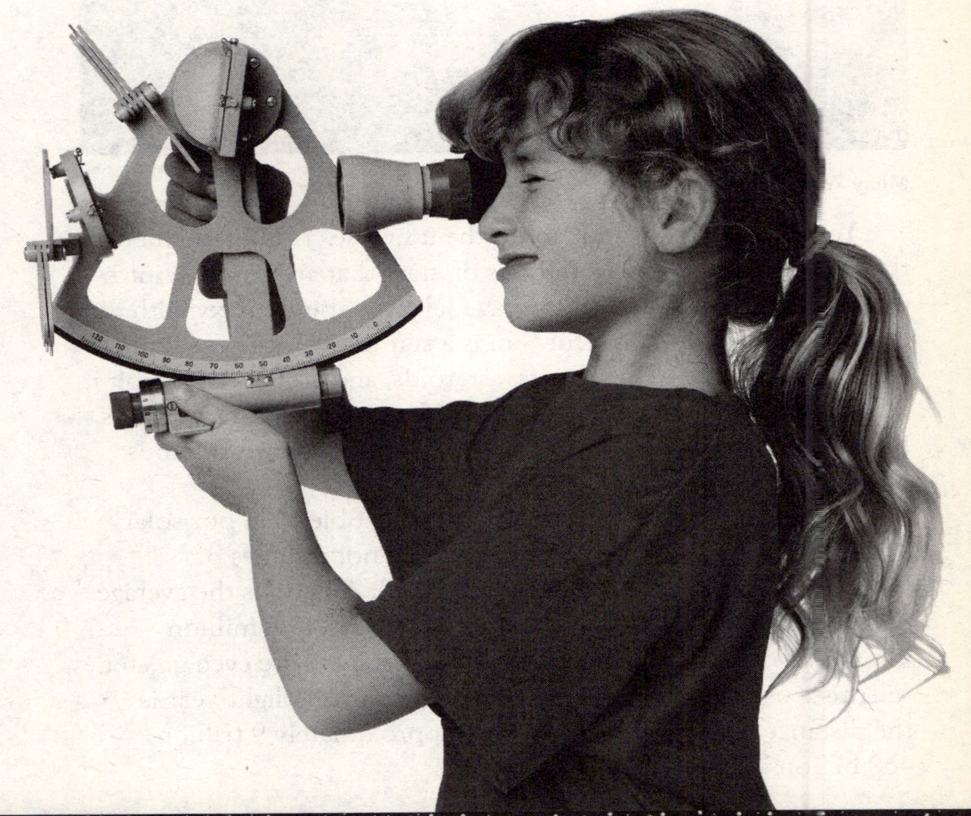

# Glossary

**altitude** — the angular distance of the Sun, the Moon, or a star above the horizon

**astrolabe** — a navigation tool invented by the ancient Greeks

**celestial navigation** — a method of navigation in which a location point is calculated by finding the position of heavenly bodies

**celestial sphere** — an imaginary sphere that has the observer as its center and that appears to enclose the universe

**horizon** — a line where Earth and the sky seem to meet

**latitude** — a distance north or south of the equator, measured in degrees

**navigator** — a person in charge of guiding a ship

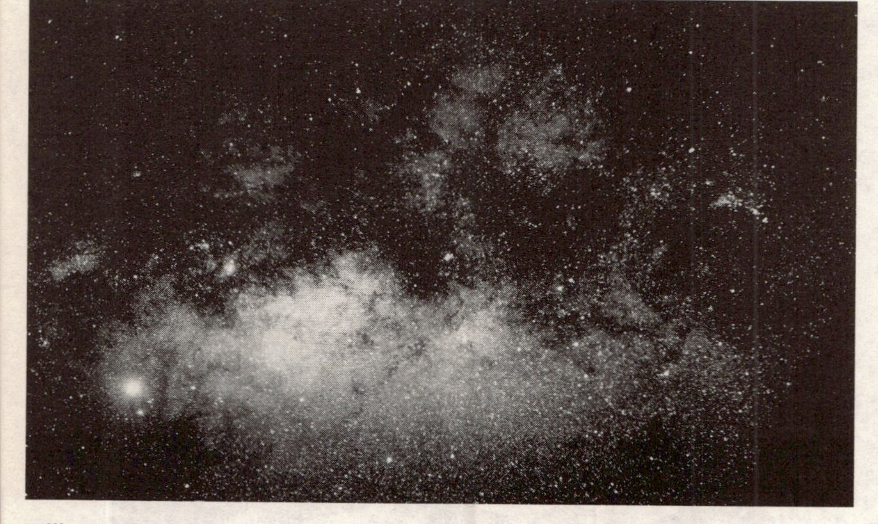

**Milky Way Galaxy**

You already know a lot about the universe. You'll remember that the universe contains billions of stars that are grouped into galaxies. We live in the Milky Way Galaxy, a spiral galaxy with long pinwheel-like arms. Our Sun is a star in one of those arms.

Our Sun and all the planets, asteroids, and comets that orbit it make up our solar system. The inner planets are Mercury, Venus, Earth, and Mars. The outer planets are Jupiter, Saturn, Uranus, Neptune, and Pluto.

The distances that separate the orbiting objects in our solar system are so great that they are measured not in miles or kilometers, but in astronomical units (AU). An AU is the average distance between Earth and the Sun, or about 149.6 million kilometers. Farther out in space, where distances are even greater, scientists use light-years as the unit of measure. A light-year is the distance light travels in one year, approximately 9 trillion, 460 billion kilometers.

GPS uses satellite technology to help people find their global position.

## Guiding Lights

In the 1900s, scientists turned away from the natural celestial bodies for navigation. But in a way, we still look to the skies to help us navigate. Today, the Global Positioning System, or GPS, is used for navigation. It relies on twenty-four satellites and many other stations on the ground to find locations anywhere on Earth. At any time, in any weather, anywhere on Earth, GPS is used to track airplanes, ships, trucks, and cars. Even hikers can use a handheld GPS to make certain they don't get lost in the woods. But celestial navigation is still an important skill. Satellites may break down, but celestial navigation always works as long as the stars shine.

# The Sextant

The sextant was developed by the English Navy in the 1750s to replace the backstaff and the cross-staff. The sextant looks similar to a quadrant, but it is one-sixth of a circle. It measures the angle between two objects by using two mirrors. The bottom half of one mirror is clear glass. The navigator uses this mirror to line up the sextant with the horizon. The other mirror is on a movable arm. The arm is adjusted so that light from the Sun reflects off it, strikes the half-clear mirror, and then travels to the navigator's eye. The navigator sees the horizon and the reflection of the Sun right on top of each other. The angle between the Sun and the horizon can then be read from a scale. The correct angle is shown where the movable arm crosses the curved bottom of the sextant. The sextant gives very accurate results. It can pinpoint a ship's location to within one-hundredth of a degree.

The sextant, invented in the 1700s, was designed to replace the cross-staff and the backstaff.



Even though the stars in the universe are huge, hot, glowing balls of gas, they still go through a life cycle. Stars are born, change as they get older, and eventually die. During their lifetime of millions or billions of years, stars produce light and other forms of energy through nuclear fusion reactions. When stars finally run out of fuel, they experience changes in size, color, and brightness. Currently, our own Sun is a yellow midsized star.

The brightness of stars is described with the term *magnitude*. Our Sun has the greatest apparent magnitude. Apparent magnitude is how bright a star appears to people on Earth. A more accurate measure of a star's true brightness is absolute magnitude. This is the measure of how bright a star would appear if every star were exactly the same distance from Earth.

The stars in our night sky are placed into groups called constellations. The constellations, such as the familiar Big Dipper, appear to move at night and during the seasons. It's really the Earth's own movement that causes these changes in position. Long ago, humans recognized the predictable movement of the stars. Sailors and explorers learned that observing these patterns could help them to find their way at sea.

Ancient astronomers made sense of the night sky by picturing certain patterns of stars as creatures from myths.

# Watching the Stars

Look up into a clear night sky. People in early civilizations did the same thing. Even 5,000 years ago, people studied the night sky and its stars. The Chinese, Egyptians, Babylonians, Greeks, and Arabs all long ago discovered they could relate their position on Earth to the Sun, Moon, and stars.

Have you noticed that the stars appear to move across the sky? Just as the Sun appears to rise in the east and set in the west every day, so do the stars. Most ancient people thought Earth was at the center of the universe and that the stars rotated around us. We now know that it is Earth turning on its axis that makes the Sun and stars appear to revolve around Earth.

As you probably know, staring at the Sun can be very dangerous. The main problem with the cross-staff was that a navigator could suffer eye damage from the bright light.

John Davis, an English navigator, invented the backstaff in 1594. It was similar to the cross-staff, except that the observer faced away from the Sun to use it. At noon, the navigator stood with his back to the Sun and looked through a sight on the backstaff. The navigator would move the backstaff until a piece called the horizon vane lined up with the horizon. Then he would move another piece called the shadow vane until it cast a shadow on the horizon vane. He could then read the Sun's altitude from two scales to determine latitude. The backstaff was popular into the 1700s.

# The Cross-staff and Backstaff

The Greeks invented the cross-staff. It was a long staff, or bar, marked with a scale and fitted with a shorter crosspiece that slid along the staff. One end of the staff was held at the navigator's eye. He would slide the crosspiece along the staff until the lower edge of the crosspiece seemed to touch the horizon and the upper edge seemed to touch either Polaris or the lower edge of the Sun. Then the angle between the object and the horizon was read from the scale to determine the ship's latitude.



The cross-staff was popular with sixteenth-century navigators.



The backstaff allowed a navigator to measure the height of the Sun without having to stare directly at it.



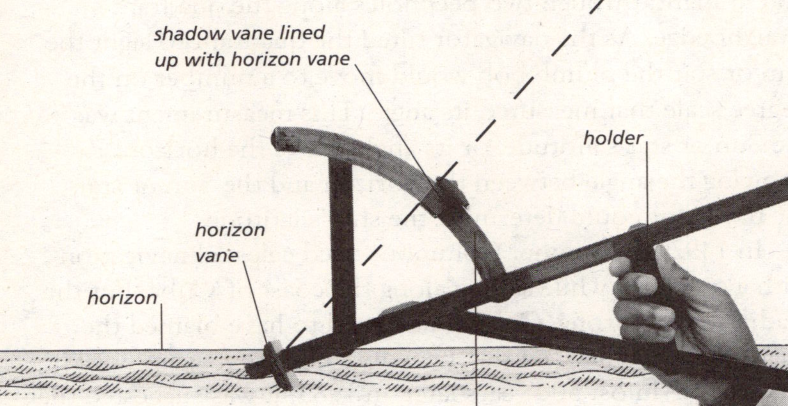

It is thought that the mysterious 5,000-year-old structure called Stonehenge in Eng and was used to observe the stars.

The ancient sky watchers also thought the stars were all the same distance from Earth. They saw the stars as tiny lights on the inside of a hollow sphere that surrounded Earth. Today we know that this is not true; there is no such sphere, and each star is a different distance from Earth. However, the ancient idea of the hollow sphere, called the celestial sphere, is a useful navigation tool. Navigators can use the celestial sphere in the same way they use a globe of Earth. The celestial sphere is a map of the night sky.

# Following the Stars

The process of finding your way by using the stars is called celestial navigation. Celestial navigation has been around for thousands of years and was used by early Greek, Chinese, Polynesian, and Viking sailors. The Phoenicians, an ancient people from what is now Lebanon, made one of the most important discoveries in celestial navigation. They found that there is one star in the sky that appears to remain still, while all the others appear to rotate around it. This is Polaris, or the North Star, which always appears due north. The Phoenicians found that the angle between Polaris and the horizon was the same as latitude on Earth. By observing their position in relation to Polaris, the Phoenicians could easily tell what direction they were traveling in.

Not only is Polaris extremely helpful for navigation, but it is also very easy to find. It is a very bright star, and it has an easily recognizable constellation pointing to it. You have probably heard of the Big Dipper. This large formation of stars is located within the constellation Ursa Major, or the Great Bear. The Big Dipper is shaped like a ladle and has a handle and a bowl. The bowl is formed by four stars that are arranged in an approximately square pattern. If you follow an imaginary line up from the end of the bowl it would point to Polaris.

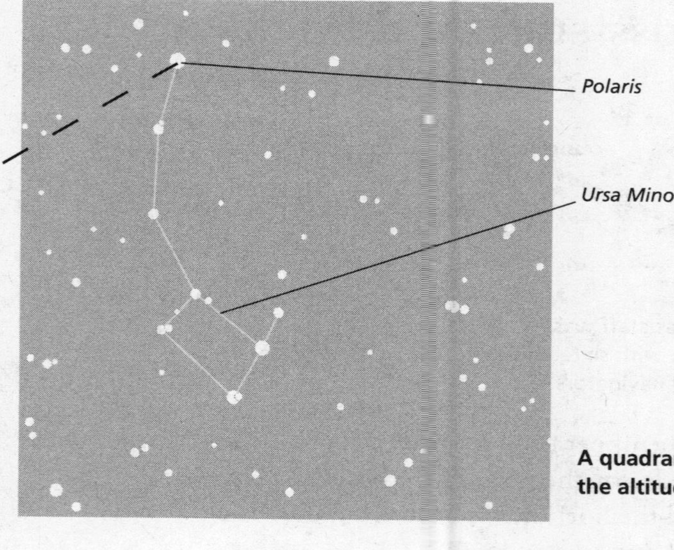


**A quadrant can measure the altitude of a star.**

The navigator would sight the Sun at noon, or the North Star at night, through two peepholes along the quadrant's straight edge. As the navigator tilted the quadrant to sight the Sun or star the plumb bob would move to a number on the degree scale that measured its angle. This measurement was the Sun or star's altitude, or its angle above the horizon. By knowing the angle between the horizon and the Sun or star, the navigator could determine the ship's latitude.

In 1492 Christopher Columbus tried celestial navigation with a quadrant while sailing along the coast of Cuba, but the readings were wrong. Columbus is said to have blamed the quadrant and remarked that he would not use it again until it was fixed. Almost 500 years later, in 1983, it was suggested that the readings were wrong because Columbus read the scale incorrectly. If he had read the quadrant scale correctly, he would have been within a few degrees of his location.

**The Phoenicians were a great seafaring people who learned to navigate by the North Star.**

# The Quadrant

The quadrant was an improvement in navigational tools
and was a bit more accurate than an astrolabe. The quadrant is
a heavy metal plate in the shape of a quarter circle. The curved
edge is divided into 90 degrees. It looks very similar to the
protractor you might use in geometry. The quadrant is used to
determine latitude, just as the astrolabe was. A weight called
a plumb bob hangs from a string at the apex, or peak,
of the quadrant and points straight down.



**Polaris is the brightest
star in the Ursa Minor
constellation.**



Polaris is found in the
constellation Ursa Minor,
or the Little Bear. This
constellation contains another
familiar grouping of stars called
the Little Dipper. Polaris is the star at
the end of the Little Dipper's handle.

As time went on, people identified and
named more and more constellations. The Greek
astronomer Ptolemy classified forty-eight constellations.
The earliest maps of the constellations date back to 1440. Until
the late 1500s, star charts included only Ptolemy's constellations.
In 1595, a Dutch navigator, Pieter Dircksz Keyser, added twelve
new constellations that are found in the Southern Hemisphere.
They were named after exotic birds: Toucan, Peacock, and
Phoenix. A complete map of the skies dates from 1930. It
includes a total of eighty-eight constellations.

# Navigators' Tools

Navigators' tools are the instruments that help determine a ship's position. Many of these tools have been around for hundreds or even thousands of years. They help navigators determine the positions of objects in the sky. This information can be used to figure out the precise location of a ship at sea.

## The Astrolabe

The astrolabe was invented by the ancient Greeks. It is one of the oldest tools for celestial navigation. It can be used to find many important pieces of information, including the heights of objects, the time of day, the positions of stars, and latitude.

An astrolabe is a metal disk that hangs from a ring. Various other disks can be stacked on top of this one. These disks have complicated star maps and other information engraved on them. There is a rotating pointer called an alidade that pivots at the center of the disk.

To use an astrolabe to find latitude of a ship, a navigator waited until noon, when the Sun reached its highest point in the sky. One sailor held the astrolabe up by its ring, while another sailor lined up the alidade with the Sun. When it was lined up with the Sun at noon, the alidade pointed to a mark on the disk that could be used to find the ship's latitude.

Once the latitude was found, a disk with a star map for that latitude was attached to the astrolabe. Using the same sighting process that was used to determine latitude, the astrolabe was then used to find the time of day, and the star map showed the position of the constellations in the sky for that specific time. Knowing the positions of constellations could help a navigator to find a ship's position at sea.

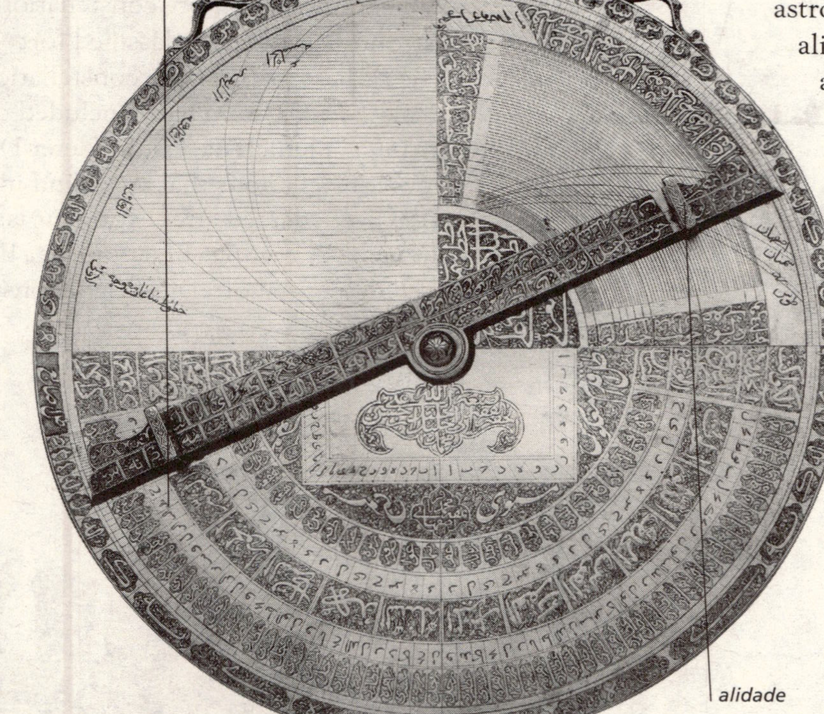



The astrolabe had different engraved disks that showed maps of the stars for various places on Earth.

Arab astronomers were highly skilled in the use of the astrolabe.

Science

Science

# The SPACE RACE

by Grace Ng



| Genre | Comprehension Skill | Text Features | Science Content |
| --- | --- | --- | --- |
| Nonfiction | Main Idea and Details | • Captions<br>• Charts<br>• Diagrams<br>• Glossary | Technology |

Scott Foresman Science 6.21

PEARSON
Scott Foresman
scottforesman.com

DK

ISBN 0-328-14032-5
90000
9 780328 140329

# What did you learn?

| Vocabulary | Extended Vocabulary |
|---|---|
| autonomous robot | Cold War |
| carbon nanotube | cosmonaut |
| industrial robot | space probe |
| nanotechnology | Space Race |
| robots | space shuttle |
| robotics | space station |
| | space walk |

1. What goal did President John F. Kennedy set for the United States?

2. Why did NASA begin the space shuttle program?

3. Why did many politicians and world leaders view space exploration as a military activity?

4. **Writing** in Science  Space exploration gained a lot of interest during the Cold War as a result of competition between the United States and the Soviet Union. Write to explain how today many countries, including the United States and Russia, work together.

5. **Main Idea and Details** The launch of *Sputnik 1* by the Soviets was the event that initiated the Space Race. One of the last events of the Space Race was the development of a reusable spacecraft. What were the most important events that link these two milestones?

**Picture Credits**
Every effort has been made to secure permission and provide appropriate credit for photographic material.
The publisher deeply regrets any omission and pledges to correct errors called to its attention in subsequent editions.

Photo locators denoted as follows: Top (T), Center (C), Bottom (B), Left (L), Right (R), Background (Bkgd).

Opener ©Bettmann/Corbis; 1 ©Bettmann/Corbis; 3 NASA; 4 (BL) ©Bettmann/Corbis; 5 ©Ed Clark/Getty Images; 6 ©Bettmann/Corbis; 7 ITAR-TASS/Sovfoto/Eastfoto; 8 (TR) ©Bettmann/Corbis, (CL) Kennedy Space Center/NASA, (BR) NASA/Science Source /Photo Researchers, Inc.; 9 (BR) ©Bettmann/Corbis; 11 (B) Corbis; 13 (B) ITAR-TASS/Sovfoto/Eastfoto; 15 (CR) Johnson Space Center/NASA, (B) NASA.

Unless otherwise acknowledged, all photographs are the copyright © of Dorling Kindersley, a division of Pearson.

ISBN: 0-328-14032-5

# Glossary

| | |
|---|---|
| **Cold War** | the ideological conflict between the United States and the Soviet Union |
| **cosmonaut** | a Russian or Soviet astronaut |
| **space probe** | an unmanned exploratory spacecraft |
| **Space Race** | the competition between the United States and the Soviet Union aimed at making discoveries in space |
| **space shuttle** | a reusable spacecraft designed to transport people and cargo between Earth and space |
| **space station** | a place where people can live and work in space for long periods of time |
| **space walk** | any kind of physical activity outside a spacecraft by one of the crew |

# What You Already Know

Technology is continually improving. Robots have become more common in science and industry because robotics has improved over time. Other technologies, such as smaller, more powerful computer systems, more precise sensors, and advanced computer programs, have helped robot designers.

Robots affect many aspects of our lives. We use robots to perform jobs that are too dangerous, boring, or repetitive for people to do. They are also useful when the work needs to be very accurate.

Almost 90 percent of robots are used in factories. They are called industrial robots. The most common type is the robotic arm. Robot arms can weld, paint, iron, assemble, pack, inspect, and test manufactured parts. Hospitals use messenger robots to carry supplies, equipment, and medications from one place to another. Robotic hands, controlled by human surgeons, are now being used in surgery.

Robots are also used to explore beyond Earth. NASA uses remote-controlled vehicles called rovers. Rovers can explore distant locations while being controlled by an operator. Robots that do not need direct supervision or specific instructions before acting are called autonomous robots. They can analyze data and decide what to do next. Robots can be used to explore places where humans cannot go and do jobs too dangerous for humans. Nanotechnology is very small-scale technology that deals with materials and processes measured in nanometers. Currently researchers believe that nanotechnology will allow people to build materials one atom at a time. With such precision, scientists should be able to make any material they want. So far scientists have not built many substances in this way. But they have had success changing some existing materials.

This marked a new era in space exploration. Different countries are now working together toward a common goal. Today sixteen countries are building another space station. Both Russia and the United States are part of the team that is building the International Space Station (ISS). New modules continue to be added to the station all the time. Once it is finished, the space station will be about the size of a football field. It will allow humans to explore space for many years to come.

## Space Linkup

On July 17, 1975, *Apollo 18* and *Soyuz 19* docked together in Earth's orbit as part of a historic joint project between the United States and the Soviet Union. Astronaut Tom Stafford and cosmonaut Aleskei Leonov shook hands in space.

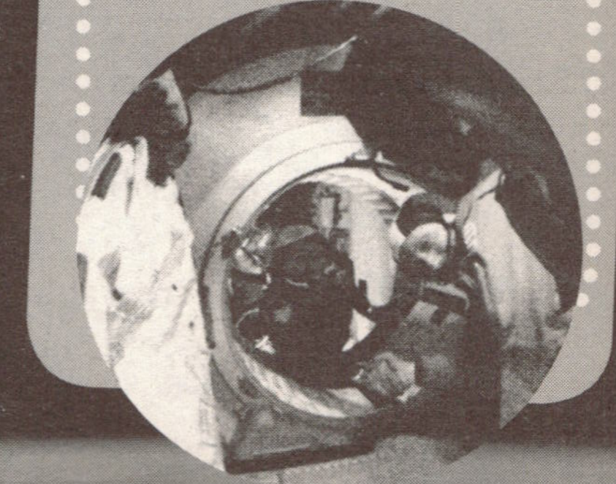

The International Space Station is being built by sixteen different countries.

# Working Together

Space exploration is no longer a competition between countries. Instead, it is an international project. Russia built the *Mir* space station from 1986 to 1996. A space station is a place where people can live and work in space. Year after year, astronauts, scientists, and researchers from all over the world used the station.

In 1995 Norman Thagard became the first American astronaut to visit *Mir*. He was aboard the space shuttle *Atlantis*, which delivered water, supplies, and equipment for medical experiments. It also delivered a docking module and two solar arrays to expand the *Mir* space station.

The space shuttle *Atlantis* is docked with the space station *Mir* in 1995.





In the future, scientists may be able to use a form of technology called nanoshells to fight cancer. These shells are injected into a tumor to kill the cancer cells using heat. Another medical application involves nanocrystals that give off specific colors of light. Researchers use these nanocrystals to locate and identify individual chromosomes. Depending on how the crystals glow, researchers can gather information about a patient's DNA.

One of the most promising breakthroughs in nanotechnology is the discovery of the carbon nanotube. Researchers think the unique properties of these molecules could be used to manufacture ultrasmall transistors and other electrical devices. These devices may be ten times smaller than what we use today!

Space exploration is one field in which technology has developed very rapidly. Political tensions between the United States and the Soviet Union after World War II fueled competition between the two countries in many areas. This competition led to many technological innovations that culminated in humans walking on the Moon!

The rovers *Opportunity* and *Spirit* have sent back images of the surface of the planet Mars.

# The Race for Space

Throughout history, people have been curious about what is beyond Earth. Such curiosity has led some to study the stars and the planets through telescopes. Others develop theories and models to explain how the universe functions. People have also been curious about space travel and exploration. It has been a topic of scientific inquiry and fictional writing for hundreds of years. However, one of the most rapid and important series of advances in space exploration began in the 1950s.

The launch of *Sputnik 1* on October 4, 1957, marked the start of the Space Race.

Two countries, the United States and the Soviet Union, led the world into an era of intense space exploration. After World War II, the two countries had strong political differences. The Cold War, a time of political disagreements and military rivalry, did not end in actual combat. However, the United States and the Soviet Union let this rivalry fuel many competitions, from sports to space exploration.

History changed on October 4, 1957, when *Sputnik 1*, the world's first artificial satellite, was launched into space. It orbited Earth in about ninety-eight minutes. This was a great victory for the Soviets because they put a satellite in orbit before the United States did.

In January 1958, the United States successfully launched a satellite, called *Explorer 1*, on a *Juno 1* rocket.

The space shuttle is a reusable spacecraft. It has been the United States' only launch spacecraft from the mid-1970s through 2004.

Some Soviet politicians thought that the United States was using the space shuttle for military purposes. So they created their own reusable spacecraft program, called the Buran program. It became the Soviet Union's largest and most expensive space program. The first and only launch of the *Buran* shuttle was on November 15, 1988. Afterwards the program ended due to a lack of money. Around this time the Cold War was ending, and the Space Race ended as a result. By the end of 1991 the Soviet Union splintered into fifteen independent countries, including Russia.

Unlike the Soviet program, America's space shuttle program grew. The space shuttle was the first spacecraft with the ability to carry large satellites from Earth to space.

After the success of America's space shuttle, the Soviets created their own reusable spacecraft, the *Buran*.

# Reusable Craft

NASA did not stop with one mission to the surface of the Moon. Between 1969 and 1972, NASA conducted more Apollo missions. But these missions were very expensive.

NASA could not afford many more missions if it did not cut down on costs. To cut costs, it developed the space shuttle, a reusable spacecraft designed to transport people and cargo between Earth and space. The space shuttle has four main components: a reusable orbiter, a large fuel tank that is used once, and two reusable booster rockets for the initial launch. On April 12, 1981, the first U.S. space shuttle flew into space. It was a great success because once again, the United States had beaten the Soviet Union by developing a reusable system.

In 1981 the first U.S. space shuttle was launched. This marked the beginning of NASA's space shuttle program.

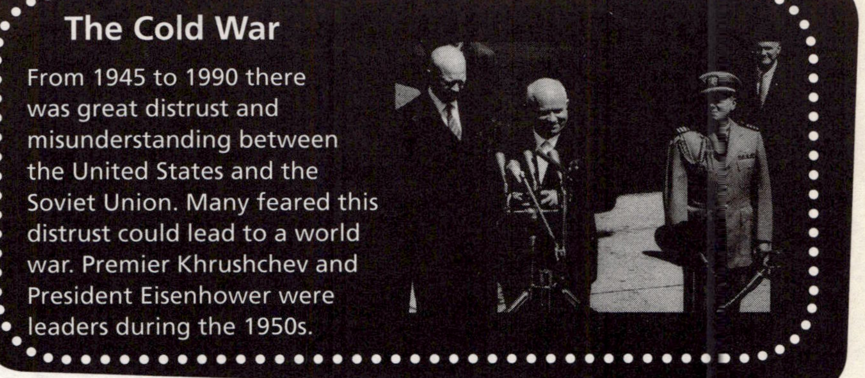



As the Soviets celebrated their success, most Americans had a very different feeling. They feared that if the Soviet Union had the ability to launch satellites, then they would also have the ability to launch missiles that could carry nuclear weapons to any location on Earth. Others thought that the Soviets' satellite was launched to get targeting information for these missiles. The public was very frightened by what could happen in the future.

Many Americans also felt shocked. They were surprised that the Soviets had technology that could rival that of the United States. When the Soviets beat them into space, Americans lost a lot of their pride. Immediately the U.S. Defense Department approved more funding for its space program. On January 31, 1958, the United States successfully launched its own satellite, called *Explorer 1*.

The launch of *Sputnik 1* marked the beginning of the Space Race. A long-term competition developed between the United States and the Soviet Union to make discoveries in space. Both wanted to be the leader in space exploration. During the Space Race, scientists and government leaders from both countries were under great pressure to meet some tough deadlines. They developed and used many new technologies in a very short period of time.

# Humans in Space

Less than a month after the success of *Sputnik 1*, the Soviet Union made another space launch. This time, *Sputnik 2* carried a dog named Laika. She was the first living creature launched into space. Scientists in the Soviet Union believed organisms could live in space. On this trip Laika proved it, though she only survived for a short time as there was no way for her to return to Earth. *Sputnik 1* weighed less than 84 kilograms. *Sputnik 2* weighed approximately 508 kilograms. It was much larger than the 1.6 kilogram satellite designed by the United States. This led many American scientists and leaders to believe that the Soviets were preparing to send a human into space.

American leaders felt that the United States was far behind in the Space Race. In 1958 Congress established a permanent government agency dedicated to space exploration. The National Aeronautics and Space Administration, or NASA, was formed. NASA's tasks were to plan and carry out space activities, to involve scientists in these activities, and to spread information about these activities to the American public.

American leaders wanted to catch up with the Soviet Union. They believed that if the United States could be the first country to send a person into space, they would catch up. However, a Soviet astronaut, or cosmonaut, beat them by a month. On April 12, 1961, Yuri Gagarin became the first human in space. He made a single orbit of Earth in his *Vostok 1* spacecraft.

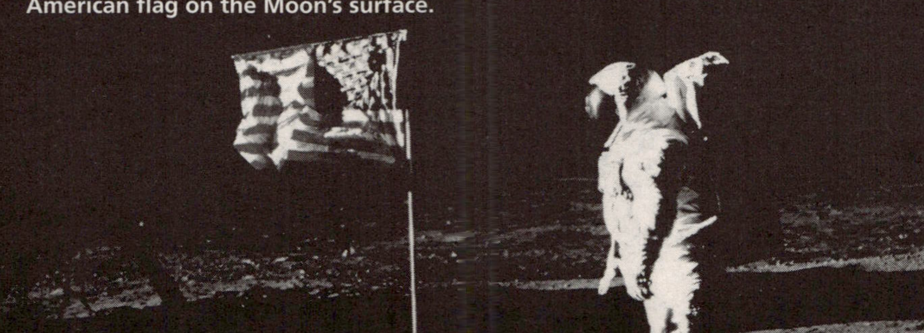

On November 3, 1957, a Soviet dog named Laika became the first living creature launched into space. She traveled in the satellite *Sputnik 2*.

On July 20, 1969, *Eagle* landed safely on the Moon, and Neil Armstrong became the first human to set foot on the Moon. He said, "That's one small step for man, one giant leap for mankind." Edwin "Buzz" Aldrin, Jr., joined him on the Moon. The two men collected rocks and soil samples, took pictures, and set up scientific experiments. They spent about two-and-a-half hours on the surface of the Moon. On July 24, all three astronauts returned safely to Earth.

Millions of people on Earth were able to watch the events on television because the astronauts had brought a camera with them. Armstrong and Aldrin even took a radio telephone call from President Richard Nixon while on the Moon's surface. It was an extremely exciting time for Americans. They had beaten the Soviets to the Moon!

The *Apollo 11* crew consisted of Neil Armstrong, Michael Collins, and "Buzz" Aldrin.

"Buzz" Aldrin stands beside an American flag on the Moon's surface.

American astronauts Neil Armstrong and "Buzz" Aldrin were the first humans to land on the surface of the Moon.



The Apollo program began on May 25, 1961. The objective of this program was to land an American on the Moon and then return him or her safely to Earth. NASA launched many different Apollo missions in preparation for its final goal. *Apollo 8* was the first manned spacecraft to orbit the Moon.

After several successful missions, the United States was ready to make history. On July 16, 1969, the crew of *Apollo 11* took off from Earth with the goal of landing on the Moon. The plan was to have a lunar module called *Eagle* separate from the main spacecraft, the command module *Columbia*. The lunar module would land on the surface of the Moon while the command module orbited the Moon.



*Vostok 1* shook wildly when it reentered Earth's atmosphere. Once Gagarin was close enough to the ground, he ejected and landed by parachute. It was a very proud moment for the Soviets. They called Yuri the Columbus of the Cosmos.

The United States celebrated a smaller milestone on May 5, 1961, when Alan Shepard, Jr., became the first American in space. He went on a fifteen-minute flight in a capsule called *Freedom 7*. He reached a high altitude but did not orbit Earth as the Soviet Gagarin had done. It was still a success for the United States.

Soviet Yuri Gagarin became an instant international hero after he became the first human in space. His orbit around Earth took place in April 1961.

# More Firsts

As the Space Race became more competitive, many milestones were achieved in a very short period of time. John Glenn, Jr., became the first American to orbit Earth, on February 20, 1962. He circled Earth three times in about five hours before returning.

Then on June 16, 1963, Soviet Valentina Tereshkova became the first woman in space. She was in space for a total of three days. Another major event was the first space walk, made on March 18, 1965, by Soviet Aleksei Leonov. A space walk is any kind of physical activity outside of a spacecraft. Leonov floated outside the spacecraft for twenty minutes.

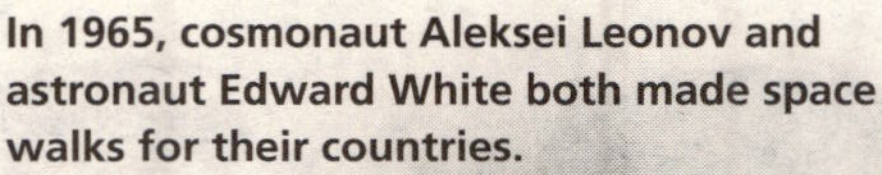
Valentina Tereshkova

In 1965, cosmonaut Aleksei Leonov and astronaut Edward White both made space walks for their countries.

In February 1962, John Glenn, Jr., became the first American to orbit Earth. He blasted off on board the *Friendship 7* spacecraft.

# Race to the Moon

Both countries began sending space probes to the Moon. A space probe is an unmanned exploratory spacecraft. The first probes were sent to pass very close to the Moon or to crash-land on it. Probes were later designed to orbit the Moon or to make soft landings on it.

Soviet-made probes were the first to accomplish each of these tasks. *Luna 1* was the first probe to fly by the Moon. *Luna 2* was the first to crash-land on the Moon, and *Luna 9* was the first to make a soft landing. *Luna 10* was the first probe to orbit the Moon.

At this point, the Soviets had beaten the Americans to every space milestone. Americans wanted to find some way to overtake the Soviets in the Space Race. Then President John F. Kennedy gave a speech to the American public. He stated that his goal was to land an American on the Moon and return him or her safely to Earth. This was a great challenge. The first country to accomplish this goal would take the lead in space exploration.

The Soviet Union was very successful in launching its space probes to the Moon. *Luna 9* was the first probe to make a soft landing on the Moon's surface.

On May 25, 1961, President John F. Kennedy gave a speech in which he set out his plan to land an American on the Moon before the end of the decade.